SHP
HISTORY
YEAR 8

SHP
HISTORY
YEAR 8

CHRIS CULPIN
IAN DAWSON
DALE BANHAM
BETHAN EDWARDS
SALLY BURNHAM

HODDER
EDUCATION
AN HACHETTE UK COMPANY

The Schools History Project

Set up in 1972 to bring new life to history for students aged 13–16, the Schools History Project continues to play an innovatory role in secondary history education. From the start, SHP aimed to show how good history has an important contribution to make to the education of a young person. It does this by creating courses and materials which both respect the importance of up-to-date, well-researched history and provide enjoyable learning experiences for students.

Since 1978 the Project has been based at Trinity and All Saints University College Leeds. It continues to support, inspire and challenge teachers through the annual conference, regional courses and website: http://www.schoolshistoryproject.co.uk. The Project is also closely involved with government bodies and awarding bodies in the planning of courses for Key Stage 3, GCSE and A level.

Although every effort has been made to ensure that website addresses are correct at the time of going to press, Hodder Education cannot be held responsible for the content of any website mentioned in this book. It is sometimes possible to find a relocated web page by typing in the address of the home page for a website in the URL window of your browser.

Hachette UK's policy is to use papers that are natural, renewable and recyclable products and made from wood grown in sustainable forests. The logging and manufacturing processes are expected to conform to the environmental regulations of the country of origin.

Orders: please contact Bookpoint Ltd, 130 Milton Park, Abingdon, Oxon OX14 4SB. Telephone: +44 (0)1235 827720. Fax: +44 (0)1235 400454. Lines are open 9.00–5.00, Monday to Saturday, with a 24-hour message answering service. Visit our website at www.hoddereducation.co.uk.

First published in 2009
by Hodder Education,
an Hachette UK company
Carmelite House, 50 Victoria Embankment,
London EC4Y 0DZ

Impression number   10   9
Year   2016

Typeset in 12/14 pt Palatino Light
Layouts by Fiona Webb
Artwork by Art Construction, Jon Davis, Peter Bull, Steve Smith, Richard Duszczak and Tony Randell
Printed in Dubai

A catalogue record for this title is available from the British Library

ISBN 978 0 340 90736 8
Teacher's Resource Book ISBN 978 0 340 90737 5

Contents

SECTION 6 POWER: DEMOCRACY: HOW DID ORDINARY PEOPLE WIN THE RIGHT TO VOTE?   178

The French Revolution

Winning the vote in Britain

CONCLUSION: WHAT HAVE YOU LEARNED THIS YEAR...?   216

Key features of *SHP History*

Before you start using this book here is a guide to help you get the most out of it.

Enquiry This book is full of enquiry questions to investigate. Some short enquiries will only take one lesson. Other longer ones – the depth studies – may spread over a number of weeks.

Quick History These are overviews that sum up long periods in a short activity.

Banner This introduces the enquiry and sums up what you are going to focus on.

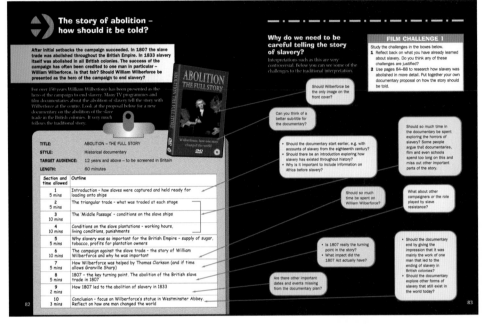

Activities These help you to build your enquiry step by step.

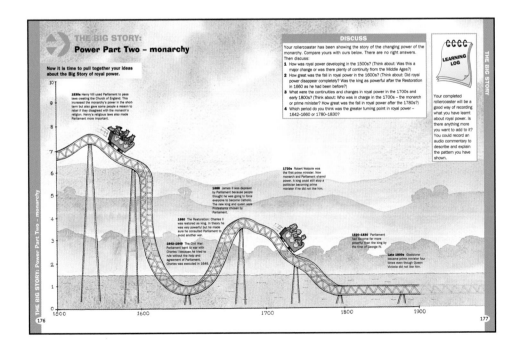

Big Story At the end of each section is a Big Story page that sums up the section and connects it with what has already been studied or with what is going to be studied. In this case, Power Part Two connects with Power Part One in the Year 7 book.

Themes Each section focuses on one thematic story. This section focuses on Power. You will probably have started this theme in Year 7 and will continue it in Year 9.

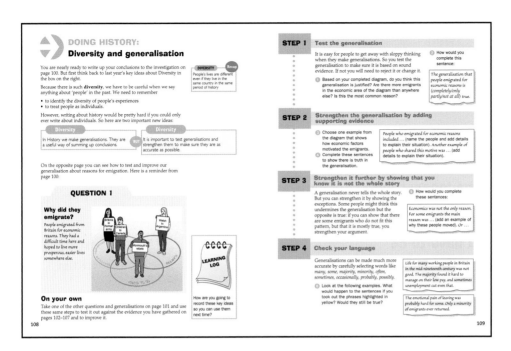

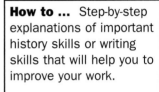

Doing History Each time you meet a new concept or process we recap the key ideas like this. If you want to get better at history this is what you focus on.

How to ... Step-by-step explanations of important history skills or writing skills that will help you to improve your work.

Learning Log This helps you to record what you have learned so you can use it next time.

Dynamic Learning For every activity you will find on-screen activities and ICT-based investigations to help you.

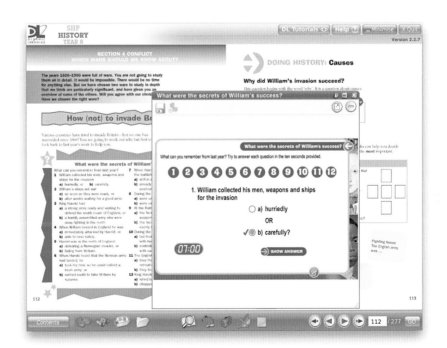

The book with no name

This book contains lots of interesting things for you to do but we are going to start with the biggest task of all. It's not the task that will take you the longest but the one that will show what you understand about the History covered in this book. In fact it's quite simple. All you have to do is – name this book!

Kings and Conquest

Religion and Renaissance

The Age of the Sword

Peasants and Pilgrims

Kings, Plagues and Priests

From Conquest to Freedom

The Middle Ages 1066–1500

The Measly Middle Ages

Medieval Realms

The Early Stuff

Battles and Buboes

From Hastings to Bosworth

STAGE 1 ▶ *Practice*

Think about **last year** when you studied the Middle Ages. Which of the suggested titles on the right do you think would be best for a book about the Middle Ages – and why? Or can you think of a better title? You may need to use the pictures opposite and the timeline below to remind yourself of what happened in the Middle Ages.

AD 1400 onwards
The Renaissance spread new ideas about art, science, geography and medicine – some of them borrowed from the Arab world.

AD 1215
King John agreed – briefly – to Magna Carta. Later kings also quarrelled with the barons but even when the barons got rid of a king they replaced him with another.

AD 650
The Angles gave England its name and many words we still use today.

AD 1066
The Norman Conquest brought castles, Domesday Book, rebellions and misery.

AD 1170
Thomas Becket was murdered in Canterbury Cathedral.

AD 1348
The Black Death arrived in Britain, killing over 40 per cent of the people.

AD 1534
Henry VIII started the Church of England then later closed the monasteries.

AD 500	AD 600	AD 700	AD 800	AD 900	AD 1000	AD 1100	AD 1200	AD 1300	AD 1400	AD 1500	AD 1600

Angles and Saxons invaded Britain after Roman legions left

AD 900
Alfred the Great and his sons united England into one kingdom for the first time since the Romans.

AD 1095
The Crusades began over who controlled Jerusalem. They continued for 400 years.

AD 1290
Edward I started the first regular Parliaments to raise money for his wars. He conquered Wales but could not conquer Scotland.

AD 1450
Gutenberg developed the first printing press in Europe and in 1476 Caxton brought printing to England.

AD 1415
The Battle of Agincourt was the latest stage in the Hundred Years War. The English were trying to conquer France. They won at Agincourt, but lost the war.

AD 1381
The peasants gathered at Smithfield to demand their freedom. They failed, but this Peasants' Revolt frightened lords into setting the villeins free.

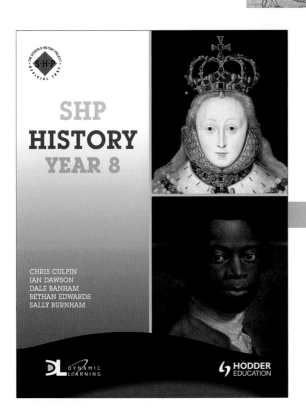

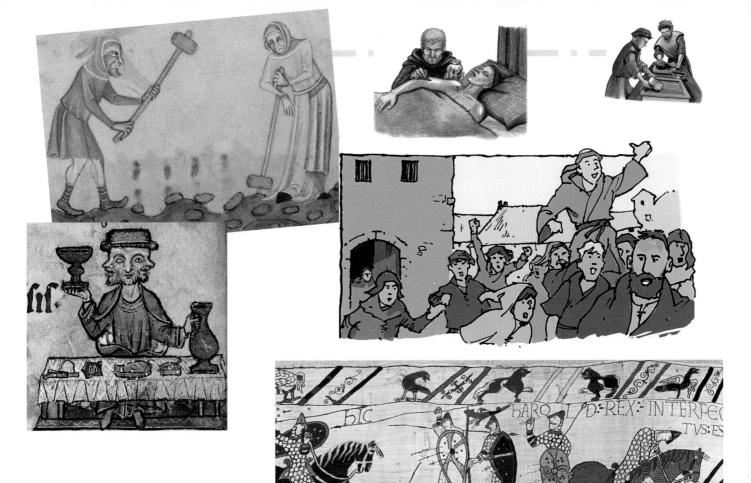

SHP
HISTORY
YEAR 8

CHRIS CULPIN
IAN DAWSON
DALE BANHAM
BETHAN EDWARDS
SALLY BURNHAM

DL DYNAMIC LEARNING

HODDER EDUCATION

STAGE 2 ▶ The Year 8 challenge

Now start thinking of possible titles for this book (left). It covers the years 1500–1900. The Quick History on the following eight pages summarises the period. What seem to be the important things that are happening? What ideas do they give you for a title?

Keep a note of your first ideas for a title and review them later – you will come back to this question at the end of the book.

3

A quick history of Britain 1500–1900

Now for a speedy overview of 400 years of British history. Think about when the greatest changes happened; which period would you most or least like to visit – and why?

A northern town in 1500

This picture is an artist's impression of a small town in 1500. Most people lived in villages, but often travelled a few miles to a town like this one. You can see some villagers selling their spare produce in the market and buying a few extras. Living conditions are quite a bit better than in 1066: most houses have fireplaces and chimneys and some have glass in the windows. In the church Roman Catholic services are held, in Latin. Everyone is free to work and live where they want. Many people own their own land now. The castle in the distance was built in the thirteenth century.

LOOK CLOSELY

1 What kinds of work are people doing?
2 What words would you use to describe their homes?
3 Does this picture suggest that England was a peaceful place?
4 What evidence is there of how people travelled?
5 Who do you think lived in the castle?

The ruler of England at this time was King Henry VII. He was the first Tudor monarch. The Tudors ruled until 1603 and were followed by the Stuarts so we often call the period 1500–1700 the 'Tudor and Stuart Period'.

A northern town in 1750

This picture is an artist's impression of the same small town in 1750. Most English people still lived in villages or small towns like this one. There have been some changes to the town since 1500. One of the most important changes has affected the church, which is now Protestant and services are in English.

LOOK CLOSELY

1 What differences can you spot between this picture and the previous one?
2 Do you think these differences are improvements, or not?
3 What similarities can you see?

The rulers of England from 1714 to 1830 were all called George:

- George I, 1714–1727
- George II (pictured), 1727–1760
- George III, 1760–1820
- George IV, 1820–1830.

Guess what this period is called?

A northern town in 1850

This is an artist's impression of the town in 1850. The Industrial Revolution has changed this place for ever. More than half the population of England now live in towns like this one and work in factories or mines. Houses have been hurriedly built for them. Some people, those who own the factories, are getting rich but life is quite hard for most people. Wages are low for unskilled workers, so their children have to work, and there are dangers from the unfenced machines in the factories and the polluted water they drink. But life must still be better than in the countryside because people are flocking to the town – more and more every year. Only a tiny handful of people – better-off men – have the right to vote: virtually all the people in this picture have no say in how the country is run.

LOOK CLOSELY

1 What differences can you spot between this picture and the previous one?
2 Do you think these differences are improvements, or not?
3 What clues can you see here that tell you about the work people do?
4 What dangers to health can you see?
5 What evidence is there of how people and goods were transported? How does this differ from earlier periods?

The monarch in 1850 was Queen Victoria, who reigned from 1837 to 1901. This period is often called 'The Victorian period' or 'The Industrial period'.

A northern city in 1900

This is an artist's impression of the same town, which has become an industrial city by 1900. Victoria is still queen and Britain is still highly industrial, so the period is still 'The Victorian period' or 'The Industrial period'. It might look like little has changed since 1850, but there are many changes you cannot see. The labels around the picture tell you about them.

LOOK CLOSELY

1 What differences can you spot between this picture and the previous one?

2 What differences in the quality of people's lives can you find?

3 What similarities can you find?

4 Do these pictures show that life has got better, or worse, from 1850 to 1900?

5 Look back over all four pictures.

   a) How have the sounds and smells in this place changed?

   b) Which time would you like to have lived in, and why?

These shops display goods from all over the world, including frozen food.

This man is home on leave from fighting in the Boer War in South Africa.

This woman has recently had a successful operation under anaesthetic.

These children are going to school. All children aged 5 to 11 have to go to school.

This man can vote in elections – he can decide who he wants to run the country.

Behind these houses is the football ground where the city's First Division football team play.

These new houses have been built well, to strict regulations, to make sure they are healthy to live in.

Many more women now work. These women have jobs working in the new telephone exchange.

LIBRARY

11

One aim of the Quick History was to help you develop your sense of chronology and particularly how history fits together. Do you remember this Doing History point from last year:

> **A sense of chronology includes**
>
> … using the correct names for periods of history

This sounds easy but there are two tricky things about the names of periods of history.

A Different people often use several different names for the same period. You can see examples on the timeline. So you have to think clearly.

1 Look at the timeline. How many different ways can you find of completing the sentence 'The defeat of the Spanish Armada took place in …'?

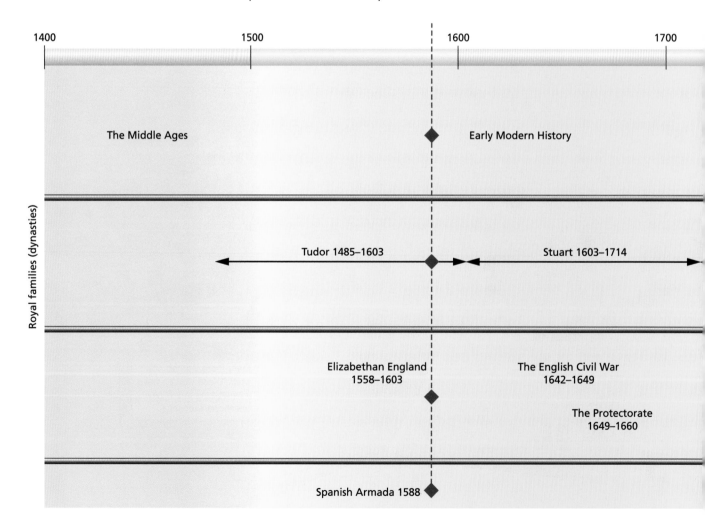

B Some of the names people give to periods of history do not mean anything. For example, have you ever heard a more boring or unhelpful name as 'Early Modern History'? It doesn't tell you anything about the important things happening at that time.

2 The Early Modern period covers 1500–1800, most of the history in this book. Look at the timeline and back to the Quick History. Which important events were happening then that the name 'Early Modern' doesn't tell you about?

3 Some periods are named after kings and queens. Can you think of any advantages or disadvantages of this?

4 Which century was 1649 in – the fifteenth, sixteenth or seventeenth century?

5 Mark on your own copy of this timeline when you think the following happened:
a) the development of printing in Europe
b) the invention of the car
c) the development of railways
d) the invention of the telephone
e) the development of photography.

6 Here are some pairs of people who lived at roughly the same time. Mark on your own copy of this timeline when you think they lived.

a) SIR FRANCIS DRAKE / WILLIAM SHAKESPEARE

b) FLORENCE NIGHTINGALE / W.G. GRACE

c) HORATIO NELSON / DUKE OF WELLINGTON

d) HENRY VIII / ANNE BOLEYN

e) CHARLES I / OLIVER CROMWELL

1800   1900

Modern History

Georgian 1714–1837   Victorian 1837–1901

The Industrial Revolution c.1750–c.1900

e French Revolutionary and Napoleonic wars 1793–1815

THE BIG STORY

Ordinary Life

Looking back

Last year you looked at what life was like in Medieval Britain and how and why it was changing. You found that after the Black Death had killed nearly half the population in Britain and ruined many lives, those who survived found life improved in many ways. By the end of the Middle Ages people lived more comfortably and had more freedom. They had more money for better homes, clothes and food.

What else does last year's Big Story Learning Log tell you about the Middle Ages?

Looking forward

This year you will be studying a period of massive change. The Industrial Revolution changed the way people worked, where they lived, and how they travelled. You will be deciding if life got better or worse for most people. What do you expect to find?

The Big Graph Challenge

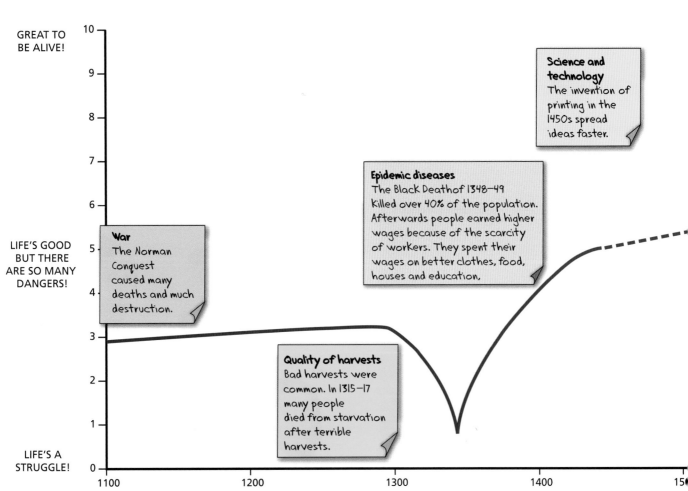

YOUR CHALLENGE

This graph tells the story of ordinary life – how good or bad it was. When the graph shoots downward the quality of people's lives has got worse and life's a struggle. When the line goes up life is getting better and more enjoyable. For example, the Black Death made life much worse for people but in the years afterwards life got a lot better.

Start by comparing this graph with the Quick History on pages 4–11.

Change

Continuity

Progress

Regress

Rapid

Slow

1500–1750

1 Describe in one or two sentences what the graph shows about ordinary life between 1500 and 1750. Use the word box on the left to help you.

2 Look back to pages 4–7. What evidence in those illustrations supports or challenges the shape of this part of the graph?

3 Write down any questions you have about these years.

1750–1900

4 Describe in one or two sentences what the graph shows about ordinary life between 1750 and 1900. Use the word box on the left to help you.

5 Look back to pages 8–11. What evidence in those illustrations supports or challenges the shape of this part of the graph?

6 Write down any questions you have about these years.

Through the rest of this section you will be asked to look again at this graph and revise your ideas.

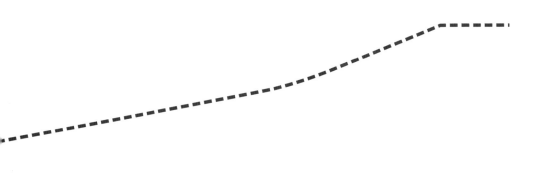

| 1600 | 1700 | 1800 | 1900 |

1500: Which home would you like to live in?

Discover a new kind of evidence – called an inventory – and see what you can infer from it about the lives of three families.

New evidence: Inventories

One of the good things about the period we're now studying is that more evidence is available. From about 1450, a new type of evidence called an **inventory** helps us find out more about people's homes.

When someone died, whether they were rich or poor, a clerk made an inventory (a list) of everything they owned and what it was worth. This was so that the people who benefited from the dead person's will got what was owed to them. The inventories which have survived are very useful to us. Reading an inventory is like looking round someone's house, just as they left it hundreds of years ago.

Here are three families from the sixteenth century, with the type of house they would have lived in. We have also added some details about other aspects of their lives.

Edward and Elizabeth, a merchant family

> We eat white bread, called manchet. We often have meat, such as lamb or beef, and have just had one of those new turkeys, brought over from America. Sometimes we have other imported items, like raisins, or dates. We drink the best beer.

Thomas and Anne, a yeoman family

> We have brown bread, made of a mixture of wheat and barley, called maslin. We eat well, with lots of our own vegetables and eggs as well as butter and cheese, and meat twice a week. We eat fish on Fridays and fast days. We drink ale.

Will and Mary, a husbandman family

> We live on a rough bread made from a mixture of rye, barley and bean flour. We have hard cheese and sometimes some saltfish. If I can poach a rabbit we have meat, but otherwise it's a bit of smoky bacon once a week if we're lucky. Weak ale is all we drink.

Look at these three inventories and use your inference skills. Remember what inference means: digging deep into a source to find out things that it doesn't obviously show or tell you.

1 Which inventory belonged to each family? Explain your choices.

2 What can you infer from the inventories about
   a) the work they did
   b) the way they lit their home
   c) how they kept clean
   d) where they slept?

3 Compare the three inventories. Which of the three had the best standard of living? Support your choice with details from the inventories.

4 What are the big differences between the contents of a house then and the contents of your home? Are these people better off than you, or less well off?

① INVENTORY
Broken counter (workbench?)
Old carpenter's chairs
Bedding
Broken brass pots and various pans
Small cupboard
Malt bundles
Large cart with 4 iron rimmed wheels for hay or corn
Cart body without wheels
Stalks of straw and a bundle of hay
Corn
Horse and mare, cows, calves, sheep, lambs, pigs, etc.

② INVENTORY
Hall
Long table, account board, iron chimney and pot, a dozen cushions, 4 carpets, 2 chairs, 2 forms,
2 tin pots and a basin.
Buttery
11 silver spoons, 2 silver pots, 3 long board cloths, 6 long towels, 6 short towels, three and a half dozen napkins, measuring pot, candlesticks.
Parlour
A chest, 7 pairs of linen sheets, 1 pair of hangings of red satin, covering of tapestry, 4 head sheets, 4 pillowcases, 2 feather beds, 6 coverlets, 4 pairs of blankets, 2 feather pillows, a mattress.
Kitchen
9 doublers (used for brewing), 10 dishes, 5 broken pots, 2 great pans and a little pan, 3 iron spits, etc.

③ INVENTORY
Hall
A table and chair, 3 pewter dishes, candlestick, brass pot, basin, pothooks, a pair of tongs, and a pair of cupboards.
Parlour
2 beds with clothes and hangings, dishes, spoons and other implements.
Outside
Loom, 5 horses and mares with 2 colts, 5 cows and three calves, sheep, iron cart with spare wheels, timber, barley, wheat, hay, corn in the field, hives, 2 ploughs.

Money.

Inventory 1 is complete but these are only a selection of entries from Inventories 2 and 3.

ACTIVITY

This investigation is not just about describing how people's lives changed. You also have to find out *why* they changed.

On pages 16–17 you saw a little of what home life was like for Edward, Elizabeth, Thomas, Anne, Will and Mary in 1500, but how would they and their families have fared in the next 250 years? Working in groups of three, choose one family and follow their fortunes through some of the key events up to 1750. You need a coin to toss and after each throw make notes on what happens. Your teacher can give you a sheet to do this.

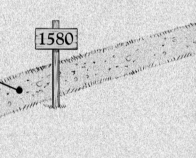

Moment of Fate 2

Religious changes, bad harvests and food prices

Edward and Elizabeth's family
Heads: This family remain firmly Catholic and refuse to attend the Protestant church services that Elizabeth I has ordered. They have to pay heavy fines and sell some land.
Tails: The family remain Catholic but live quietly and avoid trouble. They hear of the chance to trade with new lands, such as America. One of their sons joins an expedition to set up a colony in America.

Thomas and Anne's family
Heads: Harvests are bad several years running – the worst for a century – but because there is so little wheat to make bread they get a really good price for their wheat. They do very well.
Tails: Return of the plague. The eldest son visits London and goes to one of the new theatres to watch a play by William Shakespeare. That is the last they see of him because he catches the plague and dies.

Will and Mary's family
Heads: They send their sons to one of the new grammar schools, where they learn Latin and Greek. The school has plenty of books, thanks to the invention of printing. One son does well, goes to university and becomes a rich lawyer.
Tails: Bad harvests several years running mean they cannot produce enough food to live on. Life is very difficult. Two boys leave home and travel the country but cannot find work anywhere because there are too many other people looking for work. They are arrested as beggars, whipped and ordered to go back home.

The Dissolution of the Monasteries, 1536–1540

Henry VIII made himself Head of the Church in England and closed down all the monasteries.

Edward and Elizabeth's family

Heads: The family has used monasteries as resting places during travels around the country. This is no longer possible. Thieves attack the father, who is a merchant, on his next journey while he is resting at night and steal his horse.

Tails: The family buys up old monastery land. Gets richer.

Thomas and Anne's family

Heads: The father 'borrows' stones from old monastery buildings to improve the house and farm buildings.

Tails: The local monks and their knowledge of herbal cures have helped the family in the past. With the monastery closed two family members die of fever.

Will and Mary's family

Heads: The monastery is no longer there to give food to the family when harvests are bad and food prices go up. Three children die of starvation when there are bad harvests three years running.

Tails: The monks occasionally used to give the family work, so they could buy food. This is no longer available but there is more work available on land taken over by others.

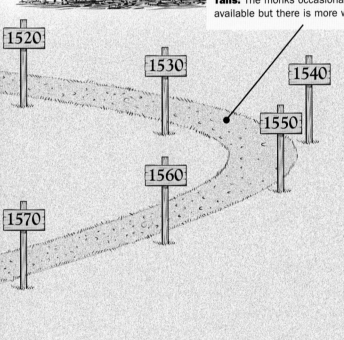

19

Moment of Fate 3

The Civil War, 1642–1649

The Civil War between King Charles I and Parliament saw battles and sieges in many parts of the country.

Edward and Elizabeth's family

Heads: The family still prefer the Catholic religion and they support King Charles who has a Catholic wife. They have to pay high fines to Parliament because they support the King. When the war ends some of the family migrate to America because they do not want to live in England without a king.

Tails: While the men are away fighting, the house and business are looted by Parliament soldiers who steal all the goods in the warehouse. The family are able to start again at the end of the war but everything has changed since the eldest son was killed at the Battle of Naseby.

Thomas and Anne's family

Heads: The family's farmyard is destroyed when a battle takes place on it. Their horses are stolen because horses are a really important piece of military equipment and all crops and animals are taken by hungry soldiers from both sides.

Tails: The family are lucky. Early on in the war, soldiers come to their area but they pay for the food they take. They move on and the family is able to farm and prosper.

Will and Mary's family

Heads: The family supports Parliament. The men join the army and are well-trained in Oliver Cromwell's New Model Army. They are promoted quickly because they are good soldiers and good church-goers who know their Bible well. At the end of the war, they return with money to buy land.

Tails: The family are split by the war as men fight for both sides. They argue most about Parliament banning Christmas and Easter, closing down theatres and wanting to punish people for drinking alcohol and swearing. The survivors never speak to one another again.

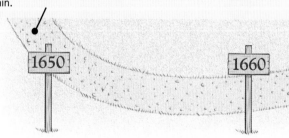

Moment of Fate 4

Plague 1665

This very dangerous disease had the same terrible outcome as the Black Death of 1347–1349, which you studied last year.

Edward and Elizabeth's family

Heads: The family has returned from America now that there is a king again in England but when the plague sweeps through the house it kills most of the family.

Tails: The problems caused by the Civil War force the family to trade more regularly with Europe. This saves many of the family, who are abroad working when plague strikes.

Thomas and Anne's family

Heads: The family give shelter to a family from London who have run away to escape the plague but one of their servants dies of the disease and it spreads through the family. Three of the children die.

Tails: The family survive but have much work to do, as there are fewer people alive to farm the land. They prosper, as food is much in demand.

Will and Mary's family

Heads: The family survive, as the plague doesn't reach their village.

Tails: Despite protecting themselves with herbal remedies, ten members of the family die.

The Flying Shuttle 1733

This invention meant that cloth could be produced much more quickly.

Edward and Elizabeth's family

Heads: Although their business is already a success they really believe in this invention and use their profits to buy machinery and employ weavers to use it. It's easy to get workers for low wages because there are plenty of people wanting work.

Tails: The family are now trading with India as well as America and Europe. They buy tea, coffee, sugar and tobacco overseas and sell it in Britain, making a lot of money. They don't see what the fuss is about this invention and ignore the change.

Thomas and Anne's family

Heads: Their farm is doing very well as they are using new techniques to grow more food and rear larger, healthier animals. This helps them produce more wool from their sheep and make more money from factories using the new machines.

Tails: They are concerned about a cousin who makes his living using the old loom. He is a real craftsman who has always made a good living but now it looks as if the new machines will do his job much faster and cheaper.

Will and Mary's family

Heads: It is hard to find work on local farms because the population is increasing and there are more people than jobs. The family thinks that the Flying Shuttle is the first of many inventions to come and decide to walk to the nearby small town to find work on these new machines.

Tails: The family is worried that new inventions could be developed for farms that will take their jobs away from them. They stay in farming but get paid less.

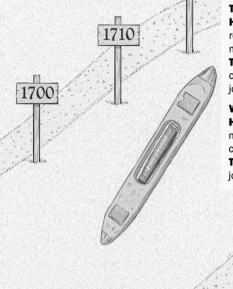

ACTIVITY

1 The word 'progress' means things getting better. Was the period 1500–1750 a period of progress for your family?

2 How much control did your family have over what happened to them?
Give one example to explain your answer.

3 People's lives were affected by the factors below. Make a Post-It note for each factor and jot down at least one example of each factor's impact on the families you have studied (you'll need these on page 23).
- Epidemic diseases
- Government laws
- War
- Science and technology
- Quality of harvests
- Communications and travel

Epidemic diseases

In 1665 plague killed many thousands of people.

The Big Graph Challenge: Part 1, 1500–1750

Monument to the Great Fire of 1666

St Magnus Church, rebuilt after the Fire

Horse-drawn wagon bringing food into London from the countryside

Tall, stone-built houses

Working people carrying goods around the city

Wide street

▲ SOURCE 1 *Fish Street Hill, London. After the Great Fire of 1666, London was rebuilt on a grand scale, as you can see.*

▼ SOURCE 2
Hay harvest in Gloucestershire in the eighteenth century.

Population of England, Wales, Scotland and Ireland

1500	3m
1550	3.5m
1600	5.5m
1650	7m
1700	8m
1750	11m

Percentage of population who lived in urban areas:

1500   5%
1600 10%
1700 15%
1750 20%

The Big Graph Challenge: Part 1, 1500–1750

1 The chart below gives a summary of life in 1500 and life in 1750. On your own copy fill in column 3, describing how much life changed between these dates.

	Life in 1500	Life in 1750	Continuity or change? A little or a lot of change? Is this aspect better or worse?
HOMES	• Houses and clothing: simple, home-made, but improving. • Food: simple, home-grown. • Education: some children went to school for a year or two.	• Houses and clothing: simple, home-made, but improving. • Food: simple, home-grown. • Education: some children went to school for a year or two.	
WORK & TOWNS	• Most people worked on the land. • There were some small towns. • The only big city was London (population 70,000).	• Most people worked on the land. • There were a few more small towns and cities but only • London had got really big (population 657,000).	
LEISURE & TRAVEL	• People had lots of Roman Catholic Church holidays, which were unpaid. • Travel was slow, on foot or horseback.	• Far fewer holidays because Protestant England banned Roman Catholic Church holidays. • Travel was slow, usually on foot, but many main roads had been improved by becoming turnpikes (toll roads). Journey times: London to Manchester 4 days; London to Oxford 2 days.	
HEALTH	• Diseases spread easily and there were few cures. • Surgery was extremely risky. • Life expectancy was about 40.	• Diseases spread easily and there were few cures. • Surgery was extremely risky. • Life expectancy was about 40.	

2 Now look at the shape of this graph for 1500–1750. Does it suggest a lot has changed or not much?

   a) Draw your own version of the graph to show how you think the pattern of ordinary life has changed.

   b) Add your Post-It notes from page 21 to show the factors that affected people's lives.

Not a lot seems to have changed in the big picture of ordinary life in Britain. Yet, as you discovered when you found out about the three families (pages 16–21), there was both change and continuity.

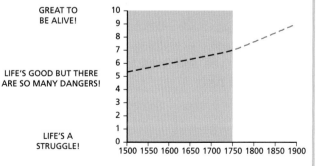

3 'At any one time in History there are usually things that are changing and things that are staying the same.' How do the pictures on page 22 provide evidence to support this idea about change and continuity?

The Industrial Revolution

What did the Industrial Revolution do for us?

ACTIVITY

Look at page 25. These students are trying to explain why the Industrial Revolution happened by linking up the factors.

1 Can you explain why they have linked Inventions to Sources of Power?
2 On your own version of this diagram draw lines to link the factors that are connected. Make sure you can explain each link that you draw.

The Industrial Revolution was the biggest change in British history. The changes that began then still affect us every day. So what was it all about and why did it happen?

Before and after the Industrial Revolution

1750	1900
There were 11 million people in Britain	There were 40 million people in Britain
20% of British people lived in towns	75% of British people lived in towns
Most people were farmers	Most people worked in factories or offices
Most goods were made by hand at home	Most goods were made by machine in factories

This chart shows just the big changes. You are going to find out about many more.

Make your own copy of the above chart and add to it as you work through pages 24–49.

The top five industries

Iron and steel – everything from trains to knives and forks to screws and nails

Pottery – plates, teapots, cups for everyone

Textiles – clothing, bedding, cloth of all kinds

Coal – to drive the machines that made everything

And there was massive growth in the oldest industry of all:
Farming – wheat for bread, vegetables, animals for meat and milk

24

A better life? Manchester in 1850

Manchester was the unofficial capital of the Industrial Revolution, the richest town in England. Tens of thousands of people travelled to Manchester to find work but what did they find when they got there?

Manchester in 1850 was the heart of the Industrial Revolution. Out of this smoking mass of chimneys, factories, warehouses, canals and railways came the cotton, cloth and other goods that made Britain the richest country in the world. Wages in the factories were higher than on farms and jobs were plentiful. But life wasn't easy. You could be laid off at an hour's notice. If there was an economic depression the whole town could face the threat of unemployment. There was no unemployment or sick pay: with no job, you got no wage, and could starve.

ACTIVITY

You are a reporter from a London newspaper, sent to Manchester to collect information for an article on how life is changing in the new industrial cities.

You have three questions you want answers to:

a) Are the homes of the industrial workers good to live in?

b) Are workers fairly treated in the factories?

c) Is life getting better for the people of Manchester?

Use the sources on pages 26–29 to find some evidence to help answer your questions.

1 Which of the sources help you answer each question?

2 Which one other question would you like to ask?

3 Which sources would help you answer your new question?

4 Which three sources will you select to quote or use in your article?
   Explain why you chose them. (The sticky notes below will help you.)

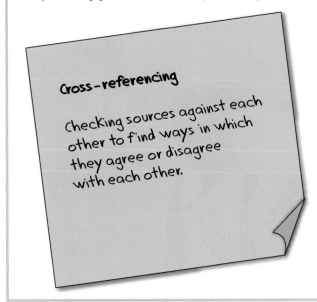

Cross-referencing

Checking sources against each other to find ways in which they agree or disagree with each other.

Selecting evidence

Selecting the sources that are most useful for investigating a particular enquiry or for telling a particular story. Make sure you aren't creating an unbalanced picture – either deliberately or not.

SOURCE 1 *A factory inspector describes what happened to a young girl in a textile mill.*

She was caught by her apron, which wrapped round the shaft. She was whirled round and round and repeatedly forced between the shaft and the carding-machine. Her right leg was found some distance away.

SOURCE 2 *Statistics from the census returns.*

Manchester's population
1750: 18,000
1851: 303,000

Preston's population
1750: 5,000
1851: 70,000

SOURCE 3 *Edwin Chadwick, writing in 1842.*

The annual loss of life from filth and bad ventilation is greater than the loss from death or wounds in any wars in which the country has been engaged in modern times.

▼ **SOURCE 6** *Manchester in 1852.*

SOURCE 4 *Some factory rules, 1840s.*

1. The door of the lodge will be closed ten minutes after the engine starts every morning and no weaver will afterwards be admitted until breakfast time. Any weaver who may be absent during that time shall forfeit 3d per loom.

2. Weavers leaving the room without the consent of the overseer shall forfeit 3d.

9. All shuttles, brushes, oilcans, wheels, windows, etc., if broken shall be paid for by the weaver.

12. If any hand in the mill is seen talking to another, whistling or singing, he shall be fined 6d.

SOURCE 5 *From 'The Factory Bell', a song from the 1830s.*

O happy man, O happy thou,
While toiling at thy spade and plough,
While thou amidst thy pleasures roll,
All at thy labour uncontrolled.
Here at the mills in pressing crowds,
The high-built chimneys puff black clouds,
And all around the slaves do dwell,
Who are called to labour by a bell.

SOURCE 7 *A description of Manchester in 1832 by James Kay-Shuttleworth, a Manchester doctor and public health reformer.*

Most of those districts lived in by the millworkers are newly built. The houses are ill-drained, often unventilated, unprovided with toilets. As a result, the streets, which are narrow, become the resting-place of mud, refuse and disgusting rubbish. In Parliament Street, there is one toilet for 380 people.

SOURCE 8 *A description of some cottages in Preston, Lancashire, in 1844 from a report by the Health in Towns Association.*

Between the backyards of the two rows of cottages, a cesspool extends the whole length of the street which receives the contents of the privies (toilets) and drains. The contents of the cesspool belong to the landlord and are taken out twice a year.

▼ **SOURCE 9** Dinner Hour, *a painting by Eyre Crowe, 1874.*

SOURCE 10 *A description of part of Manchester by Friedrich Engels, a German businessman and revolutionary who visited Manchester in the 1840s.*

Heaps of refuse, offal and sickening filth are everywhere ... A horde of ragged women and children swarm about the streets and they are just as filthy as the pigs which wallow happily on the heaps of garbage and the pools of filth ... On average 20 people live in each of these little houses of two rooms, an attic and a cellar. One privy is shared by about 120 people.

New evidence: Census and government information

From this period much new evidence is available. One example of this is the census. Since 1801, once every ten years the government has counted all the people in the country. Gradually the census has got more and more detailed. Source 11 is a page from the 1851 census. As you can see, it tells us the name of everyone living in every house, their relation to the 'Head of the family', gender, age and job. So the Wards, the Lowes and the Emerys were real people of the British Industrial Revolution.

1. Take one household each: who are the members of that household? How old are they? Who works? And what work do they do?
2. Which seems to be the most important industry in this part of Manchester? Who is the oldest worker? Who is the youngest?
3. What else would you like to know about these people?
4. How could this census information help you with your enquiry into life in Manchester in the Industrial Revolution?

New evidence: Newspapers

Daily newspapers began in the eighteenth century – the first was probably the *Norwich Post*, started in 1701. Governments did not want the lower classes reading about politics, which they were not allowed to take part in, so newspapers were taxed, putting the price up to about 6 pence – equivalent to over £5 today. However, it was the custom for people to gather in a pub or coffee house to hear someone read the whole paper to friends and neighbours. The tax was abolished in 1855, bringing the price down to 1 penny – about 35p today. The British were huge readers of newspapers: by 1850 *The Times* had a circulation of over 50,000 a day. There were seven daily papers in London, and at least one or two in most provincial cities. Apart from politics and foreign news, crime was widely reported, often in far more lurid detail than the law allows today. Sport coverage was good: from the 1880s 'football specials' came out with full reports of all the day's matches by about 7pm.

As you can imagine, old newspapers provide masses of interesting evidence for historians.

▼ SOURCE 11 *An extract from the 1851 census for Salford.*

No of House-holder's residence	Name of Street, Place, or Road, and Name or No. of House	Name and Surname of each Person who abode in the house, on the Night of the 30th March, 1851	Relation to Head of Family	Condition	Age of		Rank, Profession or Occupation
					Males	Females	
104	Bradburn's Buildings	Samuel Ward	Head	Married	45		Silk Weaver
	//	Charlotte Ward	Wife	Married		45	Silk Winder
	//	Sarah Ward	Daughter	Married		21	Silk Winder
	//	Benjamin Ward	Son		14		Silk Piecer
	//	Martha Ward	Daughter			12	Pin Winder
	//	Alice Ward	Daughter			4	At Home
105	Bradburn's Buildings	James Lowe	Head	Married	26		Log Wood Grinder
	//	Ellen Lowe	Wife	Married		31	Silk Winder
	//	Thomas Lowe	Son		2		
	//	Martha Parkinson	Lodger			16	Spool Winder – Cotton
	//	Joseph Lowe	Son		Under 1 month		
	//	Elizabeth Sant	Sister in Law	Married		28	Winder – silk
106	Ainsworth's Mill	Samuel Emery	Head	Married	27		Mechanic
	//	Charlotte Emery	Wife	Married		29	Power Loom Weaver – Silk
	//	Elizabeth A. Emery	Daughter			2	

29

The Big Graph Challenge: Part 2, 1750–1850

Now for the second part of the Big Graph Challenge. Can you improve on our graph?

▼ SOURCE 1 *Water-powered tilt-hammer, 1772.*

ACTIVITY 1

New technology was changing many aspects of life but had not yet changed everything. What can you learn from these two pictures about changes and continuities in the years 1750 to 1850?

Think about: How much iron is being made? How many people are working? Where are they working?

▼ SOURCE 2 *Steam hammer, 1840.*

ACTIVITY 2

1 Below is a summary of life in 1750 and life in 1850. On your own copy fill in column 3, describing how much life changed in this period.

	Life in 1750	Life in 1850	Continuity or change? A little or a lot of change? Is this aspect better or worse?
HOMES	• Houses and clothing: simple, home-made, but improving. • Food: simple, home-grown. • Education: some children went to school for a year or two.	• Homes in rural areas still simple. Homes in industrial cities often overcrowded, poorly built, with no running water, drains or toilets. Cheap cotton clothing available.	
WORK & TOWNS	• Most people worked on the land. • There were a few more small towns and cities but only London had got really big (population 657,000).	• Lots of people still worked on the land, but even more now worked in factories, mines and on the railways. • As well as London (now with 2.5m people) many large new cities had grown up in the industrial north and Scotland: Liverpool 376,000; Glasgow 345,000; Manchester 303,000; Birmingham 233,000; Leeds 172,000.	
LEISURE & TRAVEL	• Far fewer holidays because Protestant England banned Roman Catholic Church holidays. • Travel was slow, usually on foot, but many main roads had been improved by becoming turnpikes (toll roads). Journey times: London to Manchester 4 days; London to Oxford 2 days.	• Still very few holidays – most people worked a six-day week, with only Christmas off. • Railways connected every major town and city in Britain, making much faster travel available for all. Journey times: London to Manchester 6 hours; London to Oxford 2 hours.	
HEALTH	• Diseases spread easily and there were few cures. • Surgery was extremely risky. • Life expectancy was about 40.	• The unhealthy living conditions in the new industrial cities meant that serious diseases spread easily. There was vaccination against smallpox, but few other cures. • Surgery was extremely risky and life expectancy in some cities was only 35.	

2 Now look at the section of the graph for 1750–1850. Draw your own version of the graph to show how you think the pattern of ordinary life has changed.

3 What do you think will happen next? Will your graph go up or down?

GREAT TO BE ALIVE!

LIFE'S GOOD BUT THERE ARE SO MANY DANGERS!

LIFE'S A STRUGGLE!

10
9
8
7
6
5
4
3
2
1
0
1500 1550 1600 1650 1700 1750 1800 1850 1900

What a difference a train makes!

ACTIVITY

1 **a)** Read Sources 1 and 2. How did these people's reactions to the railways differ?

   b) What else can you learn from these sources?

2 **a)** What can you infer from Sources 3–7 about how railways changed people's lives?

   b) What does not seem to have been changed by the railways?

3 Are there any differences between what you can learn from the written sources and what you learn from photographs?

SOURCE 1 *Fanny Kemble, a famous actress, wrote this after riding on one of the first trains, around 1830.*

It is a magical machine with its flying white breath and rhythmical, unvarying pace. I stood up and with my bonnet off drank the air before me. When I closed my eyes this sensation of flying was quite delightful.

SOURCE 2 *Thomas Creevey, an MP, wrote this after travelling by train at over 36 km/hour.*

It is really flying and it is impossible to divest yourself of the notion of instant death to all. I am extremely glad indeed to have seen this miracle and to have travelled in it but I am quite satisfied with my first railway journey [being] my last.

▼ **SOURCE 3** *By 1900 the small island of Britain had 18,600 miles of railway, all built since the 1830s. This is the North Yorkshire line being built in the 1880s.*

▼ **SOURCE 4**   *A painting of Paddington Station in 1862.*

▼ **SOURCE 5**   *Teams like Bolton played in the new Football League (which began in 1888) involving teams from all over England.*

▼ **SOURCE 6**   *Paignton beach in Devon, photographed at the turn of the century. Men and women were allowed to bathe together in the sea for the first time in 1896. Before then they had to use separate beaches. It took until 1900 for Torquay to allow mixed bathing, and then only after October.*

SOURCE 7   *From* The Railway News *in 1864.*

Every morning we see the supplies for the great London markets unloaded from the night trains: fish, meat and food, fresh milk, butter and pork, apples, cabbages and cucumber.

Inside a Victorian photograph album

In 1839 there was a new invention: photography. Soon photographers were busy recording every aspect of life around them. Only the rich and famous had their portraits painted, but anyone could have their photo taken. You have already seen photos on the previous pages but now you are going to concentrate on photographs as evidence. What can you discover about everyday life for the Victorians from the pages of our photo album?

ACTIVITY

Work in pairs and choose three photographs from pages 34–39. For each photograph note
a) what it shows (look at all the details carefully)
b) any evidence of the way life was changing after 1850 (look back to the chart on page 31 for a reminder of life in 1850)
c) any evidence of things that were not changing or were getting worse.

▲ **SOURCE 1** *More people worked as servants in Victorian Britain than in any other job. Wages ranged from £45 a year for a butler to £11 a year for a 13-year-old housemaid.*

▶ **SOURCE 2** *Britain was the biggest trading nation in the world, with half the world's tonnage of ships. Many of the seamen, like these men, were Asians, called 'lascars'. There was a big lascar community, as well as Africans and Caribbeans, in east London and other port cities like Cardiff, Bristol, Liverpool and Glasgow.*

COLLIERY LASSES

▲ SOURCE 3 Women did all kinds of jobs in heavy industry, like these five at an ironworks in South Wales in 1865.

▼ SOURCE 4 By no means everyone worked in heavy industry. These skilled tailors in London, stitching men's suits by hand, worked very long hours to earn a living.

▼ SOURCE 5 Workers were given Saturday afternoons off and had a little spare money to spend. Many watched professional football and other sports. The attendance at this 1897 FA Cup Final was over 65,000.

▶ SOURCE 6 The bicycle, another late-Victorian invention, gave ordinary people freedom to travel. By 1900 it was Britain's fastest growing sport. Women were particularly liberated by joining cycling clubs, although many were shouted at because some people thought that cycling was unladylike.

▲ **SOURCE 7** *Man selling rabbits, 1885.*

▲ **SOURCE 8** *A fancy-wear dealer selling ornaments from his barrow, 1877. In the past, most people bought what they needed from markets, street-traders like this man, or hawkers. These still existed in Victorian Britain but were increasingly used only by the poor.*

▼ **SOURCE 9** *A nineteenth-century butchers, with a large display of meat for sale.*

▶ **SOURCE 10** *John Lewis store, about 1900. The great new shopping idea of the nineteenth century was the department store. They were fitted out in great luxury, with carpets, displays of goods in glass cases, uniformed doormen, elegant shop assistants, and chairs to sit down on while you were served. Standard sizes of clothes and shoes were introduced, along with a new invention, the tape measure. Department stores often had several floors, with lifts – another new invention.*

Seaside holidays

Workers were given occasional days off thanks to the 1871 Bank Holidays Act. There were plenty of northern seaside towns that were eager to welcome visitors, such as Blackpool and Scarborough. In the south, Torquay and Paignton became popular. Torquay had been visited for some time by wealthier visitors and several members of royalty had stayed there. But soon the town and nearby Paignton began to attract day-trippers. In 1897, 3000 day-trippers arrived from Rochdale in Lancashire on six special trains. A booklet 'Paignton and its Attractions', published in 1885, said:

'At the Pier Pavilion an ever-varying programme of music is provided. Everything here is quiet and refined ... I have seen the lads and lasses at Cleethorpes, Bridlington and Scarborough hugging each other cheek by jowl as they whirled frantically but here they dance with due regard to etiquette ...'

▲ **SOURCE 11** *Princess Gardens in Torquay opened in 1894.*

▲ **SOURCE 12** *Hancock's Fair at Teignmouth, 1910.*

▲ SOURCE 13 *London traffic jam, c.1900.*

▼ SOURCE 14 *Children helping with the harvest, Oxfordshire, c.1900.*

► SOURCE 15 *An operation using anaesthetic in the early twentieth century.*

◄ SOURCE 16 *The interior of a working-class home in Whitechapel, east London, c. 1900.*

🔍 New evidence: Photos

The first cameras were invented about 1840 and were difficult to use. The exposure time was several minutes, so only landscapes or static poses of people could be taken. The glass plates had to be developed as soon as they were exposed, and the whole equipment, camera and portable darkroom with chemicals weighed up to 300 kg. Progress was rapid, however. By the 1860s 10-second exposures were common and film could be used, so the photographer could travel much more easily. Photographs from the last part of the nineteenth century show the skill of these early photographers.

DOING HISTORY: Evidence

We cannot get away from sources and evidence in History. Sources give us the evidence to answer questions so this final activity asks you to use sources to create a display about the Industrial Revolution. At the same time you will practise some of the important skills involved in using sources.

SOURCES — Recap

Sources are the clues that tell us about the past.

Sources are anything from the past.

ACTIVITY

The Evidence Challenge: 'What did the Industrial Revolution do for us?'

- Working on your own or in a small group, you will create a display based on at least three pictures from the period 1500–1900. They could be pictures from this section (pages 14–49) or historical pictures of your local area.
- Your display will help to answer the question 'What did the Industrial Revolution do for us?' When you put all your class displays together this will create a really good overall answer.
- On the display explain what exactly we can learn from the pictures about how life changed between 1500 and 1900. Really show off your evidence skills using the ideas on the rest of this page to help you.
- You could create your display using paper and posters or on a computer, for example using PowerPoint.

Using sources well means

… finding out things from a source that it doesn't obviously tell you. This is called inference.

Inference Language Box

From (detail) we can infer that …
This (detail) suggests that …
We can tell from (detail) that …
It doesn't say so, but … must be so, because (detail) …

This can be fun. It's real detective work, thinking hard and making discoveries. ***In your display*** explain what each picture tells you and what you can **infer** from it. For example:

One of the main things the Industrial Revolution brought us was big cities. This picture gives us an idea of what those towns were like.

This tells me that Manchester in 1850 was a big city with lots of factories, although there was pleasant countryside nearby.

From the amount of chimneys and smoke we can infer that it would also be a dirty, smelly and polluted place although the artist has made it look so nice.

Using sources well means

… checking sources against each other to find ways in which they agree or disagree with each other before deciding on your answer. This is called cross-referencing.

You shouldn't just believe one version of a story or photograph. Even photographs can be cropped to show only part of a story. **In your display** try to cross-reference at least two pictures, explaining how you can use them together to prove a point. For example you could compare Source 1 on page 34 with Source 3 on page 35.

> One important effect of the Industrial Revolution was a change in the jobs people did.
> If you compare these two pictures you can get a much better idea of the range of jobs done by women in the period of the Industrial Revolution. Not only were they involved in housework or as servants but also they worked in heavy industry as labourers.

Using sources well means

… selecting the sources that are most useful for investigating a particular enquiry or for telling a particular story.

Always think carefully about your selection. Don't pick sources at random: pick them to make a point. For example, a picture could tell us:

a) what life was like **before** the Industrial Revolution
b) how life was changing **at a particular stage** of the Industrial Revolution
c) **why** life was changing at a particular time.

In your display explain why you have selected each source.

The Industrial Revolution did not change everything for everybody.
I chose this picture because it shows that even in 1900 life in the countryside at harvest time was much as it would have been centuries earlier, working by hand, with children helping out with the harvest.

Selection Language Box
This picture is important because …
The value of this picture is …
I chose these two pictures to show different …
The evidence from this source is convincing because …
This source is important because it is the only one that …

Cross-reference Language Box
If you compare these two pictures …
This picture shows … and you can see the same … in …
These pictures show different effects of …
This source supports the evidence of Source … by …
This source goes even further than Source … in showing … or suggesting …
This source says … but Source … doesn't mention it.
This source contradicts the evidence of Source … that …

LEARNING LOG

You will go on to do more work on sources later in Key Stage 3 History.
How will you record what you have added this year about inference, cross-referencing and selecting sources?

Now we come to a summary of what life was like in Victorian Britain and you will complete the last stage of the Big Graph Challenge.

1850

Hello. My name is Chris Culpin, and I have written most of the words in this book.

Below is my summary of life in 1850, and opposite is my summary of life in 1900.

1850 was certainly a time when there were lots of exciting changes taking place, but:

- Life was filled with hard **work**. Many people still worked in the fields, doing much the same work as they always had.

- At least they were outside in the fresh air, but **wages** were low. In the stuffy factories, where 12-hour shifts were common, they worked a six-day week.

- There were far fewer **holidays** than in the Middle Ages, when Church Holy Days provided lots of breaks from the monotony. Even children didn't escape: they didn't have to go to school but from the age of three or four onwards they worked in mills, with dangerous machines, or deep in coalmines.

- Wages in industry, although better than in farming, were unreliable. If the boss closed the factory, the workers starved. Skilled workers were being put out of business by machines.

- The biggest change was that more than half the **population** now lived in cities.

- Life in the city was freer than life in the village, where the squire and the vicar were always keeping watch. But with no money, no spare time and no political rights, the freedom meant little more than the freedom to get drunk occasionally.

- Industrial cities were very unhealthy. The crowded **living conditions**, no fresh water and no sewage disposal meant that diseases like tuberculosis, typhoid, diphtheria and pneumonia were common. Cholera was the worst: in 1848–1849, 50,000 people died of cholera in just a few weeks. Life expectancy in the cities was still under 40, no better than it had been in 1500.

- Most people lived on the edge of **poverty**. Illness or unemployment could bring disaster as income was reduced to zero and there was no help. And if someone avoided these problems, old age was harsh, with no one willing to give them a job or a pension.

You are only talking about poor people.

What about leisure and travel? There were early railways, improved roads and stagecoaches.

The population was increasing faster than ever before.

There were still no anaesthetics or antiseptics.

ACTIVITY

Use the information on these two pages to draw your own version of the Big Graph for 1850–1900 to show how ordinary life changed. Compare what I say about 1850 with what I say about 1900. But remember, this is also my interpretation of these changes. You need to make up your own mind whether life got better, got worse, or stayed the same. You don't have to agree with me. And I haven't included all the possible topics. Look at the speech bubbles around the outside. They remind you of other things that you could take into account.

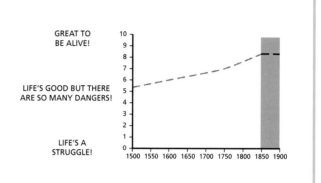

GREAT TO BE ALIVE!

LIFE'S GOOD BUT THERE ARE SO MANY DANGERS!

LIFE'S A STRUGGLE!

1900

I sometimes wish I could have been alive in 1900, when city life was booming and each year showed some new improvement.

- Better **houses** were being built. Builders had to meet strict government regulations concerning drainage, water and ventilation.

- Factories were making good, cheap **clothes**.

- From 1870 every child had to go to **school** from the age of 5 until they were 10.

- **Working hours** were still long by the standards of today, but not as bad as 1850.

- You only worked half a day on Saturday, so could go and watch professional football or cricket, or walk in the park, or dig your allotment. In the 1871 Bank Holiday Act the government introduced **national holidays** with pay on Boxing Day, Easter Monday, Whit Monday and on the first Monday in August.

- There were 18,000 miles of **railways** in Britain. You could travel quite cheaply by train to the seaside, or to visit friends.

- Scientists now understood the causes of disease. Sewers and fresh water were introduced to the industrial cities. There was **vaccination** against some killer diseases and anaesthetics and antiseptics made safe surgery possible. Life expectancy was rising: 49 for women, 45 for men.

What about the use of gas lighting in the streets, or the first cars?

You could send a message by telegraph.

Farmers still used horses.

Music halls were popular entertainment.

There were still no old age pensions, no unemployment or sick pay.

The poor were cared for by Dr Barnardo's Homes and the Salvation Army or sent to workhouses.

Why was ordinary life changing so much?

Your Big Graph has probably got lots of ups and downs on it for the years 1750–1900. Now it's time to explain why the graph leaps up and down so much – by putting all these balls into the right baskets.

WAR

GOVERNMENTS MAKING LAWS

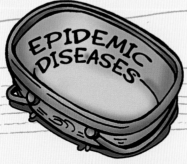

EPIDEMIC DISEASES

① In the late 1800s professional sports teams could travel the country to take part in leagues.

② Outbreaks of cholera in 1831 and 1848 led to demands for improvements in conditions in towns.

③ The development of anaesthetics and antiseptics (to stop infection) helped many more people survive surgery.

④ Michael Faraday's experiments helped him to understand electricity. Later in the 1800s Thomas Edison developed the light bulb and other electrical equipment.

⑤ In the late 1800s local councils opened libraries and public baths that were free to use.

⑥ In the 1840s a series of terrible potato harvests in Ireland led to famine. Many thousands died and more people emigrated to Britain and America.

⑦ The long wars against France (1793–1815) created many jobs because of the need for iron, weapons, cloth for uniforms and shipbuilding.

⑧ Railways brought fresh food into towns and led to workers living in suburbs and commuting into towns for work.

⑨ In the 1840s the government passed laws stopping women and children working long hours in many industries.

⑩ Isambard Kingdom Brunel, the great engineer, built railway lines, bridges and the first iron ships.

1 Each basket represents a factor that explains why life was changing. Each ball is a specific example of a factor. Your task is to put all the balls into the correct baskets.

2 Look at the number of balls in each basket and then look at the graph for 1100–1500 on page 14. How have the factors affecting ordinary life changed since the Middle Ages?

3 Add brief sticky notes to your graph to show how the factors explain the rises and falls in your graph after 1750.

Epidemic diseases

In 1848–1849, 50,000 people died of cholera in just a few weeks.

11 In the 1850s Louis Pasteur proved that bacteria cause disease. After this it was possible to develop vaccinations against common killer diseases.

12 During the early 1800s poor harvests led to food prices being very high. There were widespread protests and fear of rebellion.

COMMUNICATION AND TRAVEL

13 Gas was used for factory lighting in 1802, then for street lighting. By the late 1800s gas was supplied to most houses for lighting, heating and cooking.

14 By 1900 many migrants had arrived in Britain. Some famous businesses, such as Marks and Spencer, were started by migrants.

15 In the late 1800s governments passed laws to improve housing and force councils to provide clean water and sewers.

16 By 1900 refrigerated ships were bringing frozen meat and other foods from Australia and other distant countries.

17 The British navy was very powerful, helping to build up Britain's empire and protecting trade with other countries.

18 In the late 1700s, men like Josiah Wedgwood (pottery) and Richard Arkwright (textiles) built the first factories. Every worker had a specialist task, making production faster and cheaper.

19 In the late 1700s James Watt worked out how to improve steam engines so they could provide much more power and so drive much larger machines – from machines making clothes to railway engines.

NEW IDEAS IN SCIENCE AND TECHNOLOGY

QUALITY OF HARVEST

THE BIG STORY: Ordinary Life Part Three

Our Big Story of Ordinary Life has reached 1900. Here it is in one big diagram – it probably looks very similar to yours. Can you use the Doing History points about Change and Continuity to pick out the most important events and why they happened?

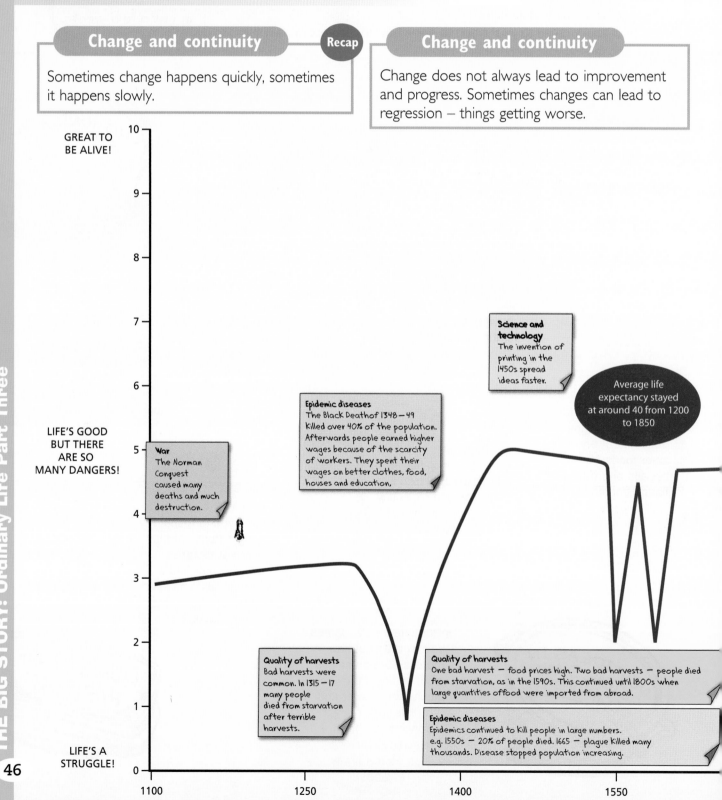

Change and continuity Recap

Sometimes change happens quickly, sometimes it happens slowly.

Change and continuity

Change does not always lead to improvement and progress. Sometimes changes can lead to regression – things getting worse.

Use these questions to sum up the Big Story so far. You could answer them by
a) writing paragraphs
b) creating a PowerPoint presentation or MovieMaker commentary
c) recording a podcast.

LEARNING LOG

1 Which two periods do you think saw the fastest improvements in ordinary life? Explain what happened in each period.
2 Choose two occasions when ordinary life got worse. Explain how quickly these changes happened.
3 Look at the factors that have affected people's lives. Are there any differences between the factors affecting life before 1750 and those after 1750?
4 What most surprises or interests you about this graph? Explain your reasons.

You will do more work on Change and Continuity later in the book in Section 5. How will you record what you have learned about Change and Continuity so you can remember it and use it later?

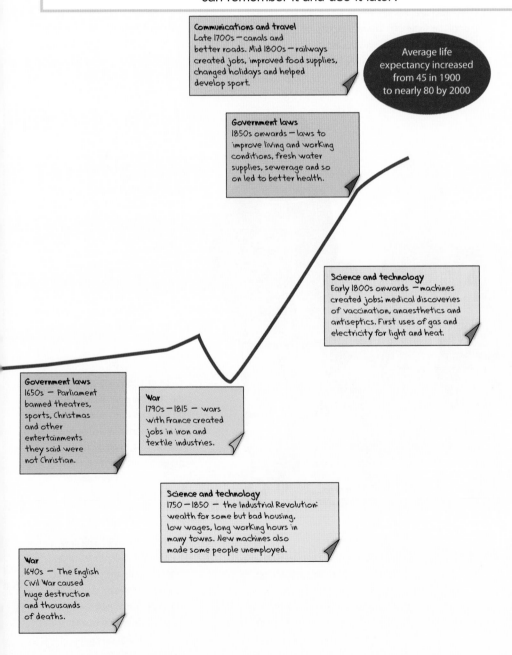

Communications and travel
Late 1700s — canals and better roads. Mid 1800s — railways created jobs, improved food supplies, changed holidays and helped develop sport.

Average life expectancy increased from 45 in 1900 to nearly 80 by 2000

Government laws
1850s onwards — laws to improve living and working conditions, fresh water supplies, sewerage and so on led to better health.

Science and technology
Early 1800s onwards — machines created jobs; medical discoveries of vaccination, anaesthetics and antiseptics. First uses of gas and electricity for light and heat.

Government laws
1650s — Parliament banned theatres, sports, Christmas and other entertainments they said were not Christian.

War
1790s — 1815 — wars with France created jobs in iron and textile industries.

Science and technology
1750 — 1850 — the Industrial Revolution: wealth for some but bad housing, low wages, long working hours in many towns. New machines also made some people unemployed.

War
1640s — The English Civil War caused huge destruction and thousands of deaths.

1700   1850   2000

What were they thinking about ... ordinary life?

You have been investigating changes in people's homes, work and health. But what did people think about their day to day lives? Ideas and beliefs changed hugely between 1500 and 1900 and those changes still affect our lives today. Your task is to fill in the ideas of our Victorian family.

The Redmans, a Tudor family from the 1520s

A
Only another week and we can get the harvest in. I pray to God that heavy rain doesn't ruin the crops. Another bad harvest like last year and people will go hungry this winter. Some may even starve to death if the harvest's really bad.

B
It will be back-breaking work bringing the harvest in but there'll soon be time off. There's plenty of Saints' days coming up. One day we'll walk into the nearby town to go to the fair.

C
Thanks be to God for the good monks at the monastery. We can depend on the monks to give us help if there is no work or food prices are high.

D
My cousin died of plague last week. Our priest says God sends plague to punish us for wickedness. Not even Goody Agnes' remedies help us. Our lives are in God's hands.

E
I would like to learn to read but that's only for boys. Father says the priest will teach my brothers for a few hours a week. Mother will teach me how to run the house, make clothes and all the other womanly tasks.

F
I'll be in the fields at sun up tomorrow – or about then. So long as I get the job done nobody minds exactly when I start. It makes for long days in summer but shorter ones in winter.

G
There are rumours that people in other countries are quarrelling over religion. At least in England we all belong to the Catholic Church. Everyone must follow the same beliefs in this country.

H
Life is very different from grandfather's time. People have more chance to get on if they work hard. Most still work in farming but there are new jobs like printing. Maybe that would be something for one of the boys?

I
We've worked hard and earned more money this year. Maybe we'll be able to buy some pewter plates and perhaps some wall-hangings to make our house more cosy.

Each family has nine thoughts. They cover nine topics so there is a pair of thoughts (one Tudor, one Victorian) for each topic.

1 a) Read the Victorian thoughts 1–3. Find the Tudor thought that is the partner of each Victorian thought.

   b) What differences can you see in each pair of thoughts?

   c) What similarities can you see in each pair of thoughts?

2 a) Look at the other six Tudor thoughts. Take each one in turn. Decide what topic it is about and on your own copy of the diagram write the Victorian thought that would fit this topic.

   b) For each Victorian thought explain what has changed and what has stayed the same.

3 Which **two** changes in thoughts do you think were the most significant? Explain the reasons for your choices.

The Coopers, a Victorian family from the 1890s

1
On Sunday mornings we go our separate ways. I am a Catholic but my husband belongs to the Church of England. My neighbours go to the Methodist church. Religion is very important to us but thank heavens we don't burn people any more for being different.

2
My brother tells me it's been another good harvest in his village. Here in the town we just go to the market to buy food. Even if our harvest's not so good there's plenty of food imported from our great empire, even frozen meat from Australia.

3
I can hear the factory bell. Everyone in the factory has to be there on time; the same time almost every day of the year. If they're late they lose a day's wages.

4

5

6

7

8

9

An extraordinary meeting

The Date:
8 November 1519

The Place:
A causeway across a lake somewhere in what is now Mexico.

▶ SOURCE 1
The meeting of Moctezuma and Cortes, painted by an unknown European artist in the nineteenth century.

ACTIVITY

This picture was painted in the nineteenth century by an unknown artist at a time when most people in Europe believed that empires were a good thing.

1 What can you tell from the picture and the text about the buildings, the weapons and the wealth of the Spaniards and the Aztecs?

2 What details in the picture tell you that the artist thought empires were a good thing?

3 Now that you know something about empires what do you think will happen next?

The Leader of the Aztecs:
Moctezuma. He was the ruler of 8 million people in the Aztec Empire, covering all of what is now southern Mexico. He lived in a beautiful palace in Tenochtitlan, which had gardens, aviaries and a zoo. He ate off gold plates and drank from gold goblets, waited on by dozens of barefoot servants, who were ordered never to look at him on pain of death.

As Moctezuma came along the causeway, he was protected from the sun by a canopy of brilliant green feathers and his noblemen put down their cloaks for him to walk on. He was wearing turquoise robes, the only person allowed to wear this colour.

The Meeting:
Both leaders bowed and exchanged gifts. Cortes gave Moctezuma a necklace of glass beads. Moctezuma gave Cortes a necklace of gold.

The People:
Coming from a city called Tenochtitlan, built on the lake, were Americans: several hundred Aztecs. Most were richly dressed, in brightly coloured cotton clothes with flashing feather headdresses in their black, glistening hair and wearing large gold ornaments.

Coming from the edge of the lake were Europeans: about 400 Spaniards. They were a rough-looking lot. Some were wearing armour; some were carrying guns; most carried long swords; a few were mounted on horses.

The Leader of the Spanish:
Cortes. He was an educated man, with a degree from a Spanish university, but had got bored with life in Spain. For some twenty years he had been living in the new Spanish colonies in the Caribbean.

THE BIG STORY

Empire

Looking back
Last year you looked at the Roman Empire and you asked the following questions:

- Why did the Romans want an empire?
- How did they get it and control it?
- What impact did the empire have?

What answers can you remember? How good was your Learning Log?

Looking forward
This year you will be studying two more European empires: the Spanish Empire and the British Empire. The stories are huge. Huge in space – virtually the whole world was involved. Huge in time – they start in about 1500 and they are not really over yet. You will be using the same three questions.

- Why did they want an empire?
- How did they get it and control it?
- What impact did each empire have?

A quick history of European empires

Spain and Portugal were the first European countries to build empires across the seas, but by 1900 several other European nations had done the same. Who were they, what happened to them and when?

What is a colony?

When the European countries were building their empires they did it by planting colonies overseas. This means they sent settlers to live there, farm there, do business there. The people who planted such colonies were called colonists. Wherever the colony was – in Africa, Australia or the Americas – it was run as if it was part of 'the mother country' and almost all the wealth went back there rather than enriching the colony itself.

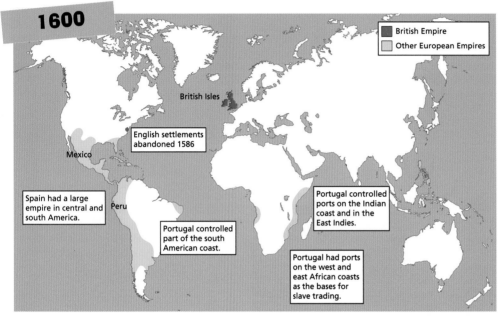

1600

British Empire
Other European Empires

British Isles

English settlements abandoned 1586

Mexico

Spain had a large empire in central and south America.

Peru

Portugal controlled part of the south American coast.

Portugal controlled ports on the Indian coast and in the East Indies.

Portugal had ports on the west and east African coasts as the bases for slave trading.

▲ SOURCE 1 *Empires in 1600. Spain and Portugal were the first European countries to develop overseas empires. Spain mined silver in south America and Portugal traded spices in India and the East Indies. England and other European countries soon joined the slave trade.*

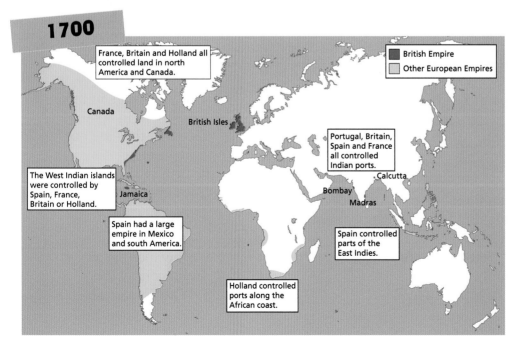

1700

France, Britain and Holland all controlled land in north America and Canada.

British Empire
Other European Empires

Canada

British Isles

Portugal, Britain, Spain and France all controlled Indian ports.

Calcutta

The West Indian islands were controlled by Spain, France, Britain or Holland.

Jamaica

Bombay

Madras

Spain had a large empire in Mexico and south America.

Spain controlled parts of the East Indies.

Holland controlled ports along the African coast.

◀ SOURCE 2 *Empires by 1700. England, France and Holland all built empires. Wars over trade and empire became common. England captured Jamaica from Spain and New York from Holland.*

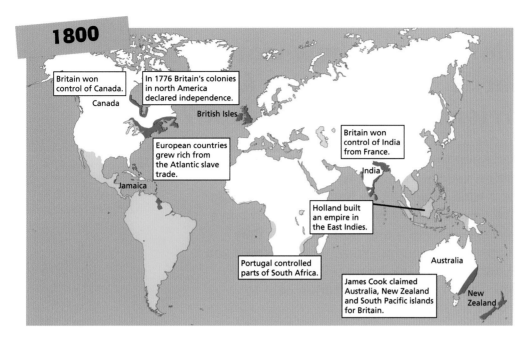

1800

Britain won control of Canada.

In 1776 Britain's colonies in north America declared independence.

Canada

British Isles

European countries grew rich from the Atlantic slave trade.

Britain won control of India from France.

India

Jamaica

Holland built an empire in the East Indies.

Portugal controlled parts of South Africa.

Australia

James Cook claimed Australia, New Zealand and South Pacific islands for Britain.

New Zealand

▲ SOURCE 3 *Empires by 1800. France and Britain developed the largest empires. They fought the Seven Years War (1756–1763, see page 132), the first worldwide war, in Europe, America and India. Britain won but in 1776 Britain's American colonies, the heart of the British Empire, declared themselves independent.*

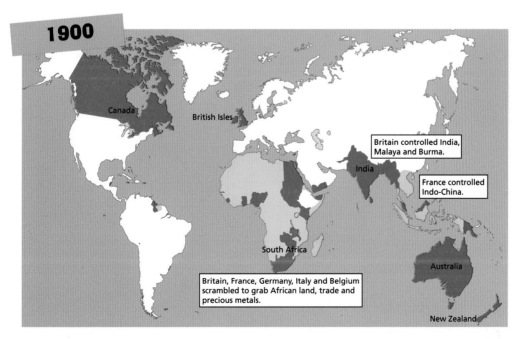

1900

Canada

British Isles

Britain controlled India, Malaya and Burma.

India

France controlled Indo-China.

South Africa

Britain, France, Germany, Italy and Belgium scrambled to grab African land, trade and precious metals.

Australia

New Zealand

▲ SOURCE 4 *Empires by early 1900s. Africa was the main focus for empire building in the late 1800s. Within 50 years nearly all of Africa was taken over by European countries. This was a time of intense rivalry, with the possibility of war often flaring up.*

DISCUSS

1 Which areas of the world were colonised first? Which later?

2 Take each map in turn. Write a single 'headline' sentence to sum up how empires were changing. You can use words or phrases from the information boxes.

3 How many reasons can you suggest to explain why so many European countries wanted empires? Think back to the work you did on the Roman Empire.

Travellers' tales: how would the Spaniards describe the Aztecs to their friends back in Europe?

After that first meeting between the Spanish and the Aztecs (see pages 50–51) Moctezuma invited the Spanish to live in the royal palace in Tenochtitlan for a while. Perhaps he hoped these strange foreigners would be so overwhelmed they would go away and leave him alone. The Spaniards were amazed – and horrified – as they found out more about Moctezuma's empire. What stories would you tell about the Aztecs to your friends back home – if you were a sixteenth-century Spaniard – and how do these stories help to explain why the Spanish built up their empire?

ACTIVITY

Over the next five pages you are going to write or record a description of the Aztecs. Part of this description will explain why the Spanish wanted to conquer the Aztecs. You are going to try to see the Aztecs not with your 21st-century eyes, but as one of Cortes' men saw them. You are going to look through a conquistador-window. Conquistador is the Spanish for conqueror.

The conquistadors were mostly interested in three things. This was their window.

WAR

The conquistador says:

My country, Spain, is the most powerful country in Europe and now we want an empire in America. We can build ships that can sail across oceans. We have swords that are light but lethal: long, sharp, pointed and made of Toledo steel, the best in Europe. We have portable handguns. We know how to fight!

▶ SOURCE 1
Aztec warriors.

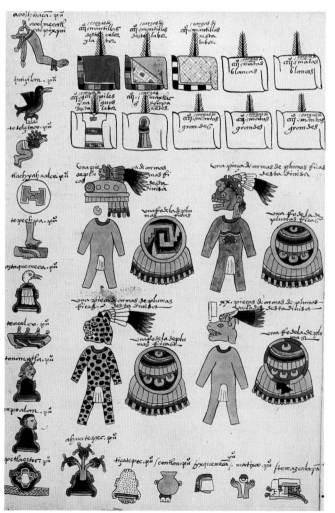

▲ SOURCE 2 *Aztec account book, showing goods to be traded.*

Cortes and Moctezuma got on well and had many long discussions. Cortes learned that the Aztecs were almost continuously at war with neighbouring peoples, and were always victorious, which was why their empire was so large. The Aztec soldiers carried spears made of sharp stones set in a wooden frame. They wore cotton armour, so thick it could stop an arrow. They ran into a battle screaming and whistling, wearing fierce warpaint and eagle headdresses. The elite squad dressed as jaguars. They danced and chanted as they fought. This was all designed to terrify the enemy.

ACTIVITY

What are you going to tell people at home about Aztec fighting? How does what you see encourage you to try to conquer the Aztecs?

For example:

I think these Aztec swords might wound us but they won't kill us. We have the best swords in Europe. The Aztecs try to be frightening but …

WEALTH

The conquistador says:

My family is poor, but I want to get rich, go home and live the life of a nobleman! I want gold!

The conquistadors marvelled at Tenochtitlan, the Aztec capital city on the lake. One of them wrote:

'Towers, temples, stone and limestone buildings, all built on the water. Our soldiers thought they were dreaming. We were seeing then what we had never seen or heard or dreamt of.'

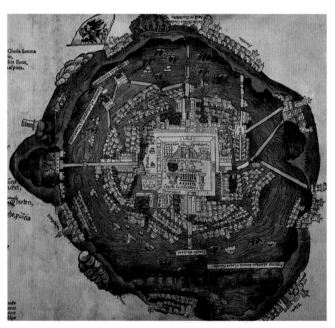

It is thought that the city was at least 8 km square and housed at least 200,000 people. It was divided into different areas for each trade – woodworkers, fishermen, mosaic makers and so on. Each area had its leader, its own temple, priests and school. Everyone paid taxes, collected by government officials. Poorer people paid by working – for example, the streets of the city were cleaned each day by 1000 sweepers.

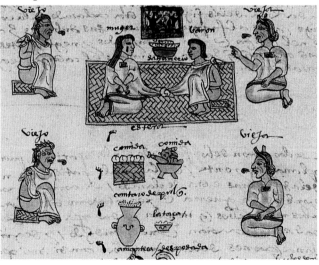

▲ SOURCE 3 *Aztec marriage ceremony: the knotted cloak symbolises the bond of marriage.*

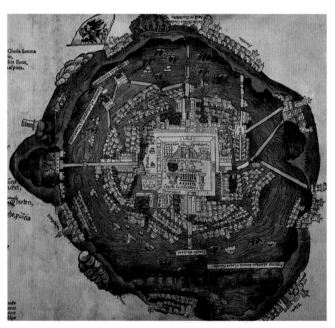

▲ SOURCE 4 *Map of Tenochtitlan.*

Everyone had their place in society, from nobles at the top, then priests, warriors, merchants, farmers and craftsmen, to slaves at the bottom. You could tell instantly what layer of Aztec society someone belonged to from the colour, quality or pattern of their clothing.

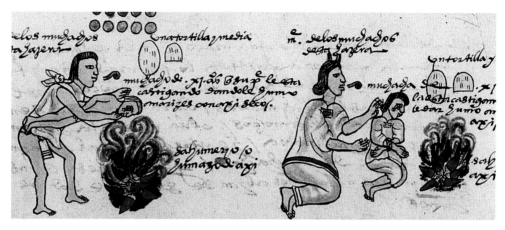

One of the conquistadors wrote: 'We saw on the lake a multitude of ships, some of which were loaded with goods … And when we had looked at it all, we turned to the great market square and the large crowd buying and selling there. The noise and the sound of the voices could be heard more than a mile away. Among us there were soldiers who had been in many parts of the world, in Constantinople, in the whole of Italy, in Rome, but they said they had never seen a market so well organised and so orderly, so large and so crowded.'

There was no democracy and the law was enforced with harsh punishments, such as strangling or burning. However, the city was quiet and orderly and people were respectful.

▲ SOURCE 6 *Aztec market.*

At the market many things on sale were new to sixteenth-century Europeans: tomatoes, squashes, chilli peppers, sweet potatoes, avocados, peanuts, popcorn, chewing gum, chocolate, tobacco, turkeys. Then there were exotic goods sent as tributes from all over the Aztec conquests: jaguar skins, hummingbird feathers, shells, precious stones – and lots of gold objects of all kinds. All these goods were carried on boats on canals into the city and then on the backs of porters: the Aztecs had no pack-animals.

◀ SOURCE 7
This gold lip ornament was worn through a hole in the wearer's lip as a sign of nobility.

RELIGION

There were temples everywhere in Tenochtitlan, with the two largest in the central square. They were stepped pyramids with flat tops. The pyramids were stained white with lime and were dazzling in the sun. On the top of the pyramids Aztec priests carried out human sacrifices.

Prisoners of war – men, women and children – were brought to the temple and led in procession up to the top. Each one was held down on the altar, then a priest cut out the victim's heart and raised it, still beating and hot, to the sun. The heart was then placed in a holy cup, while the priests coated the walls and statues, and themselves, with blood. The body was thrown back down the steps. The skull was removed and placed on a skull-rack, while the soldier who had captured the prisoner ate the rest of the body.

▶ SOURCE 8
Aztec picture of the bodies of sacrificial victims being thrown down the steps.

The conquistador says:

The Christian religion is the truth, the only truth!

58

The Aztecs believed that without this gift of human blood, the sun would not rise the next day and the world would end. Cortes calculated that 20,000 human sacrifices had taken place that year. The smell of blood was everywhere and the priests' hair was so caked with blood that it could not be combed.

This religion was nothing like the conquistadors' Christianity. They were used to Christian services with prayers, hymns and the story of Christ dying to save other people. The idea of human sacrifices to the gods was not part of their religion at all. As Christians, the conquistadors also believed that Christianity was the one true religion and all other religions were wrong. People worshipping other gods should be taught about the Christian god.

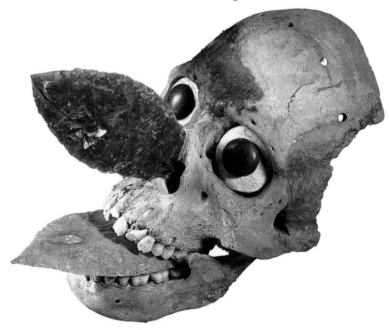

◀ **SOURCE 9** *Aztec skull with stone knives at nose and mouth. These were the knives used to cut out the victim's heart at the top of the temple.*

◀ **SOURCE 10** *This is a flint sacrificial knife with a carved wooden handle.*

ACTIVITY

What are you going to tell people at home about Aztec religion? How does what you can see encourage you to try to conquer the Aztecs?

How did the Spanish defeat of the Aztecs change Spain and Mexico?

The mighty Aztecs were fierce warriors who had built their empire by conquering other people. Yet in only a few months they were totally overthrown by a handful of Spaniards. What effects did this conquest have?

Defeat

Within a year Moctezuma was dead. When Cortes decided to leave Tenochtitlan, he had to fight his way out. He succeeded, but lost many men in battle or sacrificed on the Aztec altars. A year later, in 1521, he returned with a much bigger army, with more guns and horses. He also had support from the peoples the Aztecs had crushed. Though outnumbered by 300,000 Aztec warriors the Spaniards captured Tenochtitlan after 85 days of tough fighting. The Aztec Empire was over.

Colonisation

After defeating the Aztecs the Spanish soon conquered Mexico. Five hundred of Cortes' followers became the major landowners in Mexico. Another conquistador, Francisco Pizarro, conquered the Inca empire in Peru. By 1600, Spain ruled the empire you can see in Source 1.

From 1535 onwards Spain ruled Mexico for its own benefit.

- Spanish nobles and soldiers seized the land for themselves. They passed a law that owning a piece of land included owning the people living on it. Native Americans virtually became slaves.
- The Church sent priests to build churches and convert the Native Americans to Christianity.
- Spanish became the official language.
- A strict hierarchy was imposed with Spanish at the top and Native Americans at the bottom (see Source 3).

▶ SOURCE 1 *The Spanish Empire in North and South America.*

■ Spanish Empire
□ Portuguese Empire

Destruction

With their civilisation smashed and their religion banned, the native people were demoralised. Millions died from European diseases that were new to their world such as measles, smallpox or pneumonia. By 1568, less than 50 years after Cortes first landed, the native population of Mexico was only 10 per cent of what it had been when Cortes arrived. With so many Native Americans dying, or unwilling to work for their conquerors, the Spanish needed labourers to work the land so enslaved Africans were brought over to South America.

Although Mexico became independent in 1821, big landowners, of Spanish origin, ran the country and the poor were kept down. In 1910 a revolution began to bring democracy and progress to the country. The old rulers were thrown out, and a long civil war began. Mexicans are only now coming to value their past, helped by artists such as Diego Rivera (see Source 2).

Wealth

Meanwhile back in Spain the impact of colonisation was felt in a very different way. The empire in the Americas brought massive wealth.

Each year 500 ships arrived in Seville from the Americas laden with gold, silver and other precious goods. Seville flourished. There were 300 fountains, 40 monasteries and 30 churches. The streets were widened. The results of the flood of silver and gold can still be seen in the buildings of the city, notably the cathedral – in its day the largest in the world, 100 metres wide and 150 metres long.

▲ **SOURCE 2** *Part of a mural by Diego Rivera* America Prehispanica *which means 'America before the Spanish'.*

▶ **SOURCE 3** *Mexican society had a strict hierarchy, based on racial origin, in which colour played a large part – except for the 'Indians' at the bottom of the heap, the lighter your skin, the higher your status.*

Spaniards born in Spain

Creoles – Spaniards born in Mexico

Freed blacks – people descended from enslaved Africans who had bought or been given their freedom

Slaves – black Africans who had been captured in Africa and brought to Mexico as slaves

Mestizos – the children of mixed race – descendants of partnerships between the races

Native Americans ('Indians') – the descendants of the Aztecs and other Native Americans living in Mexico before the Europeans arrived

ACTIVITY

1 Look carefully at Source 2. It is packed full of references to ancient Aztec life. Make a list of all the features you can see.
2 Rivera wanted to give Native Americans back a sense of pride in their origins. How did he try to do this in the mural painting?

Winners and losers

3 List the winners and the losers from the Spanish conquest of the Americas.
4 In what ways did the winners show that they had won?
5 In what ways did the losers show that they had lost?

The big questions about Empire

Here are the three questions you are asking about Empire:
• Why did they want it?
• How did they get it?
• How did it affect people?

Why did the Spanish conquistadors want an empire?

Last year you found out why the Romans wanted an empire. Here are the causes, explained by Paulinus, the Roman governor of Britain.

① Which of Paulinus' reasons also apply to Cortes?
② What extra bubbles can you add for Cortes?

The taxes we collect from conquered countries make us rich.

We get food from our empire so Romans don't go hungry.

We get slaves so rich Romans don't have to work.

Our conquests bring fame and fortune to generals like me.

We bring a higher standard of living to conquered peoples, with better housing and luxuries to buy.

We bring them peace – our army keeps law and order.

How did the conquistadors take over and control their empire?

Here is what the Romans did:

How did the Romans take over and control their empire?

• Powerful army
• By helping some people to do well out of Roman rule
•
•
•

③ Which of these points also apply to the Spanish conquistadors?
④ What extra points do you need to add for the Spanish empire builders?

How did the Spanish Empire affect people?

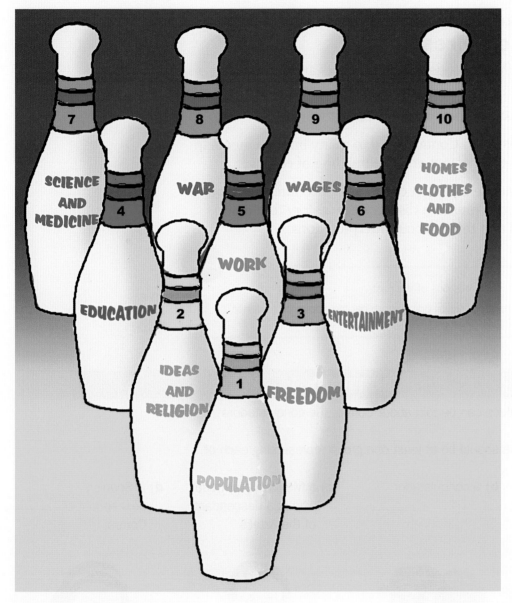

Do you remember these skittles from last year? If an event has a lot of impact it knocks the skittle over completely. If it has little impact it simply makes it totter a bit but it is still left standing.

On pages 60–61 you studied the impact of the Spanish Empire on Mexico.

5 Which skittles did the Spanish conquest knock over completely?

6 Were any skittles left standing?

Comparing empires

The Romans and the Spanish both built empires but were these empires exactly the same?

7 You have two minutes. Look back at your answers to the questions on these two pages.
  a) Jot down a quick list of similarities between the two empires.
  b) Jot down a quick list of differences.

8 Were these two empires
  a) exactly the same?
  b) mostly the same?
  c) mostly different?
  d) totally different?
  What evidence supports your answer?

DOING HISTORY: Interpretations

Why do we have to be careful when telling the stories of empires?

History contains two different kinds of things – facts and interpretations. Here are two examples:

Fact – 'The battle of Hastings took place on 14 October 1066.'

Interpretation – 'The Norman Conquest led to many improvements in England, such as better government and the building of castles.'

An interpretation is someone's version of the past. The interpretation could be in a book, a film, a museum display or in a story told aloud.

Last year you learned two things about interpretations:

INTERPRETATIONS   **Recap**

People tell different stories or interpretations of the past.

People create different interpretations by including some people, topics or evidence and leaving out or down-playing others.

ACTIVITY 1

What different interpretations can be told about Cortes, the conquistadors and the Aztecs?

1 Split into groups. There should be at least one group representing each of the following:

    a) an Aztec warrior   **b)** a conquistador   **c)** a Mexican alive today who is a descendant of the Aztecs   **d)** a Spanish descendant of Cortes.

2 Working as a group, decide how you will tell the story of Cortes and the end of the Aztec Empire. Your teacher will tell you how much preparation time you have. Remember this is your interpretation of what happened. When you are ready your group has one minute to tell your story.

3 When you have heard all the stories, stay in your role. Describe how you felt about the stories told by other groups. What are the best words to describe your feelings?

New ideas about interpretations

The activity opposite will have taught you two more things about interpretations.

> **Interpretations**
>
> … are determined by the attitudes and beliefs of the person creating the interpretation.

For example, a person's interpretation of an event could be influenced by their nationality or their political beliefs.

> **Interpretations**
>
> … can be controversial.

For example, people may not like an interpretation and may disagree with it strongly. Interpretations can even create problems and arguments between people.

And next ... the British Empire

You are now going to investigate the British Empire.

ACTIVITY 2

We have to be careful telling the story of the British Empire. Discuss why you think it is a difficult story to tell. (Think about what you have learned so far about empires and about interpretations.)

The British Empire

 ## Why were the British so worried about their empire in the 1780s?

While Spain was building its empire, England started its first colony in America in the 1580s – at Roanoke. It was a disaster – all the colonists died or left. However, by the 1660s there were British colonies and trading posts across the world and in the eighteenth century, the British Empire grew, bringing wealth back into Britain. But for many people this growth came with some big problems to worry about …

The Thirteen Colonies
British people first colonised America in the early 1600s. Many settled there hoping to grow wealthy from farming and trade. Others migrated to America so that they had the freedom to follow their religion in their own way instead of in the way the government at home ordered. Some lands were seized from the Native Americans by force and others were captured in wars with France and Spain.

Canada
The British colonies of Nova Scotia and Newfoundland began in the early seventeenth century but there was constant rivalry between Britain and France for control. In 1759 General James Wolfe captured the town of Quebec from the French. Quebec had been the centre of French power in Canada but from then on Canada was part of the British, not the French, empire.

British industry
All this trade and exploitation of other countries was funding massive expansion of industry back in Britain.

America
In 1776 the Thirteen Colonies declared independence from Britain and then, led by George Washington, won the War of American Independence against British troops. They became the 'United States of America' in 1783.

West Africa
Britain controlled coastal bases for trade, especially in slaves.

West Indies
Previously Spanish, these colonies, mostly islands, were gradually seized by Britain in the seventeenth and eighteenth centuries. Plantations were set up to grow sugar for sale in Britain and made large profits for British landowners on the islands who used enslaved Africans as their workers.

ACTIVITY

Look at the map below.

1 a) What methods had the British used to build up their empire?

b) Was this similar to or different from the ways the Romans and Spanish had built their empires?

2 Why did Britons feel that their empire was so important to them?

3 Which important part of the world did Britain lose from its empire in the 1770s?

4 Why do you think many people thought that Britain would be less powerful and wealthy in the future?

5 One of the best-selling books in the 1780s was Edward Gibbon's *The Decline and Fall of the Roman Empire*. Why do you think so many people read it?

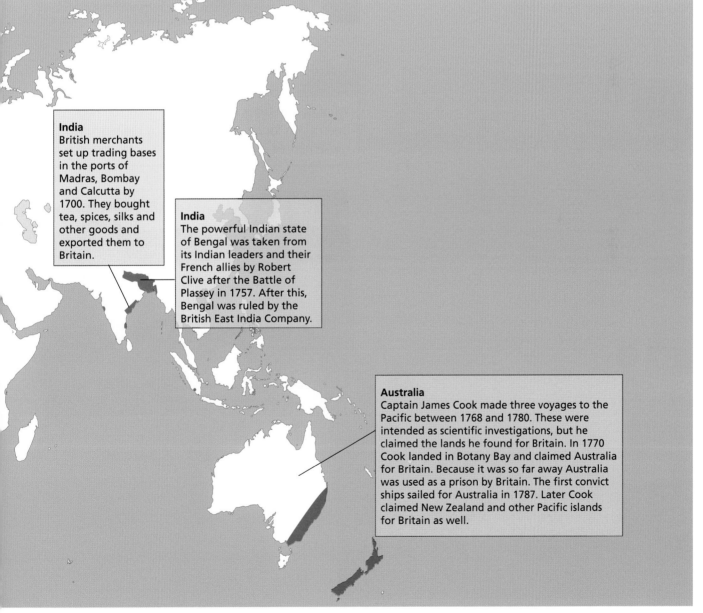

India
British merchants set up trading bases in the ports of Madras, Bombay and Calcutta by 1700. They bought tea, spices, silks and other goods and exported them to Britain.

India
The powerful Indian state of Bengal was taken from its Indian leaders and their French allies by Robert Clive after the Battle of Plassey in 1757. After this, Bengal was ruled by the British East India Company.

Australia
Captain James Cook made three voyages to the Pacific between 1768 and 1780. These were intended as scientific investigations, but he claimed the lands he found for Britain. In 1770 Cook landed in Botany Bay and claimed Australia for Britain. Because it was so far away Australia was used as a prison by Britain. The first convict ships sailed for Australia in 1787. Later Cook claimed New Zealand and other Pacific islands for Britain as well.

What made Thomas Clarkson so angry?

Thomas Clarkson was born in Wisbech, Cambridgeshire, in 1760. His father was the local headmaster and died when Thomas was just six years old. Thomas worked hard at school and won a place at Cambridge University. His aim was to join the Church but in 1785 he entered an essay writing competition that would change his life completely. As Thomas carried out the research for his essay he became increasingly shocked and angry about what he was reading.

It was but one gloomy subject from morning to night. In the daytime I was uneasy. In the night I had little rest. I sometimes never closed my eyelids for grief.

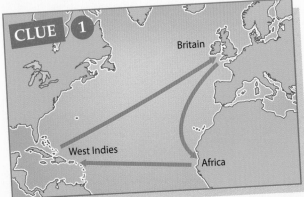

CLUE 1

Britain

West Indies

Africa

ACTIVITY

What do you think was the topic Clarkson had been given for his essay? And why did his research make him so angry? Use Clues 1–7 to work it out.

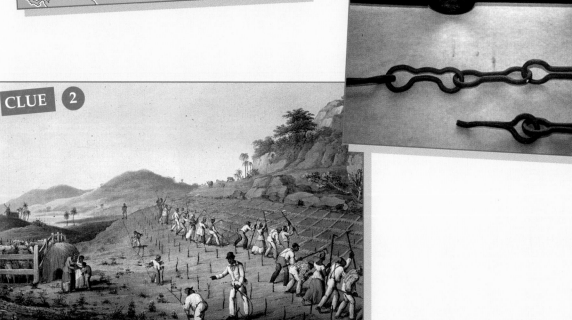

CLUE 3

CLUE 2

CLUE 4

CLUE 5

CLUE 6

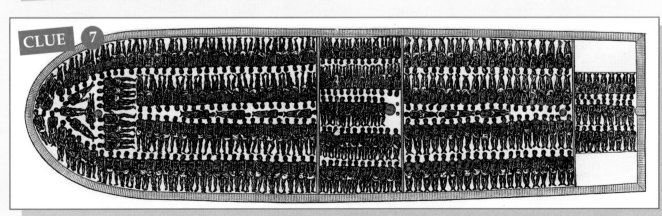

CLUE 7

69

How did the slave trade work?

The topic for Clarkson's essay was of course slavery. Clarkson, like many people in Britain, knew very little about the slave trade. Slavery had existed throughout history, in many times and in most places. The ancient Greeks, the Romans and the Aztecs all had slaves.

However, as he researched his essay, Clarkson began to learn more about the British slave trade. On these pages you can catch up with Clarkson and find out why the slave trade is often called 'the triangular trade'.

What did Thomas Clarkson's research tell him?

Look at Clarkson's map on page 70 opposite and his notes below. Tell the story of the slave trade by making notes on your own copy of the map.

a) Note what kinds of cargoes were taken on Voyage 1.

b) Now repeat this for Voyages 2 and 3.

c) The transporting of slaves was often called 'the Middle Passage'. Why?

d) Look at the clues on pages 68–69. Match each one to a stage in the triangular trade.

What was being carried round the 'Triangle'?

Sugar

The British love sugar! All classes use it in their tea and their puddings. Demand is growing: 5.5 kilos per person per year by 1800. Sugar cane grows well on plantations in the West Indian islands. Plantations owners are growing very rich from the sugar trade.

Clarkson's notes

The journey home

For the third leg of the 'triangular trade' the ships are loaded with tobacco from the southern USA or sugar from the West Indies. These fetch good prices in Britain.

Tobacco

Europeans picked up the tobacco-smoking habit from America. The British grow it on plantations in their colony of Virginia. Huge amounts are being imported into Britain now.

Profit

The ships never sail empty – at each stage the traders make a good profit on their cargo.

Plantation system

Growing and harvesting sugar and tobacco needs lots of workers. With their plantations increasingly successful, owners are buying enslaved Africans brought across the Atlantic by slave traders.

The outward journey

Ships from Britain sail to West Africa loaded with all manner of British-made industrial goods such as cloth, metal, guns and alcohol. These goods are traded for African men, women and children who have been kidnapped by slave traders or bought from African chiefs. The enslaved Africans are held in dungeons in coastal forts until a ship is ready to take them to America.

Britain's role

An estimated 80,000 Africans are taken across the Atlantic as slaves every year. Britain dominates this trade. 40,000 of those men, women and children are carried in British ships.

The Middle Passage

The slave-ships carry the enslaved Africans in chains and densely packed below decks. As soon as they arrive in the West Indies they are sold at slave auctions to plantation owners.

The Clarkson Challenge

Thomas Clarkson became so angry about the slave trade that he decided to devote the rest of his life to trying to stop it. He faced a real challenge as the slave trade had many supporters. Join Clarkson on a tour round the country and investigate the slave trade in greater detail. Your challenge is to collect evidence as you travel with Thomas Clarkson that will persuade people living at the time that the slave trade should be abolished.

As Clarkson continued his research into the slave trade he met Quakers and others who were already campaigning for an end to slavery. Clarkson saw that a national campaign was needed. In May 1787 the Society for Effecting the Abolition of the Slave Trade was formed.

However, Clarkson and his fellow campaigners faced an almost impossible task. Nearly everyone in Britain accepted slavery as completely normal. Furthermore, lots of people were doing extremely well from the slave trade.

Clarkson's responsibilities

1 Researcher/investigator Clarkson had to collect as much evidence as possible to prove how badly slaves were treated. His research could then be used by William Wilberforce, another anti-slave trade campaigner (see pages 82–84), in Parliament to raise awareness of the horrors of the slave trade.

2 Witnesses Clarkson had to find witnesses who would appear before Parliament. Very few people were willing to give evidence against the slave trade as they thought it might put their own lives in danger.

3 Persuasive writer and speaker Clarkson had to prepare speeches and pamphlets to persuade people in different parts of the country to support the campaign. Remember, few people in Britain knew about the horrors of the slave trade. Clarkson believed that human beings would always care about the sufferings of others if they knew enough about them. Therefore the way to persuade people to take action against slavery was to expose the truth.

4 Pressure groups Clarkson had to encourage people to form local pressure groups to:
• raise money for the cause
• send petitions to the government demanding that they take action against the slave trade
• organise boycotts of goods such as sugar that had been produced by slaves.

Why was Clarkson's challenge so difficult?

Clarkson and his fellow anti-slavery campaigners faced a major challenge. Nearly everyone in Britain, from farm workers to bishops, accepted slavery as completely normal. The sugar plantations in the West Indies were part of Britain's most valuable colonies. By the end of the eighteenth century £4 million came into Britain from its West Indian plantations, compared with £1 million from the colonies it controlled in the rest of the world. In Britain, those who had made much of their wealth from colonial trade built fine mansions and invested in new factories and industries.

The profits from the slave trade gave a massive boost to the economy of towns and cities throughout the country and provided jobs for tens of thousands of seamen, merchants and shipbuilders.

CLARKSON CHALLENGE 1

1 Look at the groups of people who **benefited** from the slave trade. What words would you use to describe the task faced by Clarkson and others who wanted to abolish slavery?

2 Which of these groups of people do you think was most to **blame** for the slave trade? Place the eight groups of people on a ripple diagram like this. Place those groups most to blame at the centre.

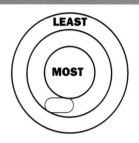

Who benefited from slavery?

African war lords who captured other Africans and sold them as slaves to Europeans. As demand for slaves went up so did their profits.

British slave ship owners who made up to 50 per cent profit on some voyages. Large sums of money were made by ship owners who never left England.

British slave traders who bought and sold the slaves.

Plantation owners who used slaves to grow their crops. They paid no wages, of course, and provided only basic food and simple huts for the slaves to live in.

Ordinary people for whom the slave trade provided many jobs back in Britain: half of Liverpool's sailors were involved in the slave trade; there were the jobs in factories making things to sell in Africa or the plantations. Slave labour made goods such as sugar cheaper for people living in Britain.

The factory owners in Britain who had a market for their goods. For example, half of all the textiles produced in Manchester were exported to Africa and the West Indies.

Bankers who did well by lending money to slave traders.

Capitalists who benefited from the profits of slavery being invested in factories and mines. It helped finance the British Industrial Revolution.

Know your enemy!

Clarkson's work was difficult, even dangerous. Powerful people made lots of money from the slave trade and were out to stop him. Clarkson needed to know the arguments they used to defend the slave trade before he could challenge them.

CLARKSON CHALLENGE 2

Look at Clarkson's notes on the right to see the arguments put forward to defend the slave trade.

1 Match each of the sources below to an argument put forward to defend the slave trade.
2 How could Clarkson challenge the reliability of Sources 1–3?
3 What do you think was the main factor that motivated people to support the slave trade? Was it greed, ignorance or racism?

Arguments put forward to defend the slave trade

1 *The racist argument:*
   Africans are less skilled than Europeans, proving that white people are superior, so they have a right to do as they wish with black people.
2 *The economic arguments:*
   The slave trade makes lots of money for Britain. It has to continue. Africa is undeveloped – no other type of trade is possible.
3 *Slaves are not captured cruelly. Most slaves are already prisoners of war. They would be killed anyway.*
4 *Conditions on the slave ships are good.*
5 *Enslaved Africans are well treated on the plantations.*

SOURCE 1 *Robert Norris, captain of a slave ship, describes conditions on the slave ships (1788).*

[The slaves] had sufficient room, sufficient air, and sufficient provisions. When upon deck, they made merry and amused themselves with dancing ... In short, the voyage from Africa to the West Indies was one of the happiest periods of a Negro's life.

SOURCE 2 *From a manual for plantation owners.*

How pleasing, how gratifying it is to see a swarm of healthy, active, cheerful, obedient boys and girls going to and returning from their puerile [childish and silly] work in the field.

▶ **SOURCE 3** *This painting was done by an artist paid by a plantation owner who wanted to hang the picture on the wall of his home in England.*

Collect your evidence carefully

Clarkson's travels would take him 35,000 miles around Britain and make him one of the best known men in the country. He spent the summer and autumn months touring the slave ports.

The rest of his time was spent in Wisbech or London doing further research, writing up his findings and keeping in touch with local anti-slavery groups.

CLARKSON CHALLENGE 3

1 Draw up an evidence collection grid with four columns:

Argument put forward to defend the slave trade	Your counter argument	Supporting evidence	Witness
1 Africans were less skilled than Europeans – white people were superior	African kingdoms before the arrival of Europeans were just as advanced as those in Europe	The kingdom of Ghana... The kingdom of Benin...	
2			
3			
4			
5			

2 Fill in the first column using Clarkson's notes on page 74.

3 Use Clarkson's notes below to help you challenge the first argument.

Clarkson's notes

Mali
From the thirteenth to the fifteenth centuries the kingdom of Mali spread across much of West and North-East Africa. At its largest the kingdom was 2000 kilometres wide and there was organised trade with gold dust and agricultural produce being exported North. Mali reached its peak in the fourteenth century. Cowrie shells were used as a form of currency and gold, salt and copper were traded.

Songhay
Between 1450 and 1550, the Songhay kingdom grew very powerful and prosperous. It had a well-organised system of government, the kingdom imported fabrics from Europe and it had a developed currency. Timbuktu became one of the most important places in the world. Libraries and universities were built and it became the meeting place for poets, scholars and artists from other parts of Africa and the Middle East.

Ghana
In the west of Africa, the kingdom of Ghana was a vast empire that spread across an area the size of Western Europe. Between the ninth and thirteenth centuries it traded in gold, salt and copper. It was like a medieval European empire, with a collection of powerful local rulers, controlled by one king or emperor. Ghana was highly advanced and prosperous. It is said that the Ghanaian ruler had an army of 200,000 men.

Benin
The kingdoms of Benin and Ife were led by the Yoruba people and sprang up between the eleventh and twelfth centuries. Studies of the Benin kingdom show that the people were highly skilled in ivory carving, pottery, rope and gum production.

Clarkson's journey 1787–1788

Clarkson's notes

My journey started in London. The first African trading ship I boarded was not a slave ship. The 'Lively' had arrived from Africa with a cargo of ivory, beeswax, palm oil, pepper and beautifully woven and dyed cloth. I soon realised that many of the goods had been produced by skilled craftsmen and was horrified to think that these people might be made slaves. I bought samples of everything and added to this collection over the following years. I kept these products in a small chest and used the contents to challenge the negative views about the African way of life held by many British people at the time. My aim was also to show that Britain could carry on a profitable trade with Africa in goods other than human beings.

▶ SOURCE 4 *This painting of Thomas Clarkson was produced by A E Chalon. On the table is a map of Africa. At Clarkson's feet is his box, containing a collection he made of the products of Africa – woods, ivory, pepper, gum, cinnamon, tobacco, cotton, and an African loom and spindle.*

CLARKSON CHALLENGE 3
continued

Use the material on pages 76–79 to fill in your evidence collection table (page 75).

Clarkson's notes

I also read a great deal. I soon realised that other people had similar views to my own. One of the few people to write positively about Africa was John Wesley, the founder of Methodism. His pamphlet 'Thoughts upon Slavery' was published in 1774. Here are some of the things he wrote.

Thoughts On SLAVERY.

By John Wesley.

THE GOLD-COAST and Slave-Coast, all who have seen it agree, is fruitful and pleasant. It produces vast amounts of rice and other grain, plenty of fruit, oil, and fish in great abundance, with much tame and wild cattle. The same is true of the kingdoms of Benin, Congo and Angola.

These three nations practise several trades; they have smiths, saddlers, potters and weavers. And they are very ingenious at their several occupations. Their smiths not only make all the instruments of iron, but also work many things neatly in gold and silver. It is chiefly the women and children who weave fine cloth, which they dye blue and black.

In London I met three people who gave me lots of information about what the slave trade was really like. **Granville Sharp** was a lawyer who helped to form the Society for Effecting the Abolition of the Slave Trade with me. Sharp was one of the few people in England at the time already campaigning against slavery. A few years earlier he had tried to prosecute the captain of one slave ship for murder.

Granville Sharp

In 1782 Collingwood, the captain of the slave ship Zong, ordered that over 130 slaves be thrown overboard. The ship had left Africa in September. By November 60 slaves had died and many were seriously ill. Collingwood knew that when he reached Jamaica he would not be able to sell the sick slaves and that the ship's owners would lose money. Collingwood thought that if they threw the sick slaves overboard the owners would be able to claim money back from the insurance company. Those slaves who put up a fight were chained before they were thrown overboard.

The owners claimed insurance money for the value of the dead slaves. I tried to prosecute the ship's captain for murder but failed. The judge said that murder was not the issue and that it was 'just as if horses were killed'.

I also met **Olaudah Equiano**. He had been kidnapped from his home in Africa and enslaved when still very young.

My brother, **John Clarkson**, was another important source of information. He had served in the Royal Navy from the age of twelve and had met sailors who had served on slave ships. When he left the navy, John became an active member of the abolition movement.

One day, when all our people were gone out to their work as usual, and only I and my dear sister were left to mind the house, two men and a woman got over our walls, and in a moment seized us both. My sister and I were separated and I ended up in the hands of a slave dealer who supplied the Atlantic slave ships.

Six months later I found myself on board a slave ship. The heat, added to the number in the ship, which was so crowded that each had scarcely room to turn himself, almost suffocated us. The air soon became unfit for breathing, from a variety of loathsome smells, and brought on a sickness among the slaves, of which many died. This wretched situation was made worse by the chains and the filth of the toilet buckets into which the children often fell and were almost suffocated. The shrieks of women, and the groaning of the dying, created a scene of horror almost unbelievable. Three desperate slaves tried to kill themselves by jumping overboard. Two drowned, the other was captured and beaten unmercifully. When I refused to eat, I too was beaten.

Olaudah Equiano

African slave dealers capture men, women and children and march them to the coast where they are traded for goods. The prisoners are forced to march long distances, sometimes hundreds of miles, with their hands tied behind their backs. The prisoners are connected by chains or wooden neck yokes.

Their journey to the coast can take months and sometimes nearly half can die on the journey.

John Clarkson

Kent

Another important witness was **James Ramsay**, an Anglican minister who had recently returned from the West Indies. Ramsay was able to give me a powerful eyewitness account. I spent a month with him at his rectory in Kent.

I was a navy doctor and minister on the West Indian island of St Christopher's, where I saw for myself what conditions were like on the plantations. I often saw beatings and weary slaves still carrying cane to the mill by moonlight. New mothers had to bring their babies to the fields, leaving them exposed to the sun and rain whilst they worked.

James Ramsay

Bristol

I realised it was time for me to get closer to the slave trade by visiting the great slaving ports of Bristol and Liverpool. Bristol first — a three-day journey on horseback.

The city had warehouses full of slave-grown products just arrived from the Americas. Each evening I searched for witnesses. Many captains and sailors were unwilling to talk to me, fearing that they would lose their jobs. However, I managed to find a doctor who worked on slave ships, called **Alexander Falconbridge**.

Notes on conversation with James Ramsay

Life on the Plantations

- *The slaves are often underfed. Their rations are so small that they are left with nothing during the second half of the week.*
- *Slaves suffer from tropical diseases such as leprosy, dysentery and yaws (a skin disease causing large red swellings).*
- *These diseases together with the slaves' bad diet and poor living and working conditions mean that life expectancy is only 26. Forty per cent of the Africans who arrive to work on the plantations die in the first year.*

Work on the Plantations

- *Children are put to work from the age of seven or eight. They have to weed, plant corn or shovel manure into cane holes.*
- *Adults start work in the fields between five and seven a.m., and continue, with meal breaks, until seven p.m., usually six days a week.*

Punishment

- *If a slave runs away for 30 days or more the punishment is death, yet an owner who kills a slave is only fined £15.*
- *Twelve lashes of the whip can be given for bad work.*
- *Slaves who run away can be given over a hundred lashes. They are sometimes branded on the face or have an ear nailed to a post.*

This is what Alexander Falconbridge told me, word for word: "The surgeon, upon going between decks in the morning to examine the situation, frequently finds several dead. These dead slaves are thrown to the sharks.

It often happens that those who are placed at a distance from the latrine buckets, in trying to get to them, tumble over their companions, as a result of being shackled. Unable to carry on, and prevented from getting to the tubs, they have to ease themselves where they lie. This situation is added to by the tubs being too small and only emptied once every day.

The deck, that is the floor of their rooms, was so covered with blood and mucus from slaves suffering from the flux [dysentery], that it resembled a slaughterhouse. It is not in the power of the human imagination to picture a situation more dreadful. At a slave market in the West Indies, one Liverpool captain disguised his slaves' dysentery by ordering the ship's doctor to plug up their anuses with rope fibre."

78

Liverpool

Clarkson's notes

From Bristol I went on to Liverpool. Liverpool, with its six miles [9.6 km] of docks, was the slaving capital of the world. This year these docks would be sending a total of 81 slave ships to Africa. Liverpool's shipyards built many of these ships, some of which could hold up to a thousand slaves each. I knew it was a dangerous place for me. And it was not long before I received death threats and a gang of sailors tried to throw me from the pier.

For the first time, I saw the 'tools of the trade' displayed in a shop window. I bought iron handcuffs, leg shackles, a hideous thumb screw and a surgical instrument with a screw device, called a speculum oris, used by doctors in cases of lockjaw. I asked why it was there and the shopkeeper told me it was for wrenching open the mouths of any slaves who tried to commit suicide by not eating. These items provided important evidence of how slaves were treated on the journey from Africa to the West Indies.

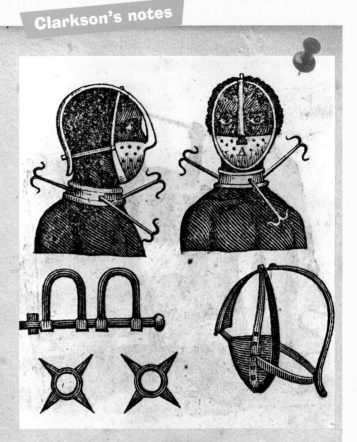

Plymouth

Clarkson's notes

My last stop was in Plymouth where I uncovered a key piece of evidence, the plan of a loaded slave ship. I reworked this when I got back to London, applying the idea to the Brookes [a slave ship from Liverpool]. The Brookes is currently allowed to carry 454 Africans by law. The Brookes used to carry as many as 609 Africans on earlier voyages. On a slave ship an adult is given a space of 6 feet (1.8 m) by 1 foot 4 inches (0.4 m).

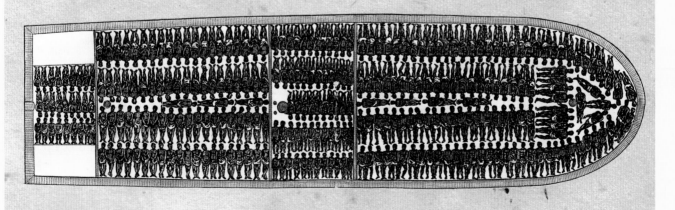

Using the evidence to win support

By the time Clarkson returned from Plymouth in 1788 he had collected a great deal of evidence. However, to run a successful campaign requires more than just collecting evidence. You have to use the evidence to win support and influence people. This is the final part of your challenge.

Members of Parliament had to be persuaded to introduce a law to ban the slave trade. Imagine you are helping Thomas Clarkson to write the parliamentary speech. You need to use the evidence you have collected to persuade Members of Parliament to abolish the slave trade. You need the MPs to do more than simply listen and agree with what you are saying. You need to persuade them to take action!

Tips from a master!

Before you start planning your speech, look at the advice below and study the techniques used by Prime Minister William Pitt to produce a powerful speech.

1 Make sure you **structure** your speech carefully.

- You need a powerful opening paragraph and a strong conclusion.
- You also need to make sure that you defeat as many of the arguments put forward to defend slavery as possible. Use your evidence collection grid (page 75). Start a different paragraph for each argument you challenge.
- Remember to support your counter-arguments with specific examples and to quote from key witnesses.

   a) Study Extract 1. How does Pitt **provide a powerful opening** to his speech?
   b) Study Extract 4. What does Pitt say is the main argument people in Britain use for keeping the slave trade? How does Pitt **destroy his opponent's arguments**?
   c) Study Extract 5. What is the **main reason** Pitt gives for ending the slave trade in his **last paragraph**?

2 Make sure you include **emotive words and phrases** to make your speech more powerful.

   a) What impact does the word 'tearing' have on the last sentence of Extract 1. Imagine that Pitt had used the word 'moving' instead. Why would this be less powerful?
   b) Can you find three other examples of emotive words or phrases in Pitt's speech? Explain the impact they would have on a person listening to the speech.

3 Use **clever techniques** to win over your audience and make your arguments more persuasive. Pitt uses all the techniques listed below. Can you spot them?

- Playing on the audience's guilt – making them feel bad about something.
- Making key points easy to follow by using short, sharp sentences.
- Creating thought-provoking images or pictures in the audience's mind.
- Clusters of three – three phrases or words used to emphasise a point.
- Raising rhetorical questions – questions that don't require an answer but make the audience think about a key issue.
- Using words like 'we', 'us' and 'you' to make the audience feel involved or responsible.
- Using repetition – saying the same word or phrase more than once for emphasis.

4 Think carefully about how to **perform** your speech. How would you perform Pitt's speech?

   a) Where would you **add emphasis** or **change your tone**?
   b) Where would you **pause** so that a key point really sinks in?

Pitt's speech

On 2 April 1792, the prime minister, William Pitt (right), stood up in the House of Commons ready to keep his promise to his close friend William Wilberforce that he would do everything in his power to abolish the slave trade. Pitt was ill and exhausted and had to take medicine before he could begin. Somehow he managed to find enough strength to deliver one of the most powerful speeches ever delivered by a prime minister. Here are some extracts:

Extract 1

Now, sir, I come to Africa. Why ought the slave trade to be abolished? I know of no evil that ever existed, nor can imagine any evil to exist, worse than the tearing of seventy or eighty thousand persons every year from their own land.

Extract 2

We ourselves tempt them to sell their fellow creatures to us. It was our arms in the river Cameroon, put into the hands of the slave trader, that gave him the means to push his trade. Can we pretend that we have a right to carry away to distant regions men of whom we know nothing? Those that sell slaves to us have no right to do so.

Extract 3

But the evil does not stop here. Do you think nothing of the ruin and the miseries in which so many individuals, still remaining in Africa, are involved as a consequence of carrying off so many people? Do you think nothing of their families left behind? Of the connections broken? Of the friendships, attachments, and relationships that are burst asunder? Do you think nothing of the miseries in consequence that are felt from generation to generation?

Extract 4

I am sure the immediate abolition of the slave trade is the first, the principal, the most indispensable act of policy, of duty, and of justice that this country has to take. There are, however, arguments set up to [defend the slave trade]. The slave trade system, it is supposed, has taken such deep root in Africa that it is absurd to think of it being eradicated. 'We are friends,' say they, 'to humanity. We are second to none of you in our zeal for the good of Africa – but the French will not abolish – the Dutch will not abolish. We wait, therefore, till they join us or set us an example.' How, sir, is this enormous evil ever to be eradicated, if every nation waits?

Extract 5

The great and happy change to be expected in the state of her [Africa's] inhabitants is, of all the various and important benefits of the abolition, the most important. I shall oppose to the utmost any attempt to postpone, even for an hour, the total abolition of the slave trade; a measure which we are bound, by the most pressing duty, to adopt.

The story of abolition – how should it be told?

After initial setbacks the campaign succeeded. In 1807 the slave trade was abolished throughout the British Empire. In 1833 slavery itself was abolished in all British colonies. The success of the campaign has often been credited to one man in particular – William Wilberforce. Is that fair? Should William Wilberforce be presented as the hero of the campaign to end slavery?

For over 150 years William Wilberforce has been presented as the hero of the campaign to end slavery. Many TV programmes and film documentaries about the abolition of slavery tell the story with Wilberforce at the centre. Look at the proposal below for a new documentary on the abolition of the slave trade in the British colonies. It very much follows the traditional story.

ABOLITION THE FULL STORY

Wilberforce: how one man changed the world

DVD VIDEO

TITLE:	ABOLITION – THE FULL STORY
STYLE:	Historical documentary
TARGET AUDIENCE:	12 years and above – to be screened in Britain
LENGTH:	60 minutes

Section and time allowed	Outline
1 5 mins	Introduction – how slaves were captured and held ready for loading onto ships
2 5 mins	The triangular trade – what was traded at each stage
3 10 mins	The 'Middle Passage' – conditions on the slave ships
4 10 mins	Conditions on the slave plantations – working hours, living conditions, punishments
5 5 mins	Why slavery was so important for the British Empire – supply of sugar, tobacco, profits for plantation owners
6 10 mins	The campaign against the slave trade – the story of William Wilberforce and why he was important
7 5 mins	How Wilberforce was helped by Thomas Clarkson (and if time allows Granville Sharp)
8 5 mins	1807 – the key turning point. The abolition of the British slave trade in 1807
9 2 mins	How 1807 led to the abolition of slavery in 1833
10 3 mins	Conclusion – focus on Wilberforce's statue in Westminster Abbey. Reflect on how one man changed the world

Why do we need to be careful telling the story of slavery?

Interpretations such as this are very controversial. Below you can see some of the challenges to the traditional interpretation.

FILM CHALLENGE 1

Study the challenges in the boxes below.
1 Reflect back on what you have already learned about slavery. Do you think any of these challenges are justified?
2 Use pages 84–88 to research how slavery was abolished in more detail. Put together your own documentary proposal on how the story should be told.

Should Wilberforce be the only image on the front cover?

Can you think of a better sub-title for the documentary?

- Should the documentary start earlier, e.g. with accounts of slavery from the eighteenth century?
- Should there be an introduction exploring how slavery has existed throughout history?
- Why is it important to include information on Africa before slavery?

Should so much time in the documentary be spent exploring the horrors of slavery? Some people argue that documentaries, film and even schools spend too long on this and miss out other important parts of the story.

Should so much time be spent on William Wilberforce?

What about other campaigners or the role played by slave resistance?

- Is 1807 really the turning point in the story?
- What impact did the 1807 Act actually have?

- Should the documentary end by giving the impression that it was mainly the work of one man that led to the ending of slavery in British colonies?
- Should the documentary explore other forms of slavery that still exist in the world today?

Are there other important dates and events missing from the documentary plan?

83

The road to abolition 1791–1838: was 1807 really the key turning point?

1791

ABOLITIONISTS DEFEATED
William Wilberforce introduces his first Bill into Parliament to abolish the slave trade. Despite the mountain of evidence that Clarkson has collected and a brilliant speech by Wilberforce, the Bill is easily defeated by 163 votes to 88 votes.

1792–1804

WAR WITH FRANCE
Public attention is focused on the war. There is a real danger of a French invasion.

1804–1807

CLARKSON RIDES AGAIN!
The Society for the Abolition of the Slave Trade expands its committee from 12 to 40 people. For the next three years they concentrate most of their efforts on Parliament. Meanwhile Clarkson tours England again building public support for the anti-slavery movement.

1807

BRITISH SLAVE TRADE ABOLISHED
The Abolition of the Slave Trade Act is passed. The slave trade is finally abolished in the British Empire. Any British captain caught with slaves on board will be fined £10 for every slave on the ship. The new Act was a major achievement for the anti-slavery movement but the law does not go far enough. It does not outlaw slavery completely. Enslaved Africans on British-owned plantations will not be set free. Only the **trade** has been abolished.

1823

A NEW ANTI-SLAVERY SOCIETY
In 1823 a new anti-slavery society is formed which aims to abolish slavery throughout the British Empire. Wilberforce and Clarkson are members but younger campaigners play a key role. Thomas Fowell Buxton, for example, takes over from Wilberforce as the anti-slavery spokesman in Parliament. Lecturers are employed for the first time to hold public meetings that expose the horrors of slavery. They also call for a new sugar boycott, urge shopkeepers not to stock slave-grown goods and call for people to only vote for MPs who support the abolition of slavery. The dramatic increase in the number of local branches and petitions being sent to Parliament means that the anti-slavery campaign can no longer be ignored.

1833

SLAVERY ABOLISHED
Slavery itself is abolished throughout the British Empire. Altogether, slave owners are paid compensation of £20 million. Enslaved Africans have to work as 'apprentices' for six years. Only then will they become truly 'free'. Apprentices have to work a 40-hour week for six years for their former masters, for no pay. This is still effectively a form of slavery under a different name. Only children under six have been given true freedom.

1838

APPRENTICESHIPS ENDED
Joseph Sturge sails to the West Indies and finds that apprenticeships have not improved life for supposedly 'free' Africans. He publishes his findings in 1837. In 1838 petitions are sent to Parliament protesting about the apprenticeship system. They are signed by 449,000 people. In the Caribbean, angry apprentices stage widespread strikes and demonstrations. Parliament finally ends the apprenticeship system on 1 August 1838.

FILM CHALLENGE 2

1 Write your own proposal for a better documentary. Use the information from this page on 'The road to abolition' to give you ideas for what each section should be about. Think about how important each part of the story is and decide on timings to reflect this. Use the sheet your teacher will give you to draft your own documentary proposal.

2 The proposal on page 82 makes 1807 the key turning point. Do you agree? If not, what are you going to use as the turning point of your documentary?

FORGOTTEN FACTORS

1 A forgotten partnership

In the 1840s a statue of William Wilberforce was placed in Westminster Abbey – an honour reserved for great British heroes. In contrast Thomas Clarkson's role has been overlooked. It was not until 1996 that a memorial stone to Clarkson was placed on the floor of Westminster Abbey. William Wilberforce and Thomas Clarkson had great respect for each other. They were a great partnership.

Clarkson himself wrote:

'What could Mr. Wilberforce have done in Parliament if I had not collected that great body of evidence … And what could the committee have done without the Parliamentary aid of Mr Wilberforce?' However, the role played by one half of this partnership has been overlooked by history.

FILM CHALLENGE 3

Use the information on pages 85–88 to explore other individuals, groups and events that are often missed from the story of the abolition of slavery in the British Empire. Make sure that you think carefully about how you use this new information in your documentary plan.

2 Forgotten campaigners

Mary Prince

Mary Prince was born to a slave family in Bermuda in 1788. She suffered terrible treatment from her owners. In 1828 she travelled to England with her owners and eventually found freedom. Mary campaigned with the Anti-Slavery Society. She was the first woman to present an anti-slavery petition to Parliament and the first black woman to write her autobiography, *The History of Mary Prince: A West Indian Slave*. The book made people in Britain aware that although the slave trade had been abolished, the horrors of plantation life continued.

Religious groups

Nine of the twelve people who set up the Society for Effecting the Abolition of the Slave Trade in 1787 were **Quakers**. They believed that slavery was against Christian teaching. Their experience as activists meant they knew how to place articles in newspapers, publish pamphlets and send petitions to Parliament. Methodists also campaigned against slavery. In 1774, **John Wesley**, founder of the Methodist Church, spoke out against slavery (see page 76).

Female anti-slavery societies

Women played an important role in the anti-slavery campaign. **Elizabeth Heyrick** (left) criticised anti-slavery leaders for moving too slowly, and supported the slave rebellions in the West Indies. Heyrick was an important figure in the formation of female anti-slavery societies. In Leicester she organised a new sugar boycott which inspired other women to set up their own campaigns.

In the 1820s there were over 70 women's anti-slavery societies, working to gain public support for the campaign. In Birmingham women's groups visited more than 80 per cent of homes, persuading people to support the cause. They also paid for lecturers to give public speeches attacking slavery.

THE
INTERESTING NARRATIVE
OF
THE LIFE
OF
OLAUDAH EQUIANO,
OR,
GUSTAVUS VASSA,
THE AFRICAN.
WRITTEN BY HIMSELF.

VOL I.

Behold, God is my falvation; I will truft and not be
afraid, for the Lord Jehovah is my ftrength and my
fong; he alfo is become my falvation.
And in that day fhall ye fay, Praife the Lord, call upon
his name, declare his doings among the people,
Ifaiah xii. 2, 4.

SECOND EDITION.

LONDON:
Printed and fold for the AUTHOR, by T. WILKINS,
No. 23, Aldermanbury;
Sold alfo by Mr. Johnfon, St. Paul's Church-Yard;
Mr. Buckland, Paternofter-Row; Meffrs. Robfon
and Clark, Bond-Street; Mr. Davis, oppofite
Gray's-Inn, Holborn; Mr. Matthews, Strand;
Mr Stockdale, Piccadilly; Mr. Richardfon, Royal
Exchange; Mr. Kearfley, Fleet-Street; and the
Bookfellers in Oxford and Cambridge.

[Entered at Stationers-hall.]

1789.

Olaudah Equiano,
or
GUSTAVUS VASSA,
the African.

Publifhed March 1 1789 by G. Vafsa

Equiano knew that his own life story was a powerful argument against slavery. His autobiography was published in 1789 and was a best seller. The book began with a petition to Parliament and ended with his anti-slavery letter to the monarch. It was a vital contribution to the abolitionists' cause.

Olaudah Equiano
Olaudah Equiano was probably born in a part of West Africa now called Nigeria in 1745. He was kidnapped when he was just eleven, forced on a long journey to the coast and taken to Barbados as an enslaved African. In 1757 a naval captain, Pascal, bought him for about £40 and named him Gustavas Vassa. Equiano spent much of his time at sea, both on warships and trading vessels.

In 1763, he was sold to Robert King, a rich merchant. During the next three years by trading and saving hard, Equiano was able to buy his freedom for £40.

Equiano eventually settled in Britain, where he started his anti-slavery activities. He worked closely with anti-slavery campaigners, trying to help slaves who had escaped from their owners and been recaptured in England. Equiano also spoke out at London debating societies and published several anti-slavery letters in London newspapers. He was a skilled writer and public speaker.

Equiano also worked with other black campaigners, such as **Ottobah Cugoano**. In 1788 he led a black delegation to Parliament in support of **William Dolben's** attempts to limit, by law, the number of enslaved Africans that ships could carry.

Equiano toured the country promoting his autobiography. He was helped by abolitionist friends, such as Thomas Clarkson, who recommended his book and wrote letters of introduction. He travelled all over Britain raising awareness of the horrors of the trade, changing attitudes towards enslaved people and inspiring others to join the abolition campaign.

There was resistance throughout the slave-trade system. There were attacks on slave ships from the shore by 'free' Africans. Perhaps as many as ten per cent of slave ships experienced revolts.

On the plantations many enslaved Africans tried to slow down the pace of work by pretending to be ill, causing fires or 'accidentally' breaking tools. Whenever possible, they ran away. Some escaped to South America, England or North America. All of these acts made slavery less profitable.

Resistance was difficult. Enslaved Africans who escaped were quickly recognised as runaways, returned and punished by their owners. Unarmed enslaved Africans had to fight overseers with guns or a trained army.

During the late eighteenth and early nineteenth centuries, slave revolts grew bigger. Slave resistance made it clear that if enslaved Africans were not set free they would soon free themselves. Slave revolts in the Caribbean averaged at least two per year during the period 1789–1815.

CASE STUDY 1: St Domingue

The largest slave revolt was on St Domingue, which was French in 1791. French soldiers were confident that they could put down the uprising. But the rebels gained control of a large part of the north of the colony. **Toussaint L'Ouverture** (left) emerged as their leader.

When the British tried to seize control of the island during their war against France they too were defeated by Toussaint's force and forced to withdraw. Britain agreed to leave Toussaint alone, and made a trade agreement.

However, Toussaint soon faced a new threat. Napoleon had seized power in France and now dreamt of recapturing St Domingue and restoring slavery. In 1802 he sent the largest invasion force ever to leave France to St Domingue. Despite capturing Toussaint, France failed to retake the colony and lost more than 50,000 soldiers. In 1804 St Domingue's leaders proclaimed the establishment of the Republic of Haiti and slavery was abolished.

CASE STUDY 2: Jamaica

On Jamaica in the 1820s more than 2500 slaves were escaping from the plantations each year. The largest slave uprising was in 1831. Enslaved Africans burnt down houses and warehouses full of sugar cane, causing over £1 million worth of damage. More than 200 plantations were attacked as 20,000 enslaved Africans seized control of large areas. The rebels were led by **Samuel Sharpe** (right), a literate and well respected deacon who was in charge of a missionary chapel in Montego Bay. It took British troops the whole of January 1832 to defeat the rebels and arrest Sharpe. Over 200 enslaved Africans were killed in the fighting. Sharpe was executed in public. Just before his death he said to a visitor: 'I would rather die upon yonder gallows than live in slavery'.

Sharpe's owners were paid £16 in 'compensation for their loss of property'.

The revolt helped to end British slavery. It reminded many of the St Domingue rebellion. It also shocked the British public and made the government see that the costs of keeping slavery in the West Indies were too high. There were fears of another major rebellion and many terrified plantation owners now accepted abolition rather than risk a widespread war.

A never-ending story?

The anti-slavery campaign was the first great human rights movement in British history. It was the first time a large number of people became so angry, and stayed angry for many years, over someone else's rights – the rights of people of another colour and on another continent. It showed that you don't have to accept the way things are: you can change them. However, equal rights for men, women and children in many parts of the world still seem a long way off.

Anti-Slavery International (whose London headquarters is named Thomas Clarkson House) argues that slavery still exists. The 1956 UN Supplementary Convention on Slavery considers anyone to be a slave if he or she is unable to withdraw his or her labour voluntarily. This includes, for example:

- bonded labourers who work for nothing to pay off money-lenders
- serfs who cannot leave the agricultural estates where they work
- exploited children who are cut off from their families to work long hours for nothing.

It has been calculated that there are at least 200 million such 'slaves' today, and probably many more. Here are just two stories:

FILM CHALLENGE 4

Use the information here to think carefully about how you will end your documentary. Do you want to make your audience aware that forms of slavery still exist today? If so, how much time are you going to allow this in your documentary plan?

DIEUSIBON, FROM HAITI

When I first moved to Port-au-Prince I cleaned dishes, the house, everything. My 'aunt' would beat me whenever I didn't get water. I worked so hard that my body ached and I couldn't move, but she would beat me if I didn't do more work. Her three children went to school … One day my aunt sent me to fetch water. I refused, so she took a pot of boiling water and threw it at me and burned my face and slammed the hot cooking pot on my hand.

Source: www.antislavery.org

AHMED'S STORY

When Ahmed was five years old he was trafficked from Bangladesh to the United Arab Emirates to be a camel jockey. He was forced to train and race camels in Dubai for three years.

I was scared … If I made a mistake I was beaten with a stick. When I said I wanted to go home I was told I never would. I didn't enjoy camel racing, I was really afraid. I fell off many times. When I won prizes several times, such as money and a car, the camel owner took everything. I never got anything, no money, nothing; my family also got nothing.

DOING HISTORY: Interpretations

Why do we have to be careful telling the story of the slave trade?

This section has not just been about the slave trade but it has also been about why there are different interpretations of events in the past. Here are the ideas from last year:

> **INTERPRETATIONS**   *Recap*
>
> People have different stories or interpretations of the past. People create different interpretations by including some people, topics or evidence and leaving out or down-playing others.

1 Look at documentary plans produced by other people in your class. How are they different? Why are they different?

2 Why might the plans look different if they had been produced for audiences in other countries? For example: the Caribbean or Africa?

Now here is a new idea.

> **Interpretations**
>
> Interpretations are determined by the attitudes and beliefs of the person creating the interpretation.

3 Look at your plan. Find an example where your own attitudes have influenced what you say or how you present it.

ACTIVITY

WHAT CAN WE LEARN FROM THE CAMPAIGN TO ABOLISH SLAVERY ABOUT HOW TO RUN A MODERN-DAY CAMPAIGN?

- **Connecting the near and the distant**
  The abolitionists' first job was to make British people understand the connection between the sugar they enjoyed, the tobacco they smoked, the coffee they drank, and the slave trade. Today, most people would be against slave labour but do they know where the goods they buy come from and the working conditions of those who made them? Are their trainers made by very young children working in a sweatshop?

- **Information is powerful**
  Clarkson and his fellow anti-slavery campaigners believed that human beings would always care about the sufferings of others.

In a small group, brainstorm the tactics you would use to run a modern campaign.
- What techniques would you use to make sure your campaign is successful?
- How many of these tactics were used 200 years ago by those people involved in the anti-slavery campaign?

Therefore the way to persuade people to take action against slavery was to educate them and provide clear evidence of the cruelties and injustices that existed in the world.

- **Small beginnings**
  In 1787, when just twelve people met in London to form a society to end the slave trade, people laughed at the thought that slavery could be stopped. Slavery looked like it would last forever. However, these individuals started a campaign that changed the world in which they lived remarkably quickly. Within the space of five years all the major towns and cities had anti-slavery groups.

Why were people so proud of the British Empire in 1900?

In the 1780s many British people believed that their empire was dying. They would have been astonished a hundred years later to know that the British Empire was larger than ever and contained a quarter of the world's population. It was the empire on which 'the sun never set': because it was so huge, it was always daytime somewhere in the empire!

Around 1900 Lord Curzon, the British Viceroy (ruler) of India, said: 'The British Empire is the greatest force for good the world has ever seen.'

Lord Curzon probably included the abolition of slavery as one of Britain's greatest achievements. But is Lord Curzon's assessment fair? The big story of the British Empire is built up using many, many small stories. These smaller stories may each give us a different impression of the empire, some good, some bad. For example, the stories we have looked at so far lead to very different verdicts. Which of these small stories deserve the thumbs up and which the thumbs down?

The stories of the British Empire

ACTIVITY

Pages 91–95 give you some more stories: some brief, some in a little more depth.

1 Make three lists:
   a) the parts of the story of the British Empire that you think get the thumbs up (meaning the empire was a force for good and helped the people within it) for example:

   The abolition of slavery

   b) the parts that you think get the thumbs down (meaning the British Empire made the lives of people within it worse) for example:

   Slavery on sugar plantations

   c) any stories that you think could be interpreted differently by different people.

2 Look at your completed lists. Why do you think people might write or tell different interpretations of the British Empire?

3 Do you think it is possible to give a completely objective history of the British Empire?

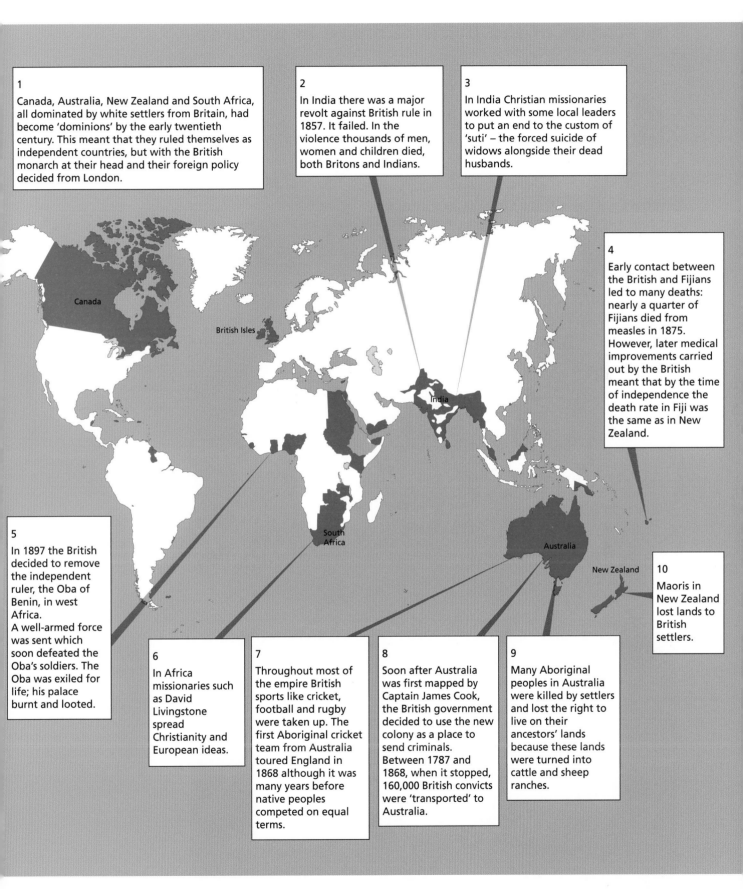

1
Canada, Australia, New Zealand and South Africa, all dominated by white settlers from Britain, had become 'dominions' by the early twentieth century. This meant that they ruled themselves as independent countries, but with the British monarch at their head and their foreign policy decided from London.

2
In India there was a major revolt against British rule in 1857. It failed. In the violence thousands of men, women and children died, both Britons and Indians.

3
In India Christian missionaries worked with some local leaders to put an end to the custom of 'suti' – the forced suicide of widows alongside their dead husbands.

4
Early contact between the British and Fijians led to many deaths: nearly a quarter of Fijians died from measles in 1875. However, later medical improvements carried out by the British meant that by the time of independence the death rate in Fiji was the same as in New Zealand.

5
In 1897 the British decided to remove the independent ruler, the Oba of Benin, in west Africa.
A well-armed force was sent which soon defeated the Oba's soldiers. The Oba was exiled for life; his palace burnt and looted.

6
In Africa missionaries such as David Livingstone spread Christianity and European ideas.

7
Throughout most of the empire British sports like cricket, football and rugby were taken up. The first Aboriginal cricket team from Australia toured England in 1868 although it was many years before native peoples competed on equal terms.

8
Soon after Australia was first mapped by Captain James Cook, the British government decided to use the new colony as a place to send criminals. Between 1787 and 1868, when it stopped, 160,000 British convicts were 'transported' to Australia.

9
Many Aboriginal peoples in Australia were killed by settlers and lost the right to live on their ancestors' lands because these lands were turned into cattle and sheep ranches.

10
Maoris in New Zealand lost lands to British settlers.

Canada

British Isles

India

South Africa

Australia

New Zealand

▲ SOURCE 1 *The British Empire in 1900.*

The stories of the British Empire in pictures

◄ SOURCE 2   *The Lansdowne Railway Bridge over the River Indus. It was designed and built by the British and opened in 1889, improving transport routes in what is now Pakistan.*

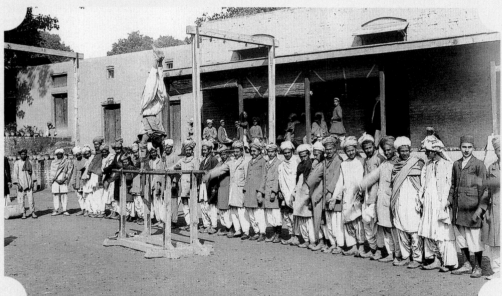

◄ SOURCE 3   *A gymnastics class at the British government high school at Pashwar, now in Pakistan.*

◄ SOURCE 4 *Indian soldiers fighting in the First World War.*

▲ SOURCE 5
Missionary preaching
Christianity to Indians.

▼ SOURCE 6 *British
soldiers auctioning loot
from the palace of King
Thibaw of Mandalay,
after he had been
defeated, 1885.*

▼ SOURCE 7 *The
18-year-old Sultan of
Zanzibar, with his
British 'Adviser', his
British 'First Minister',
and other British
officials. Although
supposedly independent,
the Sultan had to do
what the British told
him.*

▼ SOURCE 8 *British Medical
Officer of Northern Nigeria
on his rounds.*

The story of trade

This table shows not only the massive growth of commerce across the British Empire, but also that for many years exports were worth more than imports.

	Exports	Imports
1720s	£7.5 million	£7 million
1840s	£141.5 million	£79.5 million
1885	£295 million	£390 million

▲ SOURCE 9 *By the nineteenth century London was at the heart of a huge commercial empire. This picture shows the West India Docks in 1802. Entering from the River Thames, at the bottom of the picture, ships from across the globe could go to the timber dock (on the left), the export dock (centre) or the import dock (right), all surrounded by warehouses for the huge amount and variety of goods handled.*

Exports

As we saw in Section 1, Britain went through an industrial revolution in the late eighteenth and nineteenth centuries. Where was Britain going to sell all the goods that the factories were churning out? To the countries of the British Empire, of course. Coal, iron, steel and cotton textiles were all exported, as well as all kinds of manufactured goods, from teapots to railway engines. This made British industrialists rich but also did two other things. It created jobs for ordinary British people so that over time their wages increased and their living standards improved. Secondly, people in the Empire could buy many things they wanted which were made most effectively and cheaply in Britain, from clothes to railway engines.

Imports

You've already found out about sugar and tobacco but the Empire also supplied Britain with tea and coffee, chocolate, cotton and tropical foods, like bananas, oranges and pineapples. By 1900 refrigerated ships could bring in meat from Australia and butter and cheese from Canada and New Zealand. This all helped British people eat a greater variety of food and, thanks to refrigeration, fresher foods. These imports meant that money was going back to the lands of the Empire.

The story of Zimbabwe/Rhodesia

Source 10 shows the ruins of what was once a great city in central Africa called Zimbabwe. When white Europeans first saw the site in the nineteenth century, they could not believe that black Africans had built it. Only in the 1930s did archaeologists confirm that the city was built in the twelfth century, by Africans. The people who lived there mined and refined copper and gold; goods were found from Syria, Persia and even China, showing they must have traded across continents. Yet as late as the 1960s it was treason in white-ruled parts of Africa to say that Africans had built Zimbabwe.

▲ SOURCE 10 *One part of the ruins of Zimbabwe today.*

Conquest

Cecil Rhodes was the most famous British empire-builder of the nineteenth century. As a young man he said:

'I contend that we are the first race in the world. And the more of the world we inhabit, the better it is for the human race.'

Rhodes became a millionaire at the age of 27 from his diamond mines in South Africa. He was determined to use his money to make himself richer and to spread the British Empire. From South Africa he looked north, where he had heard there were rich deposits of gold to be mined. His problem was that there was a powerful black African ruler in his way: Lobengula, king of the Ndebele people. Rhodes made a deal with Lobengula, but the terms were only partly written down. Rhodes promised Lobengula, orally, that only a few mining prospectors would enter his land. Lobengula was tricked: thousands came, ignoring him and behaving as if the land was theirs.

It did not take long before conflict broke out. In 1893 Rhodes paid a force of 1200 British soldiers to deal with Lobengula. The soldiers faced 3000 of his trained warriors, but the British had a new weapon: the Maxim gun, a machine-gun that could fire 50 rounds a minute. In its first use in battle, 1500 Ndebele were killed. Only four members of the British force died. Rhodes and his British South Africa Company took over a large area of central Africa. They called it Rhodesia.

THE RHODES COLOSSUS
STRIDING FROM CAPE TOWN TO CAIRO.

▲ SOURCE 11 *Rhodes planned to create British rule 'from the Cape to Cairo'. This drawing shows Rhodes the empire-builder astride Africa, his right foot on the Cape (of Good Hope) and his left on Cairo (capital of Egypt).*

THE BIG STORY: Empire Part Two (continued)

Why were Europeans mad about empires?

You have investigated the Roman and Spanish empires and some of the story of the British Empire. But that story of the British Empire is not complete yet so we can't fully compare them. Instead we're going to look at how attitudes to empires were changing. They were all mad about empires – but 'mad' in different ways.

ACTIVITY 1

Look at the three reasons on the left. Did the Romans, Spanish and British share all three reasons or were their reasons different?

Why did they think empires were so important?

Reason 1: Empires give you wealth and power ... but you have to grab your share
People believed that the world's wealth was like a cake – there was only a certain amount of it and you had to fight to get the biggest slice. They believed the country with the biggest empire would be the wealthiest and it was the government's duty to grab as many slices as possible to help the people back home.

Reason 2: Empires help you spread your religious beliefs
Between 1500 and 1900 many people in Europe believed very strongly in Christianity and they wanted other people to share their religion. They worried that non-Christians would not be able to go to Heaven after their deaths because they hadn't had the chance to learn about Christianity. That was why Christian missionaries played a part in building the British Empire and accompanied the conquistadors to America.

Reason 3: Empires help spread up-to-date ideas and technology
Many Europeans were convinced that their way of life was the best. They were very proud of the changes that had come from the Industrial Revolution and they wanted other peoples to share in these changes. This also meant they thought people who lived differently were backward and needed to be brought up to date.

Why were they mad about empires?

ACTIVITY 2

'Mad about' can mean a range of different things.

1 Which of these people might have said each of the bubbles below? (More than one person could say a bubble.)

2 How many different reasons were there why people were 'mad' about empires?

A Roman general

A Briton who was part of the Roman Empire

An Aztec

A conquistador

A British politician in the 1800s

An Indian living in the British Empire in the 1800s

LEARNING LOG

Empires are similar in some ways but they can also be different from each other.

1 Identify one similarity between the Roman, Spanish and British empires. What evidence would you use to show this similarity?

2 Can you identify and explain any differences between these empires?

3 Empires became a very controversial issue in the twentieth century. What reasons can you suggest why people argued and fought so much about empires after 1900?

1 We rule the greatest empire the world has ever seen.

2 I wish these people had never come. My people have been slaughtered and we have lost our freedom so they can become even richer.

3 These new ideas from abroad are improving our lives.

4 They say they have come for our good but this is a lie. They came to make themselves rich.

5 We must defend our empire. It makes our people rich. We cannot afford to lose land to other people.

6 I am going to be wealthier than I ever dreamed.

7 Empires can do both good and harm. At least we abolished slavery in our empire.

97

THE BIG STORY

Movement and Settlement

Looking back

Throughout history, people have moved from place to place and country to country. This is called 'migration'. You can probably remember examples of migration from last year. You mostly looked at people who came to Britain. But it wasn't then, and has never been, one-way traffic.

Looking forward

In the period 1500–1900 millions of British people left the British Isles to start new lives elsewhere. This section focuses on these emigrants: why did they go and how were they treated in their new lands? Your big task will be to write a paragraph explaining what you discover about the stories of these emigrants.

ACTIVITY

Here are four different groups of people, from different periods in history, who were born in Britain, but emigrated. Each had different reasons.

1 Work out why each group emigrated.
   a) Were they forced or did they choose to go?
   b) If they chose to move, was it because of their beliefs or for economic reasons?
2 Emigrants are often described as 'brave' and 'adventurous'. What words would you use to describe each group of emigrants?
3 What other questions do you want to ask about these emigrants?

British Roman soldiers

In the first century AD, the Romans conquered Britain. About 12,000 British men chose to join the Roman army and once in the army they were sent all over the empire. British legionaries ended up in places such as North Africa, Syria, Germany, Turkey. Many chose to stay there when they retired from the army because they were given land in their new country to live on and to farm.

Monmouth's rebels

In 1685 the Duke of Monmouth led a rebellion against King James II. Lots of ordinary people in south west England supported the Duke's rebellion and fought on his side against the King. When the rebellion failed they were put on trial: 320 were executed, but over 800 were 'barbadosed'. That is, they were sent to the Caribbean island of Barbados as indentured labourers. They had to work for the plantation owner who only had to provide them with food, clothing and a place to sleep. They received no pay. They could not leave.

Children from British children's homes

Between 1869 and 1930 over 100,000 children from children's homes in Britain were sent to settle in Canada. They were not all orphans: some had been placed in orphanages by parents too poor to look after them and others had simply run away from bad homes. At that time it was widely believed that there were 'too many' people in Britain, particularly too many unskilled, uneducated people. It was also a time when the British Empire was at its height and new colonies were crying out for workers. Once in Canada, the boys worked on farms, the girls worked as home helps. They were usually reasonably well-treated, but given little or no affection by their hosts as they were just 'hired hands'.

Welsh families

In 1865, 153 Welsh people who were unhappy with the way Wales was being taken over by the English, decided to move 13,000 km to Patagonia, a remote part of Argentina, in southern South America. They were later joined by more Welsh emigrants. This nineteenth-century account tells you why they went:

Our Welsh souls needed independence; to gather and sing at our chapels …
It was then that the idea of emigrating started to become strong. The plan
was to leave Wales in an organised group, and find a country that would
enable the arrival of a significant number of people and where we could establish ourselves as a Welsh colony.

Today, the Welsh-Patagonian community numbers about 20,000. The picture on the right shows Welsh children going to school on horseback, photographed in Patagonia, Argentina, in 1909.

Investigating the lives of emigrants from Britain

ACTIVITY

These cards show the three questions you will use to investigate the lives of emigrants:

1 Why did they emigrate?
2 How were they received in their new land?
3 What effects did their arrival have on their new land?

For each question there is a diagram to record your findings.

Stage 1: Practice
Look back to the brief stories on pages 98–99. Discuss with a partner where each of the groups fits on each diagram. Some examples have been done for you.

Stage 2: Research
On pages 102–107 are three much more detailed case studies. Divide them up around the

class. Record your findings on your own copy of the diagrams. Make your diagrams really big so you can add notes to explain your findings.

Stage 3: Compare and collate
Compare your completed diagrams with other people doing your case study. Talk about any differences and decide on a combined diagram for your case study. Now build a whole-class set of diagrams, using evidence from all three case studies.

Stage 4: Write
Under each question on the cards is a statement. You will have to decide if this is accurate, and if not you will change it based on the evidence you have gathered. You will get more advice on this on pages 108–109.

QUESTION 1

Why did they emigrate?

People emigrated from Britain for economic reasons. They had a difficult time here and hoped to live more prosperous, easier lives somewhere else.

QUESTION 2

How were they received in their new land?

Emigrants were welcomed and helped by the people already there.

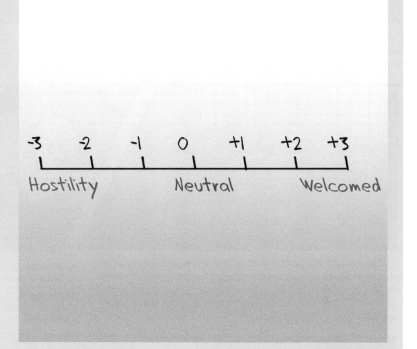

-3   -2   -1   0   +1   +2   +3

Hostility   Neutral   Welcomed

QUESTION 3

What effects did their arrival have on their new land?

Emigrants worked hard and were successful. They helped build up their new homeland.

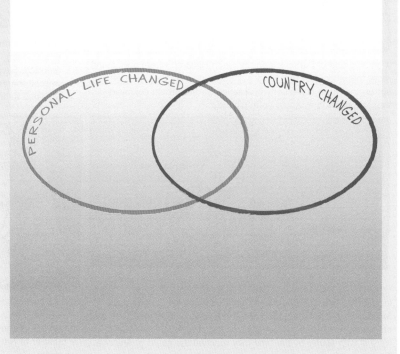

PERSONAL LIFE CHANGED   COUNTRY CHANGED

Case study 1: The Pilgrim Fathers, seventeenth century

ACTIVITY

As you research the stories of emigration, record your findings on the diagrams on pages 100–101.

In the sixteenth and seventeenth centuries everyone in a country was expected to follow the same religion, saying exactly the same prayers in churches that all looked identical. However, people did not all have the same beliefs about religion and this led to many problems and religious persecution.

Although Queen Elizabeth made England a Protestant country, some extreme Protestants, called Puritans, wanted to be allowed to worship in their own way, differently from the laws set down by the Queen. Elizabeth and her successor, King James I, would not let them.

A small group of Puritans went to live in Holland, where they found more toleration, but they were still not happy. So they decided to set up their own community in America, in the British colony of Virginia, where they could be totally free.

This was extremely brave. It involved a long Atlantic crossing in a small sailing boat. They had no idea how to make a living in America. Several attempts to set up colonies had already failed, with all the colonists dying. But these Puritans were driven by their religious beliefs so were prepared to take the risk.

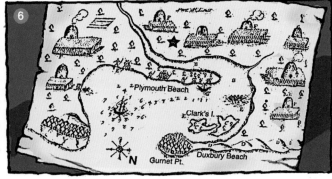

In August 1620, 102 would-be colonists crammed on board the *Mayflower*, a small boat just 29 metres long, and set off. They met storms in the Atlantic, which delayed them so much that many were ill with scurvy by the time they reached the coast of America. The storms had also driven them much further north than Virginia.

On 11 November some of the men put ashore to look around. It was bitterly cold and deep snow lay on the ground. This map from about 1608 shows where the Pilgrim Fathers landed. It also shows a number of Native American settlements, with houses and fields of maize.

By 1620, most of the Native Americans had died, probably of smallpox caught from the Europeans. A group of colonists found some Native American graves containing offerings of maize, which they ate, and some valuables, which they also took. They then found some deserted houses, from which they helped themselves.

Later the English colonists were attacked by Native Americans, but drove them off with their guns.

Half the colony died that first winter and the rest only survived because they met some Native Americans willing to help them. One of them, Samoset, had learned English from contact with traders and fishermen from England. He taught them how to build warm houses, how to fish and hunt deer and wild turkeys for food. He taught them to make birch bark canoes and moccasins, how to tap maples for syrup and when to plant maize.

The harvest of 1621 ended with a special meal, a thanksgiving. Thanksgiving is now celebrated by all Americans on the fourth Thursday in November each year, usually with a turkey dinner.

More and more Puritans left England to settle near the Pilgrim Fathers in what they were now calling 'New England'. By 1640, 20,000 people had emigrated and the city of Boston had been founded. From them grew the colonies which eventually broke away from Britain in 1783 to become the USA (see pages 178–179).

And why are they called the 'Pilgrim Fathers'? **Pilgrims** are people who go on a journey for religious reasons. **Fathers** because the colonists on the Mayflower were the first of many, the 'fathers' of the new nation of the United States of America.

DISCUSS

How would you describe the Pilgrim Fathers? Brave? Adventurous? Which three adjectives fit them best? Give a reason for each adjective you choose.

Case study 2: Canadian Scots, eighteenth century

▲ SOURCE 1

ACTIVITY

As you research the stories of emigration, record your findings on the diagrams on pages 100–101.

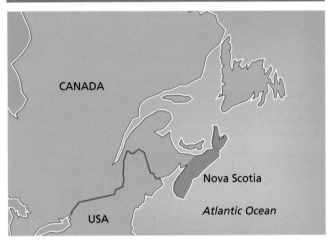

Pipers

Source 1 shows a Scottish bagpipe band, obviously, but where do you think they are? Scotland?

No, they are the St Andrew's Society Pipe Band from Winnipeg, Canada. There are far more bagpipe bands, Scottish country dancers, and Scottish clan societies in Canada than in Scotland. In fact, one in seven Canadians is of Scottish descent. How did this happen?

Settlers needed

By the eighteenth century the British Empire was growing fast as vast new colonies were added to it. But in order to benefit from all this territory, Britain needed to get people to live there. What happened in Canada was typical of what happened all over the empire.

The British government sold a huge swathe of land, 200,000 acres, in Nova Scotia ('New Scotland', see map above) to two Scottish businessmen. It was bare, unused land, never farmed. In order to attract colonists, the company owned by the pair put enticing advertisements in Scottish newspapers. It sounded great: a family of five could apply for 500 acres and live there completely rent-free for two years. After that time the cost was just £5 per 100 acres. They also offered a one-way fare across the Atlantic for £3.25.

SOURCE 2 *Verses like this also appeared in newspapers:*

There's wood and there's water, there's wildfowl and tame,
In the forest good venison, good fish in the stream,
Good grass for our cattle, good land for our plough,
Good wheat to be raised and good barley to sow,
No landlords are there the poor tenant to tease,
No lawyers to bully, no bailiffs to seize,
But each honest fellow's a landlord, and dares
To spend on himself the whole fruit of his cares.
They've no duties on candles, no taxes on malt,
Nor do they, as we do, pay sauce for our salt,
But all is as free as in those days of old,
When poets assure us the age was of gold.

The *Hector*

No wonder poor Scots, struggling with high rents and low incomes, were attracted. In 1773 a ship, the *Hector*, set off from Glasgow with 193 colonists on board. There were 119 'adults' (that meant anyone over the age of eight!), 47 aged two to eight and 27 under two.

They soon discovered that things were not quite what they had been led to expect: the ship was so rotten that the passengers could pick the wood out of her sides with their fingers. They met with a severe gale off the Newfoundland coast, and were driven back by it so far that it took them about fourteen days to return to the point at which the storm met them. The accommodation was wretched, smallpox and dysentery broke out among the passengers. Eighteen of the children died.

Harvest

Nevertheless, these first colonists survived. Breaking the land with their ploughs for the first time was tremendously hard work, but gradually they were able to grow crops. They cut the timber which grew all around them and sold it back to Britain.

They were followed by thousands more colonists: a quarter of a million Scots emigrated to Canada in the nineteenth century. They made a huge contribution to the development of Canada, in the fur trade, the timber trade, banking, industry and railways (see Source 3). Many Canadians remain deeply proud of their Scottish inheritance.

◀ SOURCE 3 *This photo shows the Canadian Pacific Railway being built, in 1886. Scots were very involved in building this important rail link across Canada as engineers, investors and directors.*

DISCUSS

Do you think 'brave and adventurous' is a good description of the Canadian Scots? If yes, give your reasons. If not, provide a better description.

Case study 3: Irish emigration, nineteenth century

ACTIVITY

As you research the stories of emigration, record your findings on the diagrams on page 100–101.

Famine

The population of Ireland rose from 5.2 million in 1801 to 8.2 million in 1841. This huge increase meant that many Irish people were getting progressively poorer as more and more of them tried to live off the same amount of land. For many, the solution to their problem was to grow potatoes, because one acre of land can produce a lot of potatoes – 6 to 8 tons a year. Many poor Irish families ate nothing else but potatoes and buttermilk, helped out by a little bacon or cabbage.

Then came disaster! In 1845 potato blight reached Ireland. The potato crops in the fields were reduced to stinking inedible rot. Soon thousands of people were starving and by 1849 1 million had died of hunger or the diseases hunger brings. The only solution was to get out.

Over 4 million Irish people left their homeland in the nineteenth century. About half moved to the British mainland. There were 150,000 Irish people in Manchester and Liverpool alone. The rest went overseas, mainly to the USA.

One-way ticket

Emigration was expensive. A one-way ticket to the USA was about £5 (equivalent to £200 today) and it cost £16–£20 to get to Australia. This was a huge sum for desperately poor people to find. So often one member of a family, usually a single young man, would emigrate first and send money home from his wages to pay the fare of the next person.

A newspaper in 1850 described the scene:

There are usually a large number of spectators at the dock-gates to witness the final departure of the noble ship, with its large freight of human beings. It is an impressive sight; as the ship is towed out, hats are raised, handkerchiefs are waved, and a shout of farewell is raised from the shore. It is then, if at any time, that the eyes of the emigrants begin to moisten with regret at the thought that they are looking for the last time at the old country – that country which, although, in all probability, associated principally with the remembrance of sorrow and suffering, of semi-starvation, and a constant battle for the merest crust is, nevertheless, the country of their fathers, the country of their childhood.

The passage was tough. For their cheap fares, the shipping companies only provided basic accommodation: bunk beds in open, crowded areas below decks, buckets for toilets, inadequate food. There was only ventilation when the hatches above were open, and during bad weather they were fastened down for days on end.

▼ SOURCE 4 *Emigrants approaching the Statue of Liberty. An inscription on the statue says: 'Give me your tired, your poor, your huddled masses yearning to be free'.*

106

Ellis Island

Migrants to the USA arrived at Ellis Island, in New York harbour – overlooked by the famous Statue of Liberty (Source 4), where they were given a health check. If they were diseased – and many immigrants were – they were turned away and put on the next ship back to Europe. If they were considered fit enough to enter the USA they headed into New York itself, or went to other cities by railroad. Most migrants did not have the spare cash to buy farm land but there were plenty of jobs available in cities as the new country grew fast and there were cheap tenements to live in.

Religion

The USA was largely a country of immigrants, so there was nothing unusual about the experience of receiving new people. Irish immigrants had some advantages. They spoke the majority language, English, and came from the dominant ethnic group, white. They were much better received in the USA than, for example, the Italians or the Hispanics who suffered discrimination. However, for the Irish there was one box that was not ticked: religion. Most Irish were Catholics. But the dominant religious belief in the USA was Protestant. Many Irish were stigmatised for their religious belief and they had to work very hard to be successful.

▼ SOURCE 5 *Shelter in New York City for newly arrived immigrants.*

▼ SOURCE 6 *'Here and There or Emigration a Remedy'. This cartoon appeared in the English magazine* Punch *in 1848.*

HERE   AND   THERE;
Or, Emigration a Remedy.

DISCUSS

Do you think 'brave and adventurous' is a good description of the American Irish? If yes, give your reasons. If not, provide a better description.

DOING HISTORY:
Diversity and generalisation

You are nearly ready to write up your conclusions to the investigation on page 100. But first think back to last year's key ideas about Diversity in the box on the right.

Because there is such **diversity**, we have to be careful when we say anything about 'people' in the past. We need to remember

- to identify the diversity of people's experiences
- to treat people as individuals.

However, writing about history would be pretty hard if you could only ever write about individuals. So here are two important new ideas:

Diversity		Diversity
In History we make generalisations. They are a useful way of summing up conclusions.	BUT	It is important to test generalisations and strengthen them to make sure they are as accurate as possible.

On the opposite page you can see how to test and improve our generalisation about reasons for emigration. Here is a reminder from page 100:

QUESTION 1

Why did they emigrate?

People emigrated from Britain for economic reasons. They had a difficult time here and hoped to live more prosperous, easier lives somewhere else.

LEARNING LOG

How are you going to record these key ideas so you can use them next time?

On your own

Take one of the other questions and generalisations on page 101 and use these same steps to test it out against the evidence you have gathered on pages 102–107 and to improve it.

STEP 1 — Test the generalisation

It is easy for people to get away with sloppy thinking when they make generalisations. So you test the generalisation to make sure it is based on sound evidence. If not you will need to reject it or change it.

1 Based on your completed diagram, do you think this generalisation is justified? Are there more emigrants in the economic area of the diagram than anywhere else? Is this the most common reason?

2 How would you complete this sentence:

> *The generalisation that people emigrated for economic reasons is (completely/only partly/not at all) true.*

STEP 2 — Strengthen the generalisation by adding supporting evidence

3 Choose one example from the diagram that shows how economic factors motivated the emigrants.

4 Complete these sentences to show there is truth in the generalisation.

> *People who emigrated for economic reasons included … (name the people and add details to explain their situation). Another example of people who shared this motive was … (add details to explain their situation).*

STEP 3 — Strengthen it further by showing that you know it is not the whole story

A generalisation never tells the whole story. But you can strengthen it by showing the exceptions. Some people might think this undermines the generalisation but the opposite is true: if you can show that there are some emigrants who do not fit this pattern, but that it is mostly true, you strengthen your argument.

5 How would you complete these sentences:

> *Economics was not the only reason. For some emigrants the main reason was … (add an example of why these people moved). Or …*

STEP 4 — Check your language

Generalisations can be made much more accurate by carefully selecting words like *many, some, majority, minority, often, sometimes, occasionally, probably, possibly.*

6 Look at the following examples. What would happen to the sentences if you took out the phrases highlighted in yellow? Would they still be true?

> *Life for many working people in Britain in the mid-nineteenth century was not good. The majority found it hard to manage on their low pay, and sometimes unemployment cut even that.*

> *The emotional pain of leaving was probably hard for some. Only a minority of emigrants ever returned.*

THE BIG STORY:
Movement and Settlement Part Two

Last year you discovered that people have always moved to and settled in other lands, and this year you've seen that many thousands of British people emigrated to make new lives elsewhere. All of us probably have an emigrant in our families, at some stage in history.

So let's sum up the Big Stories about emigration.

1 When did emigration increase?

There was little emigration from Britain in the Middle Ages but it began to speed up in the 1600s and became much more common in the 1800s.

2 Why did people emigrate?

More people wanted to emigrate, but also ships became stronger, larger and speedier and people knew more about the rest of the world so the idea of emigrating was not quite so frightening.

Even so, emigrants had to be strongly motivated: journeys were long and dangerous, the new land was often unknown and return was almost impossible. Most emigrants left because they could see no hope for a decent future where they were. Many left reluctantly.

Poverty was a very important reason, especially in the early 1800s when people were struggling to find work or their old jobs had been replaced by machines in factories. At other times people emigrated so they could follow their own religion or to avoid persecution for their religious or political beliefs. Other people had no choice – they were sent abroad as a punishment or as slaves.

3 How were people received in their new lands?

Many people were welcomed, especially in countries like the USA and Australia in the 1800s which were changing quickly and where there were plenty of jobs. However, at other times emigrants got a cautious welcome because they were strangers who might be dangerous, such as in America in the 1600s. However, even then, some Native Americans helped Europeans find food and build homes. Other people were not welcome because they seemed to be a threat, such as the sick who were turned away from the USA at Ellis Island.

4 What impact did they have on their new lands?

The impact was very mixed. Some emigrants killed many of the native peoples they met, either in wars or by accident by spreading diseases. In contrast, other emigrants contributed a lot through their work or their ideas. They built towns and railways, set up charities and introduced new sports, created jobs for other people and took part in government.

ACTIVITY 1

1 Why do you think emigrants are often described as 'brave and adventurous'?

2 Which words would you use to describe emigrants? You can choose up to five adjectives.

LEARNING LOG

Next year your work on Movement and Settlement will investigate the story of immigration to Britain.

a) Which of the points on the left will be useful to remember when investigating immigration?

b) Create your own notes or diagrams to help you remember those points for use next year.

ACTIVITY 2

Linking the Big Stories together

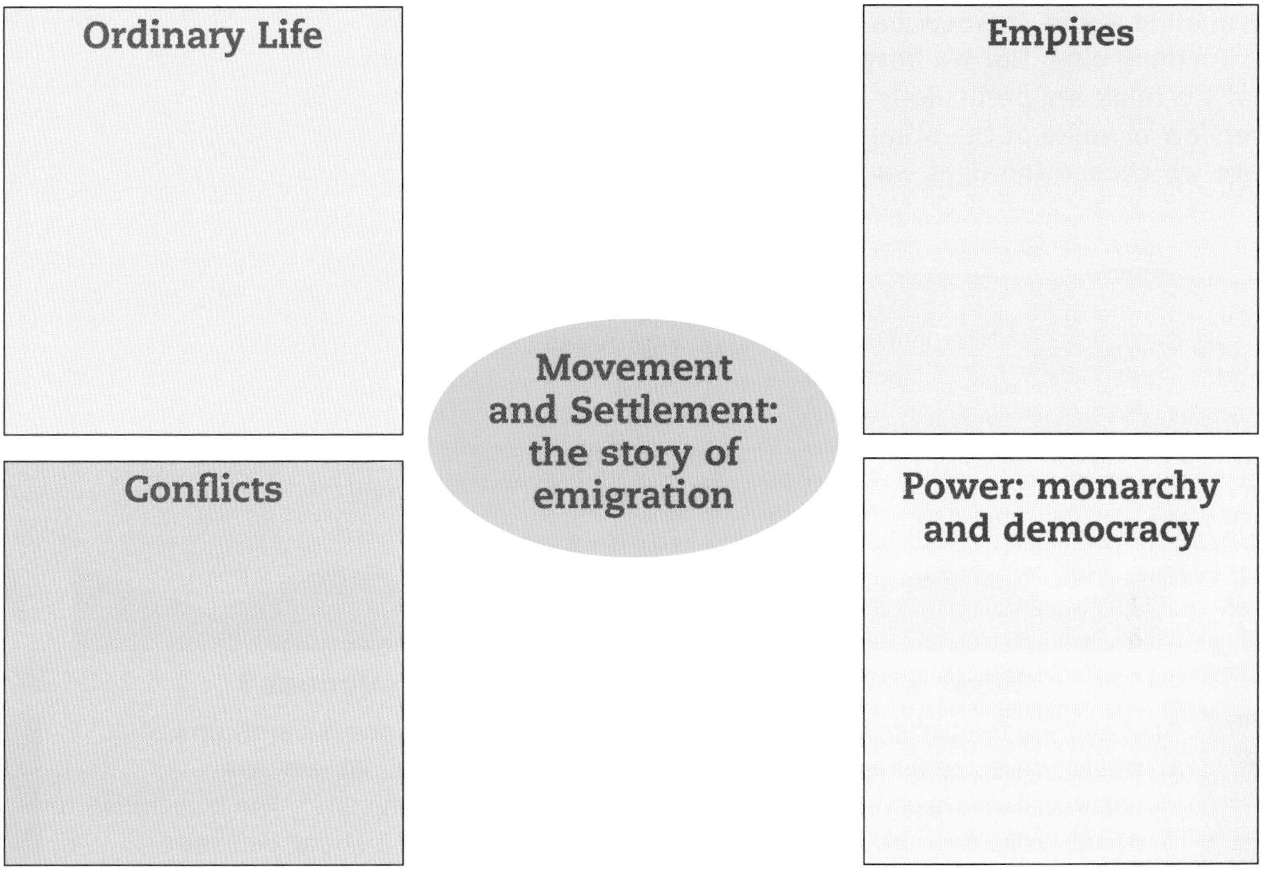

Ordinary Life

Empires

Movement and Settlement: the story of emigration

Conflicts

Power: monarchy and democracy

Some more examples of emigration 1500–1900:

A 1649–1660
After the English Civil War and the execution of King Charles I, many of Charles's supporters emigrated to America because they did not want to live in England without a king.

B
After the defeat of Bonnie Prince Charlie's rebellion of 1745 many Scots were thrown off their land. Many left for Canada.

C 1840s
During the 1840s there were many protests by Chartists who wanted all working men to have the vote. Many Chartist leaders were arrested, put on trial and sentenced to transportation to Australia for seven or fourteen years. Some stayed when their sentence ended because returning to England was difficult.

D
One of the reasons why the British wanted an empire was to provide a place for people to emigrate to. Australia, South Africa and India all offered opportunities to live better than seemed possible back in Britain.

Complete your own version of the above diagram, using evidence from this section and from examples A–D.

1 Draw lines from Movement and Settlement to any of the other Big Stories that help to explain why people emigrated.
2 Add brief notes to each line, recording evidence to show why you drew the line.
3 Colour in red the line that has the strongest links to the story of Movement and Settlement.

The years 1500–1900 were full of wars. You are not going to study them all in detail. It would be impossible. There would be no time for anything else. But we have chosen two wars to study in depth that we think are particularly significant, and have given you an overview of some of the others. Will you agree with our choice? Have we chosen the right wars?

How (not) to invade Britain!

Various countries have tried to invade Britain – but no one has succeeded since 1066! You are going to work out why but first you will look back to last year's work to help you.

What were the secrets of William's success?

What can you remember from last year?

1 William collected his men, weapons and ships for the invasion
   a) hurriedly, or   **b)** carefully.

2 William's ships set sail
   a) as soon as they were ready, or
   b) after weeks waiting for a good wind.

3 King Harold had
   a) a strong army ready and waiting to defend the south coast of England, or
   b) a hastily assembled army who were away fighting in the north.

4 When William landed in England he was
   a) immediately attacked by Harold, or
   b) able to land safely.

5 Harold was in the north of England
   a) defeating a Norwegian invader, or
   b) hiding from William.

6 When Harold heard that the Norman army had landed, he
   a) took his time so he could collect a fresh army, or
   b) rushed south to take William by surprise.

7 When Harold and his army arrived at the battlefield, William was
   a) still in camp and taken by surprise, or
   b) already in a strong defensive position on a hilltop.

8 During the Battle of Hastings, cavalry
   a) were used only by the English, or
   b) were used only by the Normans.

9 At the Battle of Hastings
   a) the Normans had more men, better weapons and better training, or
   b) the two sides were more or less evenly matched.

10 During the battle William
   a) led from the front, inspiring his men with his own bravery, or
   b) controlled the battle from a distance with carefully planned orders.

11 The English line broke because
   a) they thought the Normans were retreating and chased them, or
   b) they thought it was teatime.

12 King Harold was
   a) killed by an arrow in his eye, or
   b) chopped down by a Norman sword.

DOING HISTORY: Causes

Why did William's invasion succeed?

This question begins with the word 'why'. It is a question about causes. So what do you already know about causes from last year?

CAUSES — Recap

Most events have a number of causes

Even if there are lots of causes there's usually one that finally sets off an event

Causes are not equally important

Here is another idea to help you write good explanations:

Causes

Causes of an event are often linked

Identifying these links can help you decide which causes were the **most** important.

ACTIVITY

The quiz on page 112 reminded you about what happened in 1066. Now use that knowledge to explain why William succeeded.

1 Make five cards like those below.

2 Choose **at least** one piece of information to complete each card.

3 On a large sheet of paper, arrange your cards like the diagram on the right, with the most important cause at the top and the least important at the bottom.

4 Draw lines to link any cards that you think are connected. Write notes to explain your link.
Note: if you want to make more cause cards you can.

5 Why might an Englishman and a Norman each put a different card at the top?

Planning
William's plans were …

Weapons
The Normans had better …

Fighting forces
The English army was …

Leadership
William's leadership was …

Luck
The weather helped …

Why did the Spanish Armada fail?

One of the most famous attempts to invade England came in 1588. King Philip of Spain sent a massive Armada to remove Queen Elizabeth from the English throne. He failed. Follow the step-by-step instructions to work out why, then write a really good answer to explain the reasons.

Philip's motives

Philip was the most powerful ruler in the world. He ruled Portugal, the Netherlands, Sicily, Naples and Milan as well as an empire in America, Mexico, Peru and the Caribbean. He even had some islands in the Pacific, which were named after him – the Philippines. He wanted to invade England, remove Elizabeth from the throne and put a new ruler in place. But why?

1 The Roman Catholic faith is the one true religion. I am its greatest supporter. The ruler of England, the so-called queen, Elizabeth, is a Protestant heretic.

2 That English pirate Francis Drake has frequently attacked my towns in America and seized my gold and silver. To add insult to injury, Elizabeth has now made this pirate **Sir** Francis Drake.

3 The Dutch are rebelling against my rule in the Netherlands and Elizabeth has sent soldiers to help them in their rebellion. She must be stopped.

▲ SOURCE 1 *King Philip II of Spain.*

How to work out your answer

Here are the same five factors that you used to analyse William's success in 1066. You are now going to use them to analyse a failure.

Weapons

Fighting forces

Leadership

Luck

Planning

Philip's plan

1 I will send an Armada of Spanish warships from Lisbon up the English Channel to anchor off the Dutch coast.

2 My Spanish army in the Netherlands, commanded by the Duke of Parma, will be ready to join them in the Netherlands. They will come out in small boats to board the ships of the Armada.

3 My Armada will then sail across the Channel and land Parma's army on the north Kent coast.

4 My army will march to London repelling any attacks by the English army.

STEP 1 ▶ Your hypothesis

❶ Read about Philip's motives and his plans. Which factor do you expect to be the main reason Philip failed? Put it at the top. Which do you think was the least important? Put it at the bottom.

❷ Draw a plan of how you would arrange the cards. Jot down the reasons for your choice. For example:

Fighting forces

Planning   Weapons   Luck

Leadership

Keep a record so you can compare this with your final answer later.

STEP 2 ▶ Collect evidence

Use pages 116–119 to make notes on each card, collecting information and evidence about each factor. Begin with Philip's plan. Note down on the card examples of good or bad planning. For instance:

The English might attack before Parma got his soldiers on board the Armada.

STEP 3 ▶ Review your evidence

STEP 4 ▶ Revise your hypothesis

STEP 5 ▶ Write your explanation

When you get to page 120 you'll get more help with Steps 3–5.

Ships, guns, men and God

ACTIVITY

Continue collecting evidence of good or bad Planning, Weapons, Fighting forces, Leadership or Luck. Keep alert – there's evidence here for several of the factor cards.

Ships

The **Spanish Armada** consisted of 151 ships, of which 68 were warships. The rest were transport ships to carry equipment and Parma's soldiers. Some of these were unarmed. Philip's advisers had told him he would need 500 ships to succeed but even Spain could not afford that.

The **English fleet** consisted of about 177 ships, many of them very small – under 100 tons. 34 were royal warships.

Soldiers and supplies

Spanish: There were 7000 sailors and 34,000 soldiers on the ships of the Armada. Philip claimed that his Armada was a Roman Catholic crusade so God was on their side. There were 180 priests and monks on board and mass was said every day on every ship.

The Armada was equipped with enough ammunition, food and water for a four week campaign – which was longer than they expected to be at sea.

English: There were 16,000 sailors on board ships and 76,000 soldiers on land. Many, like Sir Francis Drake, were devout Protestants.

Elizabeth's government was mean with supplies and the English fleet did not have enough gunpowder, ammunition, food or water for a long campaign.

Guns

Both sides had cannon of different shapes and sizes on board. The largest could fire a cannonball weighing up to 15 kg about 200 metres. The main difference between the two sides was how they were used.

The **Spanish** expected to fire their cannon just once, then to come alongside enemy ships and board them. The soldiers would then fight as if they were on land. It could take up to an hour to re-load guns because of the way they were mounted. Many of the Spanish guns were probably not intended to be used at sea at all, but were being transported for land battles in England.

The **English** cannon were each mounted on a small gun-carriage, especially built for use at sea. They could be re-loaded in about ten minutes but were fired one at a time as each gun-team decided. The English had long-range guns. They did not want to get close to the enemy and risk being boarded by soldiers.

The Duke of Medina-Sidonia
He was the richest and most important nobleman in **Spain**. He had never been to sea before but many of his captains were experienced trans-Atlantic sailors. Once he had left Spain, Medina-Sidonia was completely out of touch with Philip and Parma. Remember, in those days there was no radio, satnav or telephone. They did not even have a system of ship-to-ship communication. And once the fleets were in battle every captain had to take all decisions on his own.

Lord Howard of Effingham, England
He was the queen's cousin and had only a little experience at sea. He relied on other commanders, brilliant seamen like Sir Francis Drake.

He **did not know** what the Armada planned to do. In particular he did not know about the plan to pick up soldiers in the Netherlands. He assumed the Armada would land in England, somewhere on the south coast. He also did not know how skilled the Spanish were.

He **did know** that his own seamen were skilled and experienced but that most of the English land forces were badly armed and poorly trained.

DECISION POINT

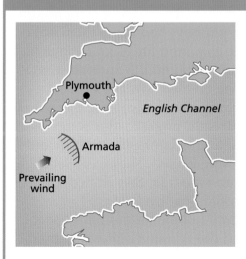

You are the English commander. The Armada has been sighted as it heads into the English Channel. Your ships are in port at Plymouth. The wind is from the west. Bearing in mind the information above, which of the following options will you choose, and why?
You could:
a) **stay in port in Plymouth** and wait for news – keeping your ships at the ready
b) go out to sea now and **attack the Armada from the front**, into the wind
c) go out to sea and **attack the Armada from behind**, with the wind behind you
d) wait for the Armada to pass and **follow at a safe distance** to see what happens.

117

What happened next?

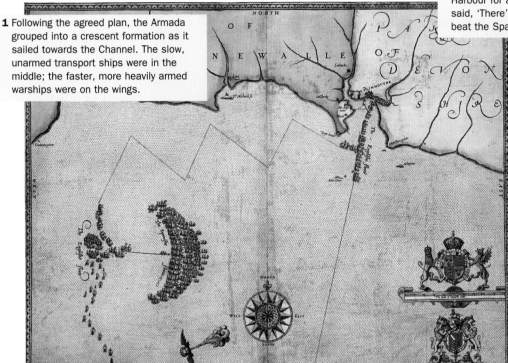

1 Following the agreed plan, the Armada grouped into a crescent formation as it sailed towards the Channel. The slow, unarmed transport ships were in the middle; the faster, more heavily armed warships were on the wings.

2 The story goes that, as the Armada was sighted off Cornwall, Drake was playing bowls on Plymouth Hoe. Knowing that the tide would prevent the English fleet getting out of Plymouth Harbour for a few hours, he is reported to have said, 'There's time to finish the game and then beat the Spaniards afterwards!'

4 Both fleets stayed in these formations for a week, as the Armada sailed slowly up the Channel with a steady westerly wind helping it.
Whenever the English ships tried to get close enough to the Armada to fire their guns the warships on the wings of the crescent closed in on them from both sides. One Spanish ship accidentally blew up, but otherwise there were no losses on either side. The English had not stopped the Armada.

◀ SOURCE 2 *A chart made at the time which shows the position of the two fleets in July.*

3 English ships separated into two fleets to get behind the Armada. You can see one route zigzags west; one goes straight south, off the bottom of the chart. Both lead to the English ships shown to the west of the Armada.

▼ SOURCE 3 *The situation on 6 August.*

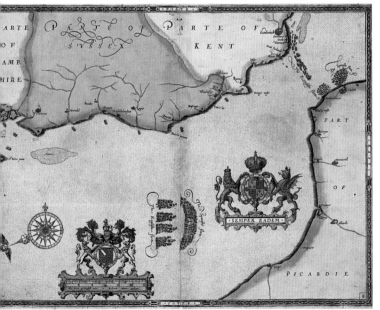

By 6 August the Armada, still intact, had anchored off the coast of France near Calais.

However, on land things had not gone well. Parma was not ready. His army was 50 km away and being attacked by the Dutch! It would take at least two weeks to assemble the army and get it on board the Armada.

Still, there was no reason for Medina-Sidonia to panic. The Spanish had kept their tight defensive formation. Their long experience on trans-Atlantic journeys had made them skilled seamen. English cannon fire at long range had made little impression on the Spanish ships.

However, the English now chose this moment to attack. Very early in the morning of 7 August 1588, eight English ships were loaded with straw, tar and inflammable rubbish and their cannon were loaded. They were set alight. On the wind and the tide, they drifted towards the tightly packed Spanish fleet.

Fire can be a terrible hazard for wooden ships. In panic, the Armada captains hurried out of the way. Some cut their anchor ropes. None of the Spanish ships was damaged but their close formation turned to chaos.

The Battle of Gravelines

The next day the two fleets went into battle. It was a confused fight, with English ships firing their cannon at a range of about 100 metres. This was enough to cause death and damage, but too far away to actually sink enemy ships. The Spanish could not return fire because their guns were not designed for a sea battle.

As night fell on 8 August, the wind strengthened. With his fleet scattered, and unable to turn back, Medina-Sidonia could see that Philip's great Armada plan was lost. He set about trying to save as many ships and lives as he could. His captains told him that the strong winds prevented them from returning through the Channel. They had cut their anchor ropes so they could not anchor. Medina-Sidonia had no choice. Their only way back to the safety of Spanish ports was the 3000 km trip around Scotland and Ireland.

The English fleet, running low on gunpowder, chased them as far as the coast of Scotland.

The end of the Armada

Some of the ships had been damaged by English gun fire but it was the weather that now took over and brought the campaign to a tragic end. Fierce storms battered the Spanish ships. The boats did not have enough food or water for this long voyage. Sailors became too ill to sail their ships properly. Nor did they have maps of these waters. Two boats were wrecked on the Scottish coast, then 25 more were lost off the coast of Ireland. Some shipwrecked Spanish sailors who made it to dry land were hunted down and killed.

Only 90 ships returned to Spain. Probably 11,000 people lost their lives.

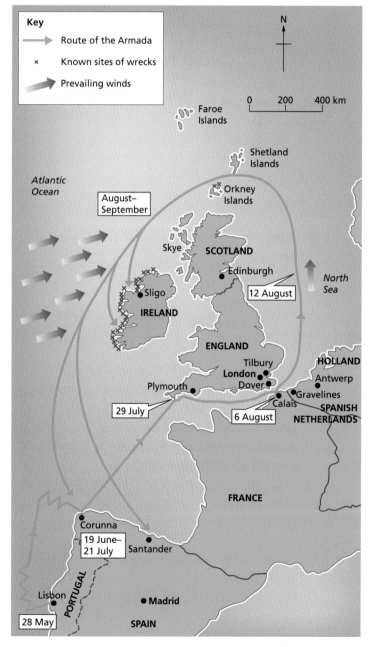

▲ SOURCE 4 *Map showing the route of the Armada and the location of known shipwrecks.*

ACTIVITY

Continue collecting evidence. These two pages will help you with all the cards.

Why did the Spanish Armada fail?

STEP 3 ▶ Review your evidence

You should have gathered lots of evidence about why the invasion failed. Your cards should be full of information and examples. For instance:

Leadership
- Both commanders inexperienced at sea – but both had experienced sailors and captains in the ships themselves so that should not matter.
- English fireships tactic worked brilliantly.
- Medina-Sidonia decided to retreat rather than fight on.
- He gave up too easily.

Weapons

Fighting forces

Luck

Planning

1. Compare your cards with other pairs or groups and improve yours if necessary.

STEP 4 ▶ Revise your hypothesis and plan your explanation

2. Arrange your cards in the order of your first hypothesis from page 115.
3. Now re-arrange them to show which factors you **now** think were the most or least important.
4. Draw lines to link any cards that you think are connected. The more links a card has the more important it probably is. Does this make you want to change your arrangement?
5. Once you are happy with the arrangement of your cards you are ready for Step 5.

STEP [5] ▶ Write your explanation

... write good explanations

There is no right answer to a typical **explanations** question like this one – but some answers are better than others! A good answer is a clear, strong argument, in which you weigh up the importance of different reasons. You will need:

- evidence to support each point you want to make. Select your evidence carefully so that it supports the point you are trying to make. Highlight the most useful evidence on each card from pages 116 to 119.
- words or phrases that drive home the argument of your explanation. You can see from the examples below what a difference it can make to choose different words or phrases.

Contribute	Allow	Prevent	This led to	Motivate
Discourage	Despite	In addition	However	
Encourage	Support	Further	Bring about	Underlying

A A **central** factor was the failure of the Spanish to keep in touch with each other.

B An **underlying** factor was the failure of the Spanish to keep in touch with each other.

C The failure of the Spanish to keep in touch with each other **prevented** the plan from succeeding.

> Writer A puts the communications problem at the heart of the explanation, Writer B also sees it as important, but it was how the situation developed that made the difference, while for Writer C it was the only factor that counted.

A The **key** difference between the two navies was that the English were fighting closer to home.

B An **important** difference between the two navies was that the English were fighting closer to home.

> Here Writer A puts more weight on the reason than Writer B.

A **Despite** the discipline of the Spanish fleet while sailing up the Channel, they panicked when the fire-ships appeared.

> This writer gives credit where it is due but links the two phases of the campaign together well by contrasting them.

A The wind direction **allowed** Drake to use fire-ships to split up the Spanish fleet. **Further,** the wind continued to favour the English.

B The fire-ships **led to** the defeat of the Armada because they **brought about** confusion in the fleet. The strong westerly gales then **contributed** to their total defeat.

> Writer B builds a stronger sequence by using 'led to', 'brought about', and 'contributed' Writer A sounds more laid back, with 'allowed' and simply 'further'.

Was Nelson the main reason why Napoleon's invasion failed?

In 1805 a huge French army waited near Calais to invade Britain. The French emperor, Napoleon Bonaparte, had already conquered most of Europe. Britain was next. He had the Bayeux Tapestry shown to his men to remind them of the last successful French invasion. But unlike in 1066, the French army never landed in Britain. Indeed it never even set sail from France. Some people give all the credit to Admiral Nelson and his famous victory at the Battle of Trafalgar. Will you agree?

ACTIVITY

Use the same process that you used to study the defeat of the Spanish Armada to investigate why Napoleon's planned invasion of Britain failed.

You are on your own this time but remember

... the five steps:
Step 1 Start with a hypothesis.
Step 2 Gather your evidence.
Step 3 Review your evidence.
Step 4 Revise your hypothesis so you are certain about your argument.
Step 5 Write up your answer.

... the five headings to gather your evidence:
Planning
Weapons
Fighting forces
Leadership
Luck

War with France

Britain was at war with France more or less continuously from 1793 onwards. Napoleon had successfully conquered all his neighbouring countries, marked in yellow on the map in Source 1, and, in 1803, he decided Britain had to be defeated too. The invasion was a serious threat: the British government made plans to evacuate southern England. They built defensive Martello Towers all along the coast.

However, those 22 miles of sea presented Napoleon with a huge problem. He ordered 2000 barges to carry a cargo of men, horses and equipment safely across. For this plan to work he also knew he had to control the Channel so that his barges would not be attacked by the British warships that were always on patrol. Napoleon either had to defeat the British warships or lure them away from defending the Channel for long enough to launch his invasion.

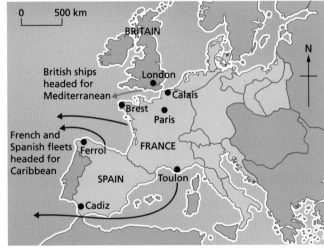

▲ SOURCE 1 *A map showing Napoleon's empire and his intentions for the battle.*

Napoleon's big advantage over the English was the number of ships. He had conquered Spain and could use Spain's navy. The combined French and Spanish fleets out-numbered the British.

Napoleon's plan

1 His fleet would cross the Atlantic to the Caribbean, where they would raid British colonies and ships.

2 This would lure the British fleet to follow them there to protect their colonies.

3 The combined French and Spanish fleets would then rush back to Europe and escort the invasion barges across to England before the British fleet returned.

The ships

The Victory

The Golden Hind

Years later Napoleon said:

I would have hastened over with my flotilla of 200,000 men, landing near Chatham, and proceeded direct to London, where I calculated to arrive in four days from the time of my landing. I would have proclaimed a republic; the abolition of nobility and the House of Lords; liberty, equality and the sovereignty of the people.

◀ SOURCE 2
Horatio Nelson was the commander of the British navy. This picture shows his flagship, the Victory, *alongside Sir Francis Drake's ship the* Golden Hind *(from 1588) at the same scale.*

The warships of Nelson's time were still wooden sailing ships, as in the time of the Armada, but were much bigger as you can see from Source 2. Nelson's flagship, the *Victory*

- cost the equivalent of £20 million today to build
- used 2000 oak trees in its construction
- was powered by 4 acres of sail and controlled by 40 miles of rope
- (most important of all) carried 104 big guns.

Warships like these had blockaded French and Spanish ports for years, preventing the French and Spanish navies from venturing out. In 1805 Nelson's second-in-command, Vice-Admiral Collingwood, had not been home for three years.

What happened?

The combined French and Spanish fleets left their ports in March 1805 and headed for the Caribbean. At first Nelson thought they were heading for Egypt and he sailed into the Mediterranean. By the time he found out his mistake, valuable sailing time had been lost. Nevertheless, Napoleon's plans began to go wrong. The journey across the Atlantic left many of the ships damaged and the sailors ill. They were in no state to raid the British Caribbean islands and had to return to Cadiz, in Spain, to recover.

Think! So what do you think of the plan? Was it any better than Philip of Spain's Armada plan?

The men, their lives and their guns

If you play any team sport you will know that a good captain can inspire an ordinary team to be great. Everyone says that Nelson was an inspirational leader, but how can we tell?

The men

Nelson's flagship, the *Victory*, was crammed with men: 821 of them. The youngest was Thomas Twitchett, aged 12; the oldest was John King, aged 56. There were 663 sailors and officers who ran the ship and the rest were marines (soldiers). It was an international crew. There were 441 English, 67 Scots, 63 Irish, 18 Welsh, 2 from the Channel Islands and 1 from the Isle of Man. Reflecting Britain's racial diversity at this time there were also 9 from the Caribbean, 1 African, 2 Indians and 22 Americans (some of whom were probably black). There were also sailors from Holland, Switzerland, Sweden, Italy, Malta, France, Norway, Germany, Portugal, Denmark and Russia. (It was as mixed as the Roman army if you can remember that from last year!)

▲ SOURCE 3
Nelson's day-cabin on board the Victory.

Life on board

Beds Sailors slept below decks in hammocks, with just 0.5 metres of space each. It was dark, smelly (soap was not issued until 1825) and damp.

Toilets Ordinary sailors used the 'heads': a plank in the bows with a hole over the open sea. Officers' toilets were the same, but enclosed.

Food was served to groups of eight sailors ('mess-mates') who shared it out between them on square wooden plates (a 'square meal'). It was difficult to provide decent food on a long voyage before refrigeration. Meat was salt-beef and hard ship's biscuits took the place of bread. It may sound revolting to us, but a good captain made it his business to see that plenty of food was provided. Sailors were probably no worse fed than poor labourers on land.

Drink Fresh water went putrid, green and slimy after a few weeks, so the men were issued with a gallon of beer (small beer, barely alcoholic, but at least drinkable) and half a pint (250 ml) of rum ('grog') per day.

Discipline was tough. Men could be flogged with the 'cat o'nine tails' – a rope whip with nine knotted ends – or put in leg-irons on deck in all weathers. A 14-year-old junior officer – a midshipman – could order a man to be 'started' – hit with a rope-end. Again, a good captain knew how to keep order without excessive cruelty.

The officers led a totally different life. Through a green baize door were their quarters, which were like a miniature version of life in an elegant London house. There were carpets on the floor, velvet-covered chairs and sash windows. They had better food, served on silver plates, with wine in fine glasses.

Think! How could Nelson as Admiral 'make a difference' to the lives of his men and keep their morale high? How important do you think this would be?

124

Weapons

Firing the guns demanded great skill and discipline. They were worked by teams of six men (see the panel on the right). It was hard, dangerous work, but a well-trained team could fire their cannon every 90 seconds. The team members had numbers. The lower your number the more skilled your job was.

The *Victory* carried 104 guns. The heaviest, on the lower deck, fired cannonballs weighing 14.5 kg. At 30 metres range they could smash through timber one metre thick, sending deadly splinters in all directions. The British were trained to aim at the hulls of enemy ships, blasting holes in them, killing men and making their guns useless.

The French and Spanish fleets

French and Spanish warships were of a similar size to the British ships, indeed some were bigger, and they carried similar guns. They had slightly more warships: 33 to Nelson's 29. However, the biggest difference was in the officers and crew.

- Many of the most experienced officers in the French navy had fled during the Revolution because they were Royalists (supporters of the King whom the revolution had overthrown – see page 188). So many of their officers were inexperienced.
- Spain was an unwilling ally of Napoleon so Spanish officers were reluctant to take orders from the French. Spanish sailors were even more reluctant to fight and many ships' crews were made up of convicts.
- French and Spanish sailors lacked sailing and battle practice as they had spent most of the war blockaded in their ports. French and Spanish gun crews could not match the speed of the British rate of fire.
- Their gunners' tactics were to aim at the mast, sails and rigging of an enemy ship, to try to make it unsailable. They also placed marksmen up in the rigging to shoot down into the decks of enemy ships.

No.4 shoved a sponge on a long handle down the barrel to put out any sparks and clean the barrel.

No.6, the powder-monkey, usually the youngest member of the team, fetched the gunpowder from the magazine.

No.3 loaded the gun with a measured amount of gunpowder and rammed a wad in after it to keep it tight. This was followed by the cannonball and another wad.

No.2 aimed the gun and then, with No.5, hauled it into position pointing through the gunport.

On the word of the gun-captain, No.1, a smouldering match was applied to the powder-hole and the gun fired. It recoiled two metres.

No.4 then started the whole process again by cleaning the barrel …

The Battle of Trafalgar

In mid-summer 1805 Napoleon gave orders to his fleet to set sail, or he would brand them cowards. He could not be disobeyed. The combined French and Spanish fleets slowly made their way out of Cadiz harbour. Most of their captains thought they were doomed. When British scouting ships passed the news to the main fleet waiting 50 miles away off Cape Trafalgar, Nelson made the signal to all his ships: 'The French and Spanish are out at last. They outnumber us in ships and guns and men and we are on the eve of the greatest sea-fight in history'.

Sea battles at that time were usually fought by bringing the two lines of ships parallel, so that they pounded each other with their guns, broadside to broadside. Nelson had discussed a dangerous but deadly new tactic with his commanders, later called 'crossing the T'. As the diagram shows, this meant sailing at right angles to the enemy fleet, during which they were under fire from enemy guns and unable to retaliate. They then raked the enemy vessel's bow or stern – the most undefended part of a warship – with the full force of a broadside attack.

Think! Why was this tactic risky for the British warships? Why was it so deadly for the enemy?

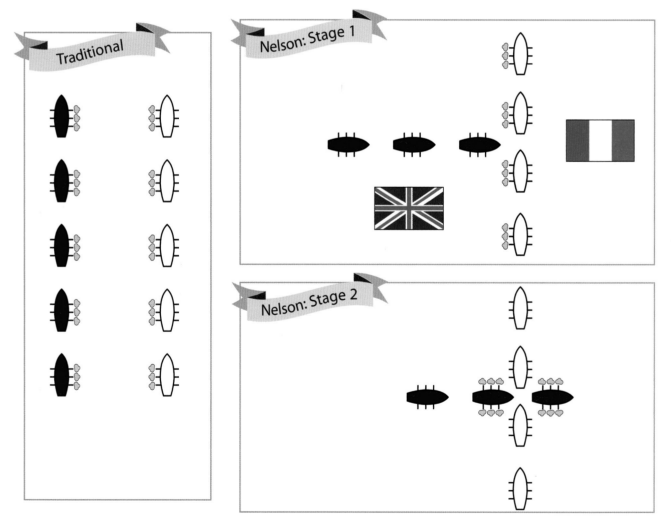

▲ **SOURCE 4** *Diagram showing stages in the Battle of Trafalgar.*

The battle

Nelson started the day, 21 October 1805, with his famous signal: 'England expects that every man will do his duty'. The wind was light, so the ships moved slowly towards each other. The first ship to make contact was the *Royal Sovereign* under Nelson's second-in-command, Admiral Collingwood. At noon he 'crossed the T' next to the Spanish ship *Santa Anna*. His first broadside killed 400 of her crew. Soon the *Victory* came under fire as it approached French and Spanish ships at right angles and was unable to fire back for fifteen minutes. Many were killed and wounded, including eight marines and Nelson's secretary.

Then the *Victory* came close under the stern of the *Bucentaure*, raking her with gun after gun along the port side. Hundreds of French sailors were killed or wounded.

More and more ships joined the battle and slowly the British fleet gained the upper hand. By the end the British victory was overwhelming: 20 French and Spanish ships surrendered and 16 more sank in the storm which followed the battle. Around 4400 French and Spanish sailors were killed, 2500 wounded and 7000 taken prisoner. There were 449 British dead and 1241 wounded.

It was a humiliating defeat for the French. Any invasion was now out of the question. The dominance of the British navy over the seas of the world lasted for the next hundred years.

Nelson dies

But the victory was hollow for the British. Their hero admiral had been killed. The *Victory* had run so close to the *Redoutable* that their rigging became locked together. As the two ships pounded one another at point-blank range, a French marksman high up on the *Redoutable* spotted Nelson on the deck and shot him. He died later that afternoon.

Nelson's body was put in a barrel of brandy to preserve it and returned to England where he was buried amid huge national grief (for his death) and celebration (that the threat of French invasion had been lifted).

▲ SOURCE 5 *Nelson's Column in Trafalgar Square, London. Nelson is probably Britain's greatest war hero, and has the most prominent memorial.*

Think! Do you think Nelson deserves this memorial? Was Nelson the one who prevented the French invasion?

127

Now for something completely different!

The last two case studies may have given the impression that the British always won their wars and always deserved to. However, read on for some contrasting examples of Britain at war ...

A bad home defeat: the Dutch raid of 1667

Britain was at war with the Dutch for much of the period 1652–1684. They were fighting for control of trade in Europe and overseas colonies. The Dutch captured Surinam, in the East Indies, from Britain. The British captured New Amsterdam, in North America, from the Dutch, and renamed it New York.

In June 1667, the Dutch admiral de Ruyter sailed his fleet into the Thames. The main British naval base was at Chatham, in Kent, where a huge chain was hung across the mouth of the River Medway to protect the warships. What happened next? Here the story is told in the famous diary of Samuel Pepys, who was Clerk to the Navy.

The *Royal Charles* was the pride of the British navy. It was named after King Charles II. It had brought him to England in triumph in 1660.

The Dutch burnt three other warships, the *Royal James*, the *Royal Oak* and the *Loyal London*, and captured several others. This is shown in the illustration below. This was deeply troubling. Pepys evacuated his wife and father-in-law from London with £1300 of gold. He was expecting an invasion, but there was more bad news to come.

The raid revealed the corruption and incompetence of Charles' government. It also revealed that the sailors were unpaid, angry and badly disciplined: no wonder they put up no fight. It was a humiliating defeat.

12 JUNE

Powell do tell me that ill news is come to Court of the Dutch breaking the Chaine at Chatham; which struck me to the heart. ... the Dutch have ... burned our ships, and particularly 'The Royal Charles' ...
I do fear so much that the whole kingdom is undone [and] went to bed full of fear and fright, hardly slept all night.

14 JUNE

Up, and to the office; where ... by and by comes ... a man of Mr Gawden's; who come from Chatham last night, and saw the three ships burnt ... But that he tells me of worst consequence is, that he himself ... did hear many Englishmen on board the Dutch ships speaking to one another in English; and that they did cry ... 'We did ... fight for tickets; now we fight for dollars!'

30 JUNE

It seems very remarkable to me, and of great honour to the Dutch, that those of them that did go on shore to Gillingham ... killed none of our people nor plundered their houses, [but] to our eternal disgrace, [the crew of the Royal Charles, who were put ashore by the Dutch raiding party that took the ship] plundered and took all away.

A terrible away win: the Opium War with China, 1839–1842

As the British Empire expanded in the early nineteenth century, British merchants tried to open up trade with China. They wanted to buy Chinese tea, silk and porcelain because there was a huge demand for them back in Britain. But what could the British sell to China in return? The Emperor had told the first British Ambassador, in 1793: 'Our Celestial Empire possesses all things in abundance. There is no need to import the manufactures of outside barbarians.'

Was there nothing the Chinese wanted? By 1800 the British had found something: opium. Opium is made from poppies and contains the highly addictive drug heroin. Poppies were grown and processed in British India; the opium was then sent in British ships to China. Opium imports to China quadrupled in the next few years and soon there were millions of addicts in China. The Chinese government tried to ban the trade, but British merchants bribed officials to ignore the ban.

The Emperor appointed a new official – Lin Tse-Hsü. Lin was so incorruptible that he was known as 'Lin the Clear Sky'. Lin wrote to Queen Victoria in 1839:

Suppose there were people from another country who carried opium for sale to England and seduced your people into buying and smoking it; certainly your honourable ruler would deeply hate it and be bitterly aroused. We have heard that your honourable ruler is kind and benevolent. Naturally you would not wish to give unto others what you yourself do not want.

...You, O Queen, can eradicate the opium plant ... hoe over the fields entirely, and sow grain in its stead. Anyone who dares again to attempt to plant and manufacture opium should be severely punished.

Lin gave the British merchants three days to hand over their stocks of opium. They refused, so Lin ordered in Chinese troops. Nearly 1000 tons of opium were seized – the biggest haul in history. He ordered it to be buried with salt and lime in huge trenches.

The British were furious. A British gunboat was sent, which fired at and sank five Chinese war-junks in 45 minutes. A bigger British fleet of steam-powered battleships arrived later and smashed the wooden Chinese sailing-ships sent to meet them (see picture above).

Lin was sent into exile. By the 1842 Treaty of Nanking the British forced the Chinese to open up more ports, including Hong Kong. British citizens in these areas were free of Chinese law. The opium trade doubled and the Chinese emperors were powerless to stop its effects on their people.

DISCUSS

1 How do you react to these two stories?
2 What do these two battles teach you about Britain at war?
3 Should these two battles be included in the school history curriculum? Why? Why not?

The long, the short and the bloody! War and peace 1066–2000

On the next three pages there are some War Top Trumps cards. All these wars involved Britain although they took place all over the world. They include four wars you studied last year and four you are going to study next year. For Activities 1 and 2 you need only the sixteen green and orange cards, 1500–1900.

ACTIVITY 1

Divide into teams. Use the Top Trumps cards for 1500–1900 and see which team can find the answers to these questions fastest.

1 In which wars did these battles take place?
  a) Waterloo   e) Balaclava
  b) Culloden   f) Blenheim
  c) Trafalgar   g) Flodden
  d) Isandhlwana
2 In which wars were these men leaders?
  a) Wolfe   c) Wellington
  b) Marlborough   d) Drake

3 Quiz time:
  a) In which century was the Crimean War?
  b) Which war is often called the 'first worldwide war'?
  c) In which war did George Washington defeat Britain?
  d) In which war did Britain win control of the city that became New York?
  e) Which war introduced the name Kop to football?

ACTIVITY 2

4 Divide the sixteen 1500–1900 cards amongst the class.
5 Look at the first three topics on your card: 'Scale', 'Impact on Britain' and 'International impact'.
6 Which four wars have the highest scores? Which four wars have the lowest scores? Place these on your living graph (see right).
7 Now place the rest of the 1500–1900 cards on the living graph.
8 Take a picture of the pattern you have made – it will be useful later on.

9 Discuss the wars that got the highest score. Do you agree they are the most significant wars?

ACTIVITY 3

This time you need all the cards 1066–present. You are going to mark all the wars on a world map.

Start with the Middle Ages. Mark those wars in one colour. Then add the period 1500–1750, and so on.

Once you have placed all your wars on a world map, photograph and discuss the pattern that you have found. What does this tell you about the changing nature of conflict from 1066 to the present day?

(see page 128)

Norman Conquest
1066–1070s

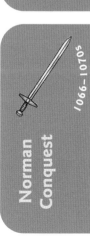

Scale: 7
England; Anglo-Saxon resistance steadily crushed by Normans after Battle of Hastings

Impact on Britain: 8
New Norman kings; castles and cathedrals built; widespread destruction and death; changes to law, language, religion

International impact: 3
England now linked to western, not northern, Europe

Memorable for: 10
The arrow in Harold's eye; last successful invasion of Britain

Crusades
1095–1400s

Scale: 7
All over Europe and Middle East; Major battles between Christians and Muslims to control Jerusalem

Impact on Britain: 4
New words from Arabic; new ideas about castles

International impact: 9
Opened up links between Christian Western Europe and Islamic Middle East for exchange of goods and ideas

Memorable for: 7
Richard the Lionheart and Saladin; long-lasting hostile memory of Christian invasion among Muslims

English wars in Wales & Scotland
1276–1500s

Scale: 4
Edward I organised three campaigns in 1200s. Lots more followed

Impact on Britain: 6
Wales, but not Scotland, conquered by England

International impact: 2
Begins rise of England as an Empire builder

Memorable for: 3
Castle-building in Wales; Robert the Bruce, Scots (and a spider) beating English at Bannockburn

100 Years War
1337–1453

Scale: 6
Fought in France; not continuous but went on a lot longer than 100 years as kings of England staked their claim to throne of France

Impact on Britain: 4
Royal need for taxes led to first regular Parliaments

International impact: 6
Longbows used by ordinary soldiers to kill rich men in armour. Development of new weapons – cannon. Disease and famine reduced population of France by two-thirds

Memorable for: 7
English victories at Crécy, 1346, and Agincourt, 1415. Joan of Arc

Henry VIII's wars with Scotland
1511–1513, 1542–1547

Scale: 2
Border wars, with English forces victorious

Impact on Britain: 1
England clearly stronger but could not conquer Scotland; caused great hardship in England because of taxes and price rises

International impact: 2
Strengthened alliance of Scotland and France

Memorable for: 2
Death of Scottish King James IV, blown up by his own cannon at Flodden, 1513

Elizabeth I's wars with Spain
1585–1604

Scale: 3
Major Spanish effort to conquer England fails utterly

Impact on Britain: 8
England's independence and Protestantism secured

International impact: 4
Leads to decline of Spanish domination of Europe

Memorable for: 4
Spanish Armada's shipwrecks; Drake supposedly playing bowls

Elizabethan wars in Ireland
1594–1603

Scale: 2
English campaigns to crush Irish leaders in Ulster (NE Ireland)

Impact on Britain: 5
Defeat of Ulster Irish lords leads to English and Scots Protestant settlement in Ulster

International impact: 0
None

Memorable for: 1
Defeat of Elizabeth's favourite, Earl of Essex

Anglo-Dutch Wars
1652–1684

Scale: 5
Series of naval wars mainly in the East and West Indies; English and Dutch fought to control trade with Europe and colonies

Impact on Britain: 6
Britain largely victorious; made commercial gains at Dutch expense; but ended with the most humiliating defeat in British naval history

International impact: 7
Britain's emergence as a world power; Dutch New Amsterdam became British New York

Memorable for: 2
Dutch sack English fleet in Medway, 1667 (see page 128)

Marlborough's Wars
1702–1713

Scale: 8
Britain's first large-scale wars in Europe; John Churchill, Duke of Marlborough, fought ten campaigns and never lost a battle

Impact on Britain: 6
Parliament increased power, seeking control of the high cost of the army; war ended with commercial benefits

International impact: 8
Monopoly of slave trade to Spanish Empire

Memorable for: 3
Blenheim House built for Marlborough by grateful nation; the Battle of Blenheim

Bonnie Prince Charlie's Rebellion
1745–1746

Scale: 4
Scottish army invaded England to make 'Charlie' king. Reached Derby

Impact on Britain: 2
Ended Stuart claims to throne; many Scots died

International impact: 0
None

Memorable for: 3
'Butcher' Cumberland's massacre at Culloden, last battle fought on British soil, 1746

War of Jenkins' Ear
1739–1743

Scale: 4
War between Britain and Spain fought mainly at sea in the Caribbean

Impact on Britain: 0
No important gains

International impact: 2
Spanish control of their empire in the Americas continued

Memorable for: 8
Cries of 'ear 'ear in Parliament when British smuggler, Robert Jenkins, claimed his ear cut off by Spanish and displayed his pickled ear in House of Commons

Seven Years War
1756–1763

Scale: 9
Britain, Prussia and Portugal against Austria, France, Russia and Spain; the first 'worldwide war', with conflicts in Europe, America, India

Impact on Britain: 7
Gained Canada, Florida, increased sense of power and empire

International impact: 6
French losses in Canada and India changed the balance of world power

Memorable for: 6
General Wolfe captured Quebec in daring attack, but was killed

War of American Independence
1775–1782

Scale: 6
The 13 British colonies in North America fought for their independence and, with French help, won

Impact on Britain: 8
National feeling of disaster as important colonies lost

International impact: 9
Emergence of USA as new nation, based on new democratic principles

Memorable for: 7
George Washington; First European colony to win its independence

Napoleonic Wars
1793–1815

Scale: 9
Three-quarters of a million British troops fought in Spain and France; navy fought all over the world

Impact on Britain: 9
Long wars helped growth of British industry; cost of wars led to first income tax; British gained South Africa, Sri Lanka

International impact: 9
French revolutionary ideas spread across Europe; British navy ruled the seas after Trafalgar

Memorable for: 5
Napoleon conquers Europe: Nelson and Trafalgar: Wellington and Waterloo

Opium Wars
1839–1842, 1856–1860

Scale: 4
British battleships easily defeated Chinese and forced China to open up its ports

Impact on Britain: 3
Trading gains in China

International impact: 3
Other European powers soon joined Chinese exploitation

Memorable for: 6
Main product British wanted to sell in China was opium

Crimean War
1853–1856

Scale: 4
Britain and France invaded Russia

Impact on Britain: 3
Change of prime minister; incompetence of army led to reforms

International impact: 4
First use of railways, trenches, telegraph, war correspondents

Memorable for: 5
Roads, pubs, etc. named after heroes and places e.g. Cardigan, Alma; the Battle of Balaclava and the Charge of the Light Brigade; Florence Nightingale and Mary Seacole

Boer War

1889–1902

Scale: 3
War between British and Boers (settlers of Dutch origin) in South Africa

Impact on Britain: 4
British rule in South Africa secure, after early defeats; unfit recruits led to health reforms

International impact: 3
Further extension of British Empire

Memorable for: 4
Spion Kop – hill gave name to football stands; British used concentration camps to defeat Boer guerrilla tactics

Zulu War

1879

Scale: 4
British attempt to take over Zulu kingdom in eastern South Africa

Impact on Britain: 4
Shock of defeat brought continuing admiration for Zulu military skills and training

International impact: 3
British took over Zulu lands

Memorable for: 5
Zulu victory at Isandhlwana; British defence of Rorke's Drift basis for film *Zulu*

Afghan Wars

1839–1842
1878–1880

Scale: 4
British attempts to conquer Afghanistan

Impact on Britain: 4
British failed to take over Afghanistan at a time when British were all-conquering

International impact: 5
Afghan determination to resist foreign rule made clear

Memorable for: 7
Massacre of entire British force of 16,000 outside Kabul

Sikh Wars

1845–1846
1848–1849

Scale: 3
Sikhs fought soldiers working for the British East India Company

Impact on Britain: 5
Empire grew

International impact: 3
British took over control of Punjab and Kashmir, valuable areas of India

Memorable for: 6
The Koh-i-noor diamond, at that time the largest cut diamond in the world, was given to Queen Victoria

Iraq War

2003–

Scale: 5
Intended as quick Anglo-US action to remove Iraqi leader Saddam Hussein, but occupying forces still there at time of printing and civil war has broken out

Impact on Britain: 7
Huge opposition to war; fear of some British Muslims turning to terrorism

International impact: 6
World opinion split; Muslim hostility to west increased

Memorable for: 5
Statue of Saddam Hussein pulled down in early days of Anglo-US invasion

Falklands War

1982

Scale: 2
Conflict over Falkland Islands, in south Atlantic, British since 1832, seized by nearby Argentina

Impact on Britain: 4
Victory helped Conservative Prime Minister Thatcher win next election

International impact: 2
Acceptance that war is a justifiable way of solving disputes

Memorable for: 3
Mrs Thatcher's defence of British tactics

Second World War

1939–1945

Scale: 10
Between: mainly, USSR, USA and Britain against Nazi Germany, Japan and Italy; fought on land, at sea and in the air over Europe, north Africa, the Pacific

Impact on Britain: 10
Severely weakened financially, but maintained pride; 'total war' – involving civilians as well as combatants, led to welfare state

International impact: 10
Emergence of 'Super-powers': USA and USSR; atom bombs changed attitudes to warfare

Memorable for: 9
Churchill; Dunkirk; heavy bombing of cities; atom bomb; Holocaust

First World War

1914–1918

Scale: 10
Large armies from most European countries and their empires; fighting in France and Belgium, eastern front, Italy, Middle East and at sea; huge death toll

Impact on Britain: 10
British debt; loss of young males; vote for most women, 1918; rise of pacifism

International impact: 10
End of Russian, Austrian and German empires; re-drawing of map of Europe with many new countries

Memorable for: 10
Trench warfare; first aeroplanes and tanks; Somme; Ypres

Which British wars should you know about?

There were obviously lots more wars than can possibly fit into a school history curriculum, so some hard choices have to be made. Which wars do you think everyone should study? To work out your answer you will have to think about significance and use our War Top Trumps cards.

ACTIVITY

A school history course has to be a selection of events from the past. So which wars between 1500 and 1900 would you choose for everyone to study – and why? Here's your guide to making your choices.

1 Read the Doing History on significance (opposite). Which significance criteria are shown around the picture below?

2 Choose the four criteria you want to use to decide which wars were most significant. You can use criteria from the opposite page or develop your own. Write them in the top row of your version of the grid opposite.

3 Decide whether you want all the criteria to be of equal importance. If not, change the numbers in the weightings row to show which ones are most important.

4 Use the Top Trumps cards on pages 131–133 to decide which **two** wars you think everyone should study.

5 Compare your choices with other groups' choices. What are the differences and why are they different?

a) Waterloo ended the war with France which had lasted 22 years and cost many thousands of lives.

b) Victory over Napoleon made the British proud again, 40 years after Britain had felt humiliated by losing its American colonies.

c) Waterloo was not just a British victory. The wars were won by an alliance of countries, co-operating to defeat Napoleon, who wanted to dominate the whole of Europe.

d) The long wars helped develop British industries and affected many people's lives, especially when they feared invasion.

e) The Duke of Wellington, the British commander, was a brilliant general who played a vital role in defeating Napoleon in Spain and then at Waterloo.

f) The bravery of the soldiers was astonishing as they stood up to cannon-fire and charging cavalry.

Why was the Battle of Waterloo significant?

DOING HISTORY: Significance

Last year we decided that we need criteria to help us decide if an event is significant. The criterion we used to think about the significance of the Black Death and the 1381 Revolt was:

SIGNIFICANCE   **Recap**

Events are significant if they change lots of aspects of people's lives

This year we are going to look at two more ideas about significance:

Significance

Comparing events against the same criteria helps us decide which events are the most significant

For example, you will be choosing criteria against which to measure all the wars so your group can decide which ones everyone should study.

but

Significance

People choose different criteria because they have different attitudes and values. This then means they disagree about who and what is significant

LEARNING LOG

You will do more work on significance later in the course. How will you record what you have learned about significance this year so you can remember it and use it again in the future?

You'll find out whether every group chose the same criteria and how different criteria lead to different choices.

So what criteria would you choose? Here are some ideas:

1 The scale of the wars (their geographical spread and how long they lasted)

2 The ways they changed life or affected the people of Britain

3 The ways they affected people around the world

4 They make interesting and dramatic stories

5 They make us proud of people in the past who risked their lives in a good cause to help others

6 British victories make us proud of being British

7 It is important to know about heroic British leaders from History

8 People's behaviour and attitudes in the past have something to teach us about behaviour and attitudes today

Criterion	1	2	3	4
Weighting	5	5	5	5
Henry VIII's Wars				
The Armada				
Elizabeth's Irish Wars				

THE BIG STORY:
Conflict and Co-operation Part Two

Last year you learned a lot about conflict in the Middle Ages and now you've completed the story up to 1900. Use this page to sum up the really Big Story in your Learning Log, identifying the similarities and differences in warfare from 1066 to 1900.

Your task is to produce your own version of the information on this page, identifying

a) what had changed in warfare since the Middle Ages

b) what stayed the same after the Middle Ages

c) why people have different ideas about which wars should be remembered.

Take each question in turn and decide how you want to record the key points. You could use a different method for each question – bullet points, a PowerPoint screen, a mind map, a diagram, a podcast – it's up to you to choose the method that you think will be best for recording and remembering these ideas.

1 Warfare: Where? Why? How?

2 Why were wars won?

God was on our side against France.

I admit the weather helped a little because the wet ground slowed down their cavalry.

Great leadership from King Henry and the nobles and we archers were well-trained.

The alliance with Burgundy helped us in the long war with France.

And we believed in our cause – that kept us going.

You need good leadership from men like the Duke of Wellington. At Waterloo the sight of his long nose among us was worth 10,000 men any day of the week. And you need well-trained men. Wellington called us the 'salt of the earth'.

Naval power helps to win wars, making sure the men are well supplied with food and equipment.

The weather can play its part, especially at sea.

Our industries at home supply the best equipment. A wealthy country like Britain should beat a poorer country.

And we believed in our cause – that kept us going.

An archer from Agincourt

A soldier from Waterloo

3 Which wars should we remember?

People have different ideas about which wars and war heroes we should remember, commemorate and study.

a) What reasons can you find that are making these people disagree?

b) What other reasons explain why people have different ideas about which wars should be remembered?

Our glorious English victory over France at Agincourt should always be remembered. It was a triumph for the English archers, ordinary men but great fighters.

Trafalgar and Waterloo should always be remembered. They saved Britain from invasion and made sure France could not conquer the whole of Europe.

We should always commemorate World War Two. Winston Churchill was an inspirational leader and so many people risked their lives to put an end to the evils of Hitler and the Nazis.

We like to remember when we burned the English ships in the 1660s. It was a great victory for the Dutch.

Conflict and co-operation: how were ideas and beliefs changing?

Nowadays we think of war as the last resort, something to be avoided if at all possible, but is that what people thought between 1500 and 1900? Play Mix and Match to summarise their attitudes, ideas and beliefs about conflict and co-operation.

ACTIVITY

1 Read the ideas about conflict and co-operation on the timeline. Each idea can be supported by evidence from this page. Which evidence would you use to support each statement? Some of the links are clear in this evidence. Some you will have to think about or check details on other pages, including the Top Trumps cards (pages 131–133). You could use a piece of evidence to support more than one statement.

2 Which attitudes continued to be of great importance into the twentieth century?

Attitudes

It is important to stop one country taking control of the whole of Europe. If necessary we will make alliances and go to war to stop any country dominating Europe.

We have a right to build up an overseas empire and trade all over the world. There is only so much wealth in the world to share so we will fight other countries to defend and increase our share of empire and trade.

Having a strong navy is vital for defending Britain against invasion and for defending our Empire and trade throughout the world.

England needs to go to war to take control of the rest of Britain.

The King needs to go to war to show his people how powerful he is and to win himself glory and fame.

Britain has become the richest nation in the world because of its empire and its trade, so it needs to fight wars to protect its trading empire.

We cannot afford to let other countries build up industrial strength to match our own. This will threaten the British Empire and make us weaker in wars.

We do not want another country to tell us what our religion should be. We will go to war to defend our religion.

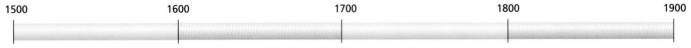

| 1500 | 1600 | 1700 | 1800 | 1900 |

▲ SOURCE 1 *Timeline showing attitudes to war 1500–1900.*

Evidence

A England successfully fought off the Spanish Armada in 1588.

B Britain won the Opium Wars against China in the mid-nineteenth century.

C John Churchill, Duke of Marlborough, commanded the British forces who, with their allies, defeated the French in the late 1600s and 1700s.

D The Seven Years War (1756–1763) between Britain and France was the first worldwide war with battles in North America and India as well as Europe.

E Henry VIII invaded France, wanting to be as famous a hero as Henry V. He failed.

F Nelson's victory at the Battle of Trafalgar in 1805 ended the threat of French invasion.

G During the French Revolutionary Wars and Napoleonic Wars (1793–1815) Britain made a series of alliances with other countries in Europe.

H During the 1800s Britain produced far more iron and steel than any other country. The industries were able to make weapons in wartime and the textile industries produced uniforms and other equipment. Britain's wealth played a big part in defeating Napoleon's France.

I The key turning point at the Battle of Waterloo in 1815 was the arrival of the Prussian army to fight alongside the British forces.

J Twice in the 1800s Britain tried to take control of Afghanistan in order to stop Russia threatening Britain's empire in India.

K By the late 1800s Germany, France and the USA were matching Britain's industrial strength and were developing new methods for producing goods more cheaply and efficiently.

L Henry VIII spent a great deal of money on his wars with Scotland.

Would you have signed Charles I's death warrant?

In 1649 King Charles I was put on trial. He was charged with treason against the people of England. He was found guilty and he was executed. Yet many people were deeply unhappy about this. You are going to investigate why Charles was on trial and examine the evidence for and against him. You can make your own decision about whether the outcome was the right one. Would you have signed Charles I's death warrant?

The charges

John Bradshaw read out the charges against the man he called simply Charles Stuart:

> Trusted to govern England according to the law, he has in fact tried to rule according to his own will.
>   He has wickedly made war on his own subjects, and so is responsible for all the murders, rapings, burnings, damage and desolation caused by the wars.
>   He called in help from France and the Dutch against his own subjects.
>   He started the war after being defeated.

▼ **SOURCE 1** *For fear of being shot by one of Charles's supporters the judge John Bradshaw wore this bullet proof hat.*

Charles' response

Charles did not answer the charges. Instead he argued that the court had no right to try him:

> 'I wish to know by what power I am brought here – by what lawful authority. Remember I am your king, your lawful king. I have a trust committed to me by God, by old and lawful descent.'

Charles argued so much that Bradshaw ordered him to be taken away and the witnesses gave their evidence without him.

The verdict

The sentence of the court was obvious from the start:

> 'The said Charles Stuart, as a Tyrant, Traitor, Murderer and a public enemy, shall be put to death by the severing of his head from his body.'

Although Charles had earned many enemies only 80 of the 135 men appointed to be judges actually turned up. Of these, 68 voted that he was guilty, but only 59 were prepared to sign the death warrant.

Three days later Charles was executed.

► **SOURCE 2** *Contemporary picture of Charles I's trial.*

1 Look at Source 2. Find:
- the benches for the judges
- the raised bench of John Bradshaw, President of the Court
- the King, in the dock with his back to us
- spectators in the main part of the hall
- important spectators in galleries at each side at the back.

2 Why do you think there were so many soldiers in the court?

ACTIVITY

Charles was not defended at this trial. He did not accept the authority of the court. No one had ever put a king on trial before. But if he had been defended, there are many points that could be made in his defence. Your task is to weigh up the evidence and consider whether you, if you had been there at the time, would have been prepared to sign the death warrant and why.

STAGE 1 ► Gather evidence

Choose one of the charges and on your own or with others use the next eight pages to gather evidence using a table like this.

Charge	Evidence against Charles	Charles' defence

CHARGE 1: 'That he did ignore the will of Parliament and ruled according to his own will'

King *v.* Parliament

Charles had very strong beliefs about the role of the king. He believed in the Divine Right of Kings. Kings were appointed by God and ruled by the authority of God. So Charles expected complete obedience from his subjects. He did not think he had to consult anyone, even his Parliament, over important decisions.

In practice of course a king could not rule the country by himself. He needed Parliament to help him. For example, he needed their permission to raise taxes. Parliament included all the most powerful people in the country. In the House of Lords there were nobles and bishops; in the House of Commons there were elected MPs who were mostly rich landowners but included some merchants. A successful king had to earn Parliament's trust and keep all these powerful people on his side. Members of Parliament were prepared to obey their king. But only if he earned their trust by consulting them, listening to their advice and ruling the country well.

But instead of listening to Parliament, Charles preferred to take the advice of a small group of people whom he trusted and liked. Parliament particularly distrusted Charles' favourite the Duke of Buckingham.

Parliament and the King disagreed over three key issues.

ACTIVITY

You are gathering evidence for and against Charles. Use your table from page 141 to record what you find.

Charge	Evidence against Charles	Charles' defence
1		

MONEY

Parliament's main task was to grant taxes to the king. It was usual for Parliament to meet at the beginning of a new king's reign to vote to grant the king customs duties (taxes on goods coming in and out of the country) for life. Because they did not trust Charles or his advisers, Parliament voted to give him these taxes for just one year! They hoped this would ensure that Charles would call Parliament once a year.

ISSUES

RELIGION ✝

In those times religion was a hot topic. England was a Protestant country and most English people thought that Catholics were their enemies. Some could still remember what happened 60 years before when the King of Spain had sent the Spanish Armada to try to force England to have a Catholic ruler. Even more people could remember only 35 years before when the Catholics, allegedly, attempted to blow up the King and Parliament in the Gunpowder Plot.

Yet one of the first things that Charles did was to marry a Roman Catholic French princess, Henrietta Maria. She brought her own priests with her to court and Roman Catholic services were held there. Charles also appointed William Laud as Archbishop of Canterbury. Laud was not a Catholic, but to many Puritans (extreme Protestants) it looked as if he was because he wanted to increase the amount of ceremony and decoration in churches. There were many Puritans in Parliament.

It looked to them as if Charles might turn England Catholic again.

PERSONAL RULE

So Charles decided to rule without Parliament. From 1629 to 1640 he did not call Parliament at all. Instead he found other ways to raise money. Many thought that he was exceeding his power in most of the money-raising systems he used. For example, he demanded everyone paid 'ship money', a tax usually only paid by coastal towns to pay for warships to defend traders against pirates.

Charles was not the first king to do this. There were no laws about how often the king had to call Parliament. But twelve years was a very long time to go without a Parliament. And many landowners resented not being allowed to meet to express their views on how England was being ruled.

Do you remember Magna Carta, the Great Charter the barons made King John agree to back in 1215? One of the things it said was that the king should not demand taxes without first getting the agreement of barons and bishops. Charles' opponents quoted from Magna Carta to justify their opposition to him, saying he had broken this agreement, already 400 years old by that time.

Charles should have known he would have to call Parliament eventually. When Charles and Laud tried to introduce their religious ideas to Scotland, the Scots formed an army and invaded England. Charles had to buy them off, paying them £850 a day. He could not afford this, so was forced to call Parliament in 1640. Many MPs rode to London furious with Charles and determined to bring him under control.

CHARGE 2: '... that he did wickedly make war on his own subjects ...'

None of the MPs who rode to Westminster for the Parliament of 1640 was planning to wage war on Charles. It was very far from their minds. And it was equally far from the King's mind too. So why did the war begin? Parliament blamed the King – but were they right? Or was it, as Charles claimed, the fault of the unreasonable MPs?

> We can no longer trust this king. He must be forced to realise he has to rule with Parliament.

John Pym

April–May 1640
The Short Parliament
The MPs tried to start discussions but ...

November 1640
The Long Parliament
Charles was forced to call Parliament again when his war against the Scots continued to go badly. MPs took their chance to discuss all the grievances they had against Charles.

February 1641
The Triennial Act
Parliament passed the Triennial Act, which said that Parliament had to meet at least every three years, whether the king called it or not.

May 1641
The execution of Strafford
The Earl of Strafford was Charles' most important minister. Parliament put him on trial and demanded that he should be executed for treason.

> Parliament must let me rule my own country. That is what I am appointed by God to do. All they are interested in is religion.

Charles I

... Charles dismissed Parliament after only 22 days as soon as MPs were critical and got onto the topic of religion.

May 1641
The Army Plot
Some of the King's supporters in the army hatched a plan to capture the Tower of London and force Parliament to close. Charles went along with the plot but they failed to capture the Tower.

Under great pressure, with angry crowds outside the windows of Whitehall Palace where he and his family lived, Charles agreed to the execution of the Earl of Strafford.

November 1641
The Grand Remonstrance
Roman Catholics in Ireland rebelled against English Protestant rule. This scared the MPs: an army would have to be raised to crush the rebellion but would Charles then use it against Parliament? John Pym (the most important leader of the opposition) played on their fears to pass the Grand Remonstrance, a list of all the grievances against Charles, including the need for Parliament to control the King's ministers.

And Pym tried to get those outside Parliament involved in the struggle. He published the Grand Remonstrance as a pamphlet and had it given out on the streets of London! Gangs of Londoners gathered outside Parliament and MPs who did not support Pym were jeered at and jostled.

June–August 1641
The removal of the King's special powers
All the powers that Charles had used in his attempt to rule without Parliament from 1629 to 1640 – special taxes, special royal courts – were abolished one by one.

ACTIVITY

You are gathering evidence for and against Charles. Use the table to record what you find.

Charge	Evidence against Charles	Charles' defence
2		

March 1642
Militia Ordinance
Parliament gave orders to the local militia, the only trained troops in the country. Monarchs had always controlled the army and this was the first time in English history that Parliament issued a law without the monarch's consent.

July–August 1642
War!
With outbreaks of fighting in several parts of the country, Parliament raised an army.

The Grand Remonstrance was a turning point. This turned many moderate MPs towards the King. They believed it stripped him of many of the powers English monarchs had always had, like calling Parliament and choosing their own ministers. They even wanted to control the education of the king's children! It looked as if Parliament wanted to rule England with the king as a figurehead with no real power.

January 1642
The Five Members
Charles, in person and with an armed guard, came to Parliament, sat in the Speaker's chair and tried to arrest five key Parliamentary leaders, starting with John Pym. He failed because they had all slipped away by boat to a safe house in the City of London.

January 1642
Charles leaves London
Charles left London for York. He began to collect supporters and weapons. His French wife Henrietta Maria went to France to raise money for war.

The King raised his standard at Nottingham on 22 August 1642, and called on all loyal men to join his army.

Charles didn't fight the Civil War on his own: thousands of supporters joined him, including 119 Members of the House of Commons and most of the House of Lords.

CHARGE 3: ... that he was responsible for all the murders, rapings, burnings, damage and desolation caused by the wars

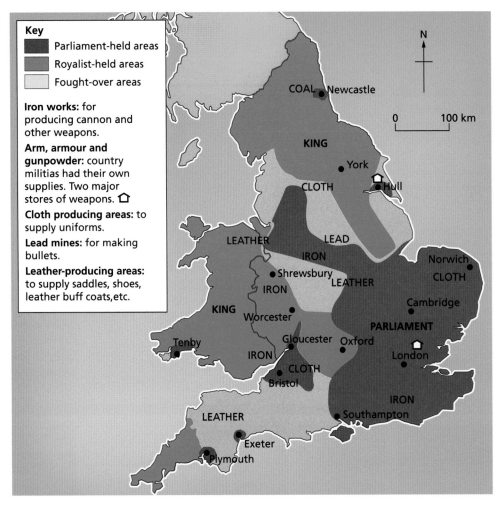

Key

Parliament-held areas

Royalist-held areas

Fought-over areas

Iron works: for producing cannon and other weapons.

Arm, armour and gunpowder: country militias had their own supplies. Two major stores of weapons. ⌂

Cloth producing areas: to supply uniforms.

Lead mines: for making bullets.

Leather-producing areas: to supply saddles, shoes, leather buff coats,etc.

N

0   100 km

COAL • Newcastle

KING

• York

CLOTH ⌂ Hull

LEATHER   LEAD

IRON   Norwich •

• Shrewsbury   CLOTH

IRON   LEATHER

KING   Cambridge

Worcester   PARLIAMENT

Tenby •   Gloucester Oxford ⌂
          •   •   London •

IRON

CLOTH

Bristol •

IRON

LEATHER   • Southampton

        • Exeter
• Plymouth

▲ SOURCE 3 *Map of England and Wales showing regions supporting Parliament and King Charles I.*

Parliament's supporters controlled the richer and more densely populated south east, with some other important towns. The King held the north, Wales and south Midlands, and Cornwall. This was a larger total area, but meant his support was split into three.

At the start the Royalists were more organised. Their leaders were usually landowners, used to giving orders, running their estates. Parliament had to set up its own system for collecting taxes. This later became very efficient, but it took time to get under way.

Major events 1642–1646

October 1642 Battle of Edge Hill. Royalist victory but Charles did not take the chance to win the war by taking London.

July 1644 Battle of Marston Moor. Parliament's victory won them control of the north but Charles still controlled most of the west and the Midlands.

1644–1645 Oliver Cromwell and Thomas Fairfax set up Parliament's New Model Army, the first national army, better trained and equipped.

June 1645 Battle of Naseby. Parliament won a decisive victory: 5000 Royalists were killed or captured.

May 1646 Charles I surrendered.

Violence and hatred

The Civil War was not mainly a war of battles. It was a war of sieges and skirmishes.

By no means everyone had joined up on one side or the other. Most ordinary people simply wanted to get on with their lives. But if they were in the wrong place at the wrong time they suffered terribly. War can brutalise those who take part and both sides plundered the towns and villages they passed through. Houses were set on fire and soldiers looked for food to eat and valuables to steal.

The Souldiers in their passage to York turn unto reformers pull down Popish pictures, break down rayles, turn altars into Tables

▲ SOURCE 4 *The caption to this picture is often given as 'soldiers sacking a church'. In fact it was published by a Puritan who approved of the actions of these Parliamentary soldiers.*

SOURCE 5 *Parliamentary account of what happened when Prince Rupert's Royalist troops captured Birmingham. Prince Rupert was Charles I's nephew and his leading cavalry commander.*

They ran into every house cursing and damning, threatening and terrifying the poor women most terribly, setting naked swords and pistols to their breasts. They fell to plundering all the town, picking purses and pockets, searching in holes and corners and every other place they could suspect for money and goods. They beastly assaulted many women's chastity, and bragged about it afterwards, how many they had ravished. The next day in every street they kindled fire with gunpowder, match, wisps of straw, hay and burning coals.

▲ SOURCE 6 *The Bilton Snake. This curious snake is carved on the door of Bilton church, near Marston Moor, Yorkshire, scene of a great Civil War battle in 1644 that Parliament won. It has a crown and a letter 'R' (for Rex, meaning King). It is probably meant to be King Charles, as seen by a Parliamentarian soldier.*

ACTIVITY

You are gathering evidence for and against Charles. Use the table to record what you find.

Charge	Evidence against Charles	Charles' defence
3		

CHARGE 4: ... that he restarted the war after being defeated

Nobody had expected a war and even when they were fighting people expected it to end with an agreement between King and Parliament about how to govern the country. But an agreement was never reached. Why?

The situation in 1646

Because of the war the situation had become more polarised. And a new power had emerged: the Parliamentary Army. It was no longer just King against Parliament.

ACTIVITY

You are gathering evidence for and against Charles. Use your table to record what you find.

Charge	Evidence against Charles	Charles' defence
4		

The King

Although the Royalists had lost and he had surrendered, Charles was determined to preserve as much royal power as possible. He still hoped his enemies would fall out amongst themselves, and he could benefit from their disagreements.

The Army

The soldiers saw Charles as the enemy. During the war, many vowed that if they met Charles in battle they would shoot him as readily as any other Royalist. Further, many were Puritans who saw their victory as a sign that God thought they were right.

Parliament

Almost all MPs still believed in government by King, Lords and Commons. They did not intend to get rid of Charles and expected to persuade him to work with them.

1646

May–June Charles surrendered to the Scots. Parliament offered him a peace agreement in which Parliament ruled but kept the monarchy. Charles delayed his reply and then refused.

1647

January Charles was handed over to the English.

November Charles escaped from imprisonment to the Isle of Wight.

December Charles was recaptured and imprisoned but made a deal ('The Engagement') with the Scots to side with him and invade England. This started the second Civil War.

1648

August The Parliamentary Army won the Battle of Preston.

November Parliament reopened negotiations with the King.

December The Parliamentary Army removed 231 MPs from Parliament, leaving just the 240 MPs who were Army supporters.

1649

January Charles was taken to London and put on trial.

ACTIVITY

STAGE 2 ▶ **Consider your verdict**

Having collected and read the evidence, which of these charges do you think Charles is guilty of?

What happens next?

Consider your options.

a) **If you execute** the King will it create even more hatred among the King's supporters – will there be another war some day because of it?

b) **If you execute** the King what will happen next? Who will rule England? Will you choose another king?

c) **If you let the King go** as a free man what do you expect will be his next actions? And his supporters' next actions?

STAGE 3 ▶ **Cast your vote**

Make your decision: to execute the King or not. Note down the **two** main reasons for your choice. Then cast your vote.

How well can you explain the Medieval Royal Rollercoaster?

In the Middle Ages the monarch decided whether to go to war and what the laws said. Today our king or queen is a lot less powerful. Over the next 20 pages you are going to examine when, how and why this changed.

THE MEDIEVAL ROYAL ROLLERCOASTER

ACTIVITY

This Royal Rollercoaster tells the story up to 1500. The higher the climb the more powerful the king is. The bumpier the ride the more troubled his reign is.

Using what you can remember from last year and the Information Box opposite, explain the numbered features of the Medieval Royal Rollercoaster.

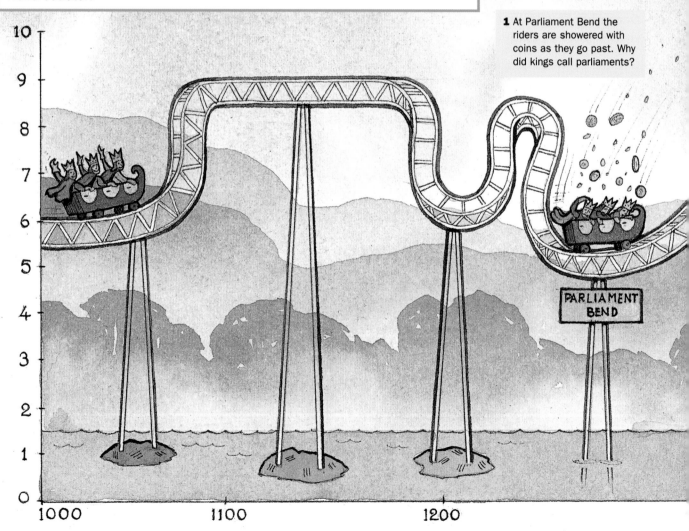

1 At Parliament Bend the riders are showered with coins as they go past. Why did kings call parliaments?

In **1215** King John agreed to rules set out in Magna Carta.

Kings began calling parliaments in the **1240s** to get money for wars. Edward I used them a lot from the **1280s** when he was fighting in Wales and Scotland.

In **1327** and **1399** Edward II and Richard II were deposed and replaced by new kings.

The Wars of the Roses (**1455–1487**) led to several changes of king in a short time.

THE BIG STORY

Looking back

By the end of the Middle Ages, royal power was still high despite all the ups and downs.

Looking forward

So you've had a reminder of the Middle Ages. Between 1500 and 1900 kings and queens went on a rollercoaster ride of highs and lows, of glories and disasters. Your main task will be to design the Royal Rollercoaster Ride to tell the story of royal power from 1500 to 1900.

Royal Power

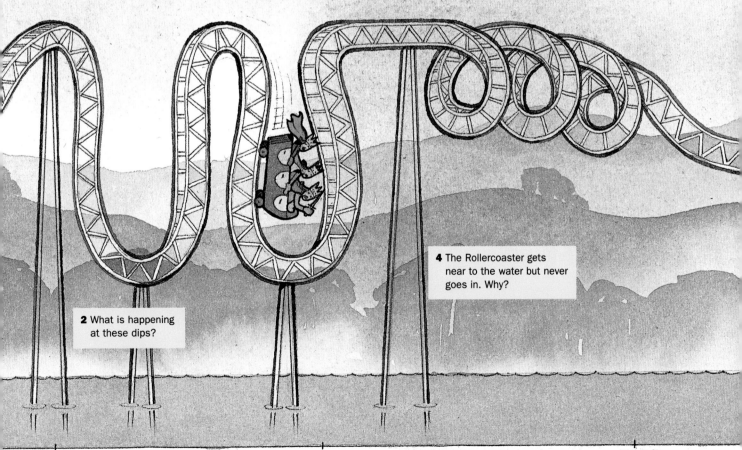

3 One king is waving an object to symbolise his main task in the Middle Ages. What does it mean? What else could the other kings carry to symbolise their other roles?

4 The Rollercoaster gets near to the water but never goes in. Why?

2 What is happening at these dips?

1300

1400

1500

The Royal Rollercoaster: your hypothesis!

Before you look at the detail you are going to get an overview of the period and create your own hypothesis to test.

15 November 1539

The wind whipped across the marshes and plucked at the clothes of the little crowd of people on the top of Glastonbury Tor. It ruffled the white hair of an old man, well over 70, closely guarded by a small squad of soldiers. He looked out across the wide Somerset Levels, to the fields, farms and fishponds he knew so well. Then he looked up to the gallows waiting for him.

The old man was Richard Whiting, the Abbot – or head – of Glastonbury Abbey. He had been put on trial the previous day in Wells, condemned to death and brought the ten miles to Glastonbury that morning. He was tied to a hurdle – a fence used for penning sheep – and dragged through the streets, then taken up the Tor to be hanged.

Once he was dead, his body was cut into four pieces. On the King's orders, each piece was displayed in a different Somerset town, while his head was jammed on a spike over his own Abbey gate.

Whiting wasn't alone. Two other monks died with him on the orders of the King, Henry VIII. Henry was a man who dealt ruthlessly with anyone who angered or opposed him. Over 300 people were executed in the 1530s for daring to disobey him.

30 January 1649

It was a freezing cold morning in London but the crowds had gathered very early in Whitehall. They had watched as a man was led on foot through streets lined with soldiers. On arrival at the Banqueting House, he was led upstairs and through a window to the high platform. In front of him was the huge, silent crowd, held back by armoured cavalry. On the scaffold was a wooden block, an open coffin and a masked executioner, holding a broad-bladed axe. The area around the block had been scattered with sawdust to mop up the blood.

The man was Charles I, King of England for the last 24 years. Determined to die bravely, he was wearing two shirts because he did not want anyone to see him shiver in the cold and think he was shivering with fear.

Charles made a short speech. He blamed Parliament for the Civil War that caused so many deaths but said he forgave them. Then he said a final prayer, knelt down and stretched out his hands. At that signal, the executioner cut off Charles's head with one blow. As the axe fell, the crowd let out a huge groan. Then the executioner held up the King's head for all to see. The King was dead!

April 1827

It was two months since Lord Liverpool, the Prime Minister, had fallen ill. A new Prime Minister was needed to lead the government. It was the King's duty to choose the new Prime Minister, one of the few important decisions left to him. But King George IV was not interested in making the choice. 'Let the politicians decide,' he said.

ACTIVITY

These three stories span 300 years. Your task is simple.

1 On a scale of 1–10 how powerful do you think each king is at the time of the story?
2 Use these stories to sketch what you think might be the rough shape of the Royal Rollercoaster Ride 1500–1900.

ACTIVITY

Here's our artist's first sketch of the Royal Rollercoaster Ride after 1500.
Is this what the Royal Rollercoaster should look like?

1 Describe the shape of royal power shown by the Rollercoaster:
- **a)** When was royal power at its strongest?
- **b)** When was royal power at its weakest?
- **c)** When was the most important turning point in royal power?

2 Look at your sketch from page 153.
- **a)** What are the similarities and differences between your sketch and this one?
- **b)** Do you think there are any mistakes in this sketch that will need to be put right?

1700   1800   1900

Put your ruler in the Hot Seat!

To decide what the Royal Rollercoaster Ride should look like you are going to work in teams. Each team will research one section of the Rollercoaster and then tell everyone about their discoveries from the Hot Seat.

ACTIVITY

1 Divide into groups. Each group should take one of the six rulers below.

1500		1600		1700		1800		1900

Tudors 1485–1603 | Stuarts 1603–1714 | Georgians 1714–1837 | Victoria 1837–1901

English Civil War 1642–1651

Henry VIII (pages 158–159)

Queen Elizabeth I (pages160–161)

Charles I (pages 162–163)

Oliver Cromwell (pages 164–165)

George II (pages 166–167)

George IV (pages 168–169)

2 Read the brief opposite. It's not about finding out as much as possible about your person. You have to practise the skill of **selecting** the right information for each part of the task.

3 Complete your research, using the pages in this book and other books or sources. Then plan your presentation carefully.

4 When it's your turn in the Hot Seat, explain what you have found out – then be ready to answer any difficult questions that the class throw at you!

Presentation brief

Your group is going to make a short presentation to the rest of the class. You have a maximum of two minutes. In the presentation you will tell everyone about your ruler. You should include:

1 **Who** you are and **when** you ruled England.

2 **Two interesting stories** or pieces of information about yourself – things that you think everyone would be interested in. You could include some 'famous quotations'.

3 At least **one thing** you did that affected people greatly at the time – and make sure you explain how it affected people.

4 **What the rollercoaster ride should look like** at your time in history.
   Don't forget:
   a) Who was in charge – the monarch, Parliament or Prime Minister?
   b) What was happening to royal power? Was it changing – going up or down, changing slowly or quickly? Was this an important turning point?

Think how you are going to make your presentation interesting.

Do you want to use props – a crown, a wooden sword? Are you going to show any pictures? Are you going to sketch your section of the rollercoaster or act out a scene from history?

Henry VIII (1509–1547)

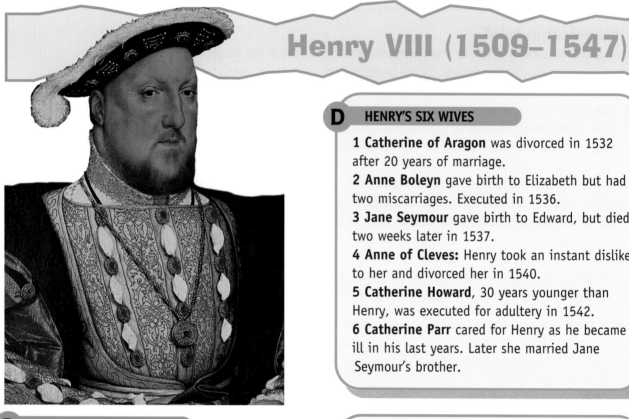

D   HENRY'S SIX WIVES

1 Catherine of Aragon was divorced in 1532 after 20 years of marriage.

2 Anne Boleyn gave birth to Elizabeth but had two miscarriages. Executed in 1536.

3 Jane Seymour gave birth to Edward, but died two weeks later in 1537.

4 Anne of Cleves: Henry took an instant dislike to her and divorced her in 1540.

5 Catherine Howard, 30 years younger than Henry, was executed for adultery in 1542.

6 Catherine Parr cared for Henry as he became ill in his last years. Later she married Jane Seymour's brother.

B   THE NEW KING

Henry was born in 1491, the second son of the first Tudor king, Henry VII. He was expected to become a bishop but became Prince of Wales when his elder brother, Arthur, died. Henry was 17 when he became king.

C   YOUNG HENRY

In 1515 an ambassador from Venice described Henry, then aged 24, like this:

The King is the handsomest prince I ever set eyes on, above the usual height, with an extremely fine calf to his leg, his complexion very fair and bright ... He speaks French, English and Latin, with a little Italian; plays well on the lute and harpsichord, sings from a book at sight, draws a bow with greater strength than any man in England and jousts marvellously.

E   RELIGION

Henry changed England's religion – because he wanted to marry Anne Boleyn and have a son. Henry had expected the Pope, the head of the Roman Catholic Church, to agree to end his marriage to Queen Catherine but the Pope refused. That gave Henry a huge problem. He was a Roman Catholic at heart but he wanted to marry Anne.

He was so uncertain that it took several years to decide what to do but he eventually set up the Protestant Church of England with himself as head of it. England had been part of the Roman Catholic Church for 1000 years. Now it was entirely separate.

Henry had more power over religion than any previous king. He gave himself a divorce and married Anne. He could also decide what church services were like, what people should believe about God, even how churches were decorated. Henry had changed the religion of everyone in England.

F PARLIAMENT

Henry held only one Parliament between 1515 and 1529. However, in the 1530s, he held eight Parliaments, mostly to pass his laws making religious changes and closing the monasteries. Henry made sure Parliament agreed with him, watching who voted for or against his plans. However, something important was changing. Parliament was meeting more often than ever before. Some members of Parliament began to think they should carry on meeting regularly to discuss important decisions made by the King. Henry himself said:

We at no time stand so highly ... as in the time of Parliament, wherein we as head and you as members are joined together into one body.

G WARS

Henry dreamed of being a great soldier-king like Henry V. He went to war with France several times but was never very successful. The most famous event is when his ship, the *Mary Rose*, sank. Henry's wars cost many lives and millions of pounds, paid for by English taxes.

H MONASTERIES

In the 1530s there were about 800 monasteries in England and Wales. Many of them were very rich. The monks and nuns all thought of the Pope as their leader and they had strong links with monasteries in Catholic countries such as France and Spain. Henry and his advisers decided to close the monasteries. He was afraid the monks would encourage people to rebel against him or support a foreign invasion. He also had plans for the wealth of the monasteries. He could use it to make himself more powerful, to pay for his wars and to win the support of the nobles who could be bribed with land not to oppose his religious changes.

I OPPOSITION

Henry dealt ruthlessly with anyone who opposed him. Two days after he became king, he had two of his father's unpopular advisers arrested, imprisoned and executed. Sir Thomas More told his son-in-law: *The King favours me as much as any subject in the kingdom but if my head could win him a castle in France then he would cut it off.*

In the 1530s Henry executed religious leaders like Richard Whiting and even two of the chief advisers who helped him, Sir Thomas More and Thomas Cromwell.

In 1536, 30,000 people joined a rebellion in the north, called the Pilgrimage of Grace, against Henry's religious changes. Henry tricked them: he agreed to their demands, but the next year, he arrested and executed all the leaders. He ordered the Duke of Norfolk:

Cause such dreadful executions upon a good number of the inhabitants, hanging them on trees, quartering them and scattering the quarters in every town, as shall be a fearful warning.

J HENRY IN OLD AGE

Elizabeth I (1558–1603)

A ELIZABETH PAINTED IN 1602

B THE NEW QUEEN

Elizabeth was the daughter of Henry VIII and Anne Boleyn. She was only two when her mother was executed. She was no longer addressed as 'Princess', but just as 'Lady Elizabeth', and was sent away from court. Later she was kept in prison during part of her sister Mary's reign.

C DANGER FROM SPAIN

Some Catholics wanted to make Elizabeth's cousin Mary, Queen of Scots, queen instead of her. The Pope encouraged Catholics to assassinate Elizabeth. She had no police force and no regular army. In 1588 the King of Spain sent his great Armada to invade England. Many people expected the Armada to win but instead it was a great English success, partly thanks to English commanders such as Sir Francis Drake.

D ROYAL PROGRESSES

Every summer Elizabeth left her London palaces and went on a 'progress', a journey round the country for several weeks. She believed in showing herself to the people as much as possible. The Spanish ambassador was amazed: *She was received everywhere with great cheers and signs of joy. She gave me to understand how much her subjects loved her, and how glad she was about this ... She ordered her carriage to be taken where the crowd seemed thickest, and stood up and thanked the people.*

E THE VIRGIN QUEEN

Why did Elizabeth never marry?
She had seen how marriage brought disaster and death to her mother and stepmothers.

Her sister Mary had married King Philip of Spain. England had been pulled into Spain's war with France and so lost the last English possession in France, Calais.

She would probably have liked to marry Robert Dudley, Earl of Leicester. But who would rule England then: herself, or her husband?

Elizabeth made the most of not marrying: she was the boss, no one ordered her about; she did not have to take special notice of anyone.

F LEISURE

She loved dancing, played a variety of musical instruments, read and wrote in Latin, Greek and French. She also spent many hours riding and hunting.

G RELIGION

She inherited a big problem. Her brother Edward VI (1547–1553) made England even more Protestant. Then her sister Mary (1553–1558) made England Roman Catholic again. Mary arrested and burned 284 Protestant men and women as heretics.

Elizabeth was a Protestant but she chose a 'middle ground' policy that won lots of support. *'I will not make a window into men's souls,'* she said. *'There is only one Christ, Jesus, and all else is a dispute over trifles.'* By the end of her reign most people in England were moderately Protestant, like Elizabeth.

J SPEECHES

Elizabeth was known as 'Gloriana' and 'Good Queen Bess'. John Hayward, who knew her well, wrote that: *'None knew better than Elizabeth the art of commanding men.'* At the time of the Spanish Armada in 1588 she spoke these famous words to the assembled troops: *'I know I have the body of a weak and feeble woman but I have the heart and stomach of a king.'*

In her last speech to Parliament, made in 1601, she said: *'Though God has raised me high, yet this I count the glory of my crown: that I have reigned with your love'*.

H PARLIAMENT

Elizabeth did not allow Parliament a big part in running the country. She only called it thirteen times in the 45 years of her reign, mostly to grant the taxes she needed. However, MPs sometimes took the chance to question her decisions, about whether to marry, whether to go to war or whether to execute Mary, Queen of Scots. When Members of Parliament tried to tell her what to do she became angry. *'It is monstrous that the feet should direct the head,'* she said on one occasion.

One MP objected to the way Elizabeth's councillors tried to control elections and what Parliament talked about. In 1576 Peter Wentworth said, *'There is a rumour runs about the House and it is "Take heed what you do, the Queen likes not such a matter. Whoever [speaks for it] the Queen will be much offended with him."'* He was right. Elizabeth ordered that Wentworth spend six months in prison for daring to criticise her.

K THEATRE

During Elizabeth's reign the great writer William Shakespeare wrote comedies, tragedies and histories – and laid on performances for the Queen herself.

I PORTRAITS

All images of the Queen had to be approved by her and her council. The 'Rainbow Portrait' (see opposite) is an example of an approved portrait. It was painted almost at the end of Elizabeth's reign, in 1602, when she was 68. Some items in the picture had special meanings.
- The Latin words mean 'No rainbow without the sun': the rainbow is a symbol of peace.
- The eyes and ears on her dress show that she can see and hear everything.

L POVERTY

There was a massive increase in the number of poor people. Elizabeth and her ministers had the sense to see that there were two kinds of poor people who needed treating differently: scroungers who ought to be set to work; and needy people who needed looking after. They passed a Poor Law that lasted for more than 200 years.

Charles I (1625–1649)

CHARLES I

IDEAS ABOUT BEING KING

Charles' father, James I, had written a book about the Divine Right of Kings. This was the theory that kings were appointed by God alone. King James said: *'It is not lawful to argue with the king's power. It is contempt in a subject to say that a king cannot do this or that ... Kings are the makers of laws ... he has power of life and death over every person.'* Charles followed his father's ideas and expected complete obedience from his subjects.

CHARLES, PARLIAMENT AND TAXES

MPs expected Charles to consult Parliament regularly but Charles ruled without calling Parliament for eleven years from 1629 to 1640. However, this gave him a problem. Charles did not have enough money to run the country so in the end he had to call Parliament to ask for taxes. When Parliament met, many MPs were very angry that Charles had tried to rule without them. You can find out more about this on pages 142–145.

THE STUARTS

Kings of England and Scotland. Charles I became king in 1625. He was the second Stuart king. His father James had been King of Scotland before he also became King of England and Charles ruled both countries too. Charles was a quiet, shy, obstinate man. He was interested in art and began the Royal Collection of paintings. He did not travel around the country but preferred his happy marriage and his orderly life at court.

E RELIGION

Charles married a Roman Catholic French princess, Henrietta Maria. She brought her own priests with her to England and held Roman Catholic services at the royal court. Charles appointed William Laud as Archbishop of Canterbury. Laud wanted to increase the amount of ceremony and decoration in churches. He was not a Catholic, but to many Protestants it looked as if he was. They feared that Charles might make the whole country Catholic again.

F THE CIVIL WAR

The Civil War began in 1642 and lasted until Charles was executed in 1649. Charles and his Royalist supporters (the Cavaliers) fought against Parliament (the Roundheads). The whole country was split between the two – even Parliament. 119 Members of the House of Commons and most of the House of Lords fought for Charles.

G CHARLES' TACTICS

Even when Charles had been beaten in battle he refused to negotiate with Parliament. In 1646 he surrendered and was offered a peace agreement which said that in future Parliament would rule but Charles would stay as king. He delayed his reply and then refused to agree. In 1647 he was imprisoned at Carisbrooke Castle on the Isle of Wight but still made a deal with the Scottish army to invade England.

H THE IMPACT OF THE CIVIL WAR

At least 150 towns and many villages suffered considerable damage during the Civil War, often while being captured in attacks or sieges. Liverpool, for example, was described as '*in great part destroyed and burnt*'. At Taunton the local church minister described his own town as '*heaps of rubbish, houses consumed by fire standing in their own ashes, here a poor forsaken chimney, there a fragment of wall*'.

I TRIAL

In January 1649 Charles was brought to London and put on trial. Charles did not answer the charges against him. Instead he argued that the court had no right to try him.

Charles argued so much that Bradshaw, the President of the Court, ordered him to be taken away. The witnesses gave evidence without him. The sentence of the court was obvious from the start: '*The said Charles Stuart, as a Tyrant, Traitor, Murderer and a public enemy, shall be put to death by the severing of his head from his body.*' However, it had not been easy to convict him: 135 men were appointed judges but only 80 actually turned up. Of these, 68 voted that he was guilty, but only 59 signed the death warrant.

J EXECUTION

At his execution Charles wore two shirts because he did not want anyone to see him shiver in the cold and think he was shivering with fear.

Oliver Cromwell, Lord Protector (1653–1659)

A CROMWELL AS A SOLDIER

B CROMWELL'S FAMILY

Cromwell was born in Huntingdon in 1599. His father was a farmer, well off but not rich. He studied law but when his father died he returned home to look after his mother and sisters. Cromwell was a loving father and husband. He was happily married to Elizabeth for 38 years. They had eight children, three of whom died before Oliver and he was devastated each time. In 1640 he was an ordinary local landowner when he was chosen to be one of the MPs in the new Parliament.

C RELIGIOUS BELIEFS

Cromwell was a Puritan (an extreme Protestant). Puritans believed that the Church should be based on the Bible and nothing else and that, as God's servants, Parliament had a duty to introduce laws to make people behave in a more Godly way, for example:
- 1642 Theatres in London were closed.
- 1644 Sunday had to be observed as the Lord's Day, at church and family prayers.
- 1647 Christmas and Easter were banned. New holidays once a month replaced them.
- 1650 Swearing and adultery were banned.

D WHAT DID HE ENJOY?

Cromwell had a deep love of music and songs. As Lord Protector, he employed an organist and a violinist and held dances at court. He also enjoyed horse-racing, hawking and hunting – and practical jokes.

E THE SOLDIER

Cromwell had not been trained as a soldier but in the Civil War he turned out to be a brilliant cavalry commander. He controlled his men on and off the battlefield. He took them into battle in a close, tight formation. When they broke through the enemy's ranks, he did not allow his men to chase after them for plunder. Unlike other cavalry commanders, he regrouped his men and attacked the enemy from behind. These tactics proved devastatingly effective.

Cromwell took special care to get religious men into his troop. This helped avoid disorder, mutiny and plunder. If a man swore, he paid a 12 pence fine. If someone was drunk, he was set in the stocks.

F THE NEW MODEL ARMY

Cromwell played a huge part in Parliament's victory in the Civil War by creating a national army, the New Model Army. All its soldiers wore the same red uniform and were paid regularly. In 1645, the New Model Army won the decisive victory at Naseby, near Leicester. Cromwell's brave cavalry charges helped Parliament win a crushing victory. 5000 Royalist soldiers were killed or captured. Afterwards, Cromwell told Parliament, 'This is the hand of God, and to Him alone belongs the glory.'

G LORD PROTECTOR – AND KING?

After Charles I was executed in 1649, Parliament ruled England but there were quarrels amongst the leaders. In 1653, Cromwell took charge as Lord Protector and ruled efficiently. In 1657 Parliament offered him the Crown. He thought long and hard but turned down the chance to be king.

H CROMWELL AS RULER

Cromwell made England stronger abroad. The navy defeated the Spanish and won control of Jamaica in the West Indies. Less popular were some of his religious changes: in 1653, he banned horse races, cock fighting, bear baiting and plays.

I A CONTEMPORARY CARTOON OF CROMWELL AS A KING C. 1649

WITHAL

J CROMWELL'S EXECUTION

Cromwell died naturally but two years later, after Charles II had become king, he was declared a traitor. His dead body was hanged, cut down and then his head was cut off and put on show outside Parliament.

K CROMWELL AND IRELAND

Cromwell made sure England kept control of Ireland. There had been an Irish Catholic rebellion against Protestant landowners and Cromwell also feared that Royalists would use Ireland as a base to invade England. In 1649 he took his army to Ireland and captured the town of Drogheda. Many thousands of Irish people were killed – soldiers and civilians. In England Cromwell was hailed as a hero but in Ireland he has always been remembered as a villain who slaughtered thousands of helpless people after the town had surrendered.

L THE RETURN OF THE MONARCHY

Cromwell died in 1658. His son, Richard, took over as Lord Protector but did not want to rule England. Besides, the idea of having a monarch was still very popular and Charles I's son, also called Charles, was soon invited back to be king. The monarchy was restored in 1660 when Charles II became king but with more limited powers. Charles II had to make sure that he stayed on good terms with Parliament. He did not have to call Parliament but he did, every three years. He was able to choose his own advisers and decide if the country went to war – but he needed Parliament to give him taxes to pay for those wars. He also stayed a Protestant because that was what Parliament wanted, even though at heart he was a Catholic. He did not dare change the country's religion back to Catholicism or Parliament would have deposed him, just as they did his father.

George II (1727–1760)

A PORTRAIT OF GEORGE II

B WHO WERE THE GEORGIAN KINGS?

The Georgians are also called the Hanoverians because they came from Hanover in Germany. George II was (surprise, surprise) the second Georgian king.

His father had been chosen by Parliament to be king just because he was a Protestant. As a result of all the problems in the 1600s over religion, Parliament had passed a law saying the monarch had to be a Protestant. Therefore, when Queen Anne died in 1714, Parliament chose George I as king because he was Anne's nearest Protestant relative. Over 50 members of the Stuart family were more closely related to Anne but they were all Catholics.

C HANOVER

Both George I and his son, George II, spent a lot of time back in Hanover. It was their home, after all, and they continued as rulers of Hanover. They could speak English but life was a lot more enjoyable speaking their own language in their own country among people they knew well.

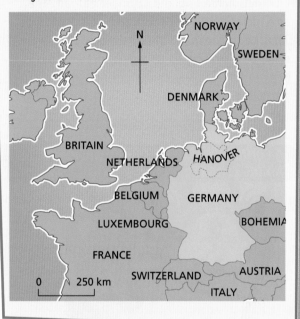

D KING GEORGE'S TEMPER

George II was a short, bustling man, keen on playing cards and stag-hunting but was famously bad-tempered. One story tells how 'His Majesty stayed about five minutes in the gallery, criticised the Queen, who was drinking chocolate, for always stuffing, and told off Princess Emily for not hearing him, Princess Caroline for growing fat, the Duke for standing awkwardly, and then took the Queen to walk, and be criticised again, in the garden.'

E GEORGE II IN BATTLE

George II was the last English king to lead his men, sword in hand, onto the battlefield. He was aged 60 when he commanded his army at the Battle of Dettingen where British and Hanoverian forces beat the French.

F THE FIRST PRIME MINISTER

George I and George II spent large amounts of time in Hanover. So who was left in charge in England? The answer was the King's chief minister who became known as the prime minister. Robert Walpole was the first prime minister, from 1721 to 1741. Walpole made the job of prime minister more and more important until it rivalled the importance of the king.

G POWER

When George II was young he was more involved in taking government decisions. He was interested in war and took the important decisions on alliances and wars. However, George did not control other government decisions as he was too lazy to read government papers.

At times George could not even get his way about who the prime minister was and at the end of his reign George even let William Pitt the Elder, as Prime Minister, take the key decisions in the Seven Years War with France.

H THE END OF THE STUARTS

The Stuart family made two attempts to win back the crown from the German Georges. Their first effort, in 1715, was pathetic but the second, in 1745, was a greater threat. The invasion was led by Charles Edward Stuart, also known as Bonnie Prince Charlie. The Stuart army marched south from Scotland until it reached Derby but then suddenly gave up and headed back north. It was finally beaten and butchered by the royal army at the Battle of Culloden. Bonnie Prince Charlie had proved to be as bad a leader as all the other Stuarts. In London a new song was written to inspire people to fight against the invaders. It was called 'God save the King'.

I THE ROYAL FAMILY AND CRICKET

George's son, Prince Frederick, was an early cricket fan and organised his own team. Unfortunately he wasn't any good at actually playing cricket and was once hit on the head while batting – or trying to bat.

George IV (1820–1830)

PORTRAIT OF GEORGE IV

C **THE PRINCE REGENT**

All that changed when George III fell ill. In 1810 he became insane and so his son George became Prince Regent – the stand-in king – at the age of 57. Prince George spent ten years as Regent but did not seem to learn anything about how to be a successful king. One politician described him as *'a madman, doomed from his personal character alone, to shake the throne.'*

D **THE QUEEN CAROLINE SCANDAL**

George IV finally became king in 1820 but there were no national celebrations. He was already a figure of fun, mocked by cartoonists for being hugely fat, extravagant and lazy. Then the scandal of his queen made this even worse. George and Caroline had disliked each other immediately they met. On first seeing his future wife, George had gasped *'I feel faint, a glass of brandy if you please.'* Soon after they married, Caroline left England. Now she wanted to come back to be crowned queen. George tried to get Parliament to agree to a divorce but Parliament refused. To stop Caroline attending the coronation George had the abbey doors locked and employed bouncers on the doors to prevent her getting in.

B **HAD GEORGE III BEEN A SUCCESS?**

George IV's father, George III, reigned for 60 years, 1760–1820. He did his best to play his full part as king because he worked hard and had a strong sense of duty. However, times were changing and many politicians felt that George III was too powerful and he was heavily criticised after Britain lost its American colonies. Even then, George showed that a king could still control the government. In 1783 he chose 24-year-old William Pitt the Younger to be prime minister. Opponents mocked Pitt's 'mince-pie administration' – they said he would be gobbled up over Christmas – but, with the King's support, Pitt stayed as prime minister for 18 years.

E **WILLIAM PITT THE YOUNGER**

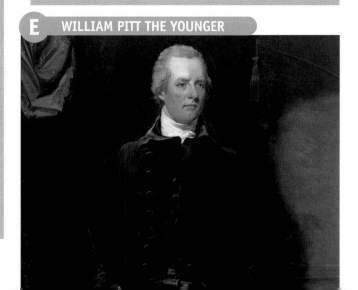

F | WHY WERE PRIME MINISTERS TAKING OVER THE POWER OF THE KING?

In the 1700s the power of the king and prime minister were often evenly balanced but the balance shifted heavily in favour of the prime minister between 1780 and 1830. Why?

- George III's long illness and George IV's laziness and lack of interest left a gap in the government.
- At the same time two very effective prime ministers dominated politics – William Pitt the Younger (1783–1806) and Lord Liverpool (1812–1827).
- This was also the time of the long wars with France (1793–1815) when good leadership was needed. The kings did not provide leadership. The prime ministers did.
- Britain was changing rapidly with towns and industries growing swiftly. Governments had to do more and the business of running the country was becoming more complicated.
- The royal family was unpopular. George IV especially was disliked for his gambling, drinking and extravagant laziness.

H | MILITARY HEROES

George IV's brother was the 'Grand Old Duke of York' who marched his men to the top of the hill and marched them down again. This rhyme was originally a rude verse criticising the Duke for leading an unsuccessful invasion of Holland in 1799 during the wars with France. King George himself boasted that he had been at the Battle of Waterloo even though everyone knew he had never left the comfort and security of his palaces.

I | CHOOSING A NEW PRIME MINISTER

In April 1827 George IV should have chosen the new prime minister after Lord Liverpool fell ill. It was one of the few important decisions left to the king but George was not interested in making the choice. *'Let the politicians decide,'* he said. The new prime minister was George Canning, a man the King hated but could not stop becoming prime minister.

G | AT THE SEASIDE

Earlier kings had led their armies to France and on Crusade. George IV led his people to the seaside and helped to create the fashion for seaside holidays. He loved going to Brighton and the Brighton Pavilion was built as a royal palace for his visits.

J | THE END

When George IV died in 1830, one newspaper wrote: *'Never was there a human being less respected than this late king ... what eye weeps for him?'*

Why were ideas and attitudes to monarchy changing?

Between 1500 and 1900 ideas about monarchy changed a huge amount. Decide which reason you think was most important in explaining this change.

ACTIVITY

1 Compare ideas about monarchy in the Middle Ages and 1800s. Choose one and explain in your own words how it has changed.

2 One factor is important for explaining **when** the power of the monarchy changed. Which one is it?

3 Which factor is the most important in explaining why the power of the monarchy grew less? Give at least one reason to explain your choice.

Ideas about monarchy in the Middle Ages

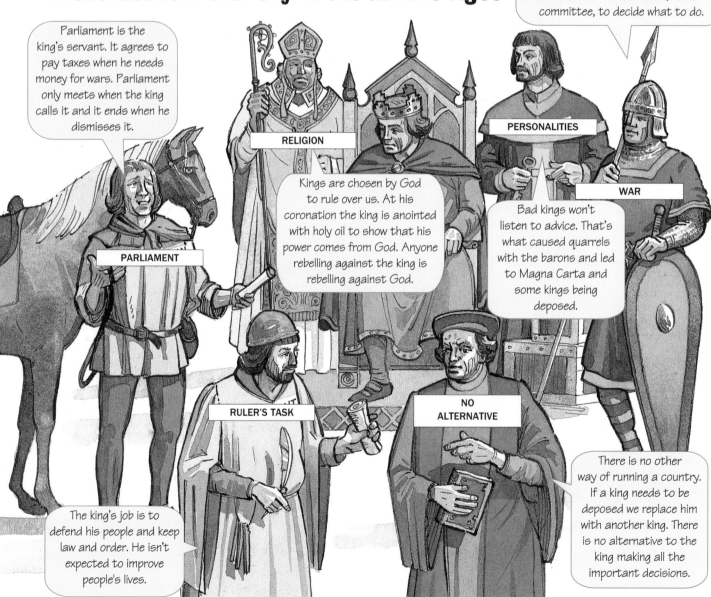

We are often at war. We need one man to lead us and organise our armies. We need an heroic leader, not a committee, to decide what to do.

Parliament is the king's servant. It agrees to pay taxes when he needs money for wars. Parliament only meets when the king calls it and it ends when he dismisses it.

RELIGION

PERSONALITIES

WAR

Kings are chosen by God to rule over us. At his coronation the king is anointed with holy oil to show that his power comes from God. Anyone rebelling against the king is rebelling against God.

PARLIAMENT

Bad kings won't listen to advice. That's what caused quarrels with the barons and led to Magna Carta and some kings being deposed.

RULER'S TASK

NO ALTERNATIVE

The king's job is to defend his people and keep law and order. He isn't expected to improve people's lives.

There is no other way of running a country. If a king needs to be deposed we replace him with another king. There is no alternative to the king making all the important decisions.

Ideas about monarchy in the 1800s

In Cromwell's day they could not think of a practical alternative to having a king. Now we have a prime minister who leads the government and makes the important decisions. We can change him if he doesn't do a good job. You can't do that easily with a king or queen.

Now Parliament is in control, discussing and voting on all important laws. Parliament said the king has to be a Protestant – and it won a civil war and executed a king. The prime minister has to have the support of Parliament – but he can do without the support of the king or queen.

THE ALTERNATIVE

PARLIAMENT

RELIGION

Since the religious changes in the 1500s some people have put their loyalty to religion before their loyalty to the monarch. People do not believe any more that monarchs are chosen by God to rule over us. The monarch has to be a Protestant – that was decided by Parliament, not God.

Some monarchs wanted everything their own way or were too sick or lazy to rule properly. That's when Parliament gained power from the monarch.

WAR

PERSONALITIES

RULERS' TASK

Nowadays wars last many years and need careful planning by many generals and officials. We can't win a war these days just because a king charges heroically at the front of his army. Just as well – some of our monarchs have been too fat and old and some have even been women!

Everything is changing fast – growing towns, new jobs, new machines. One man or woman cannot make all the decisions any more. It needs a team of people – and we want to vote to choose those people.

Hero or villain? Why do reputations change over time?

In your Hot Seat activity on pages 156–157 you gave your verdict on the importance of individual rulers. That was your verdict, today in the early 21st century. But the reputations of many people change over the years. Here you are going to consider why they change, using the example of one of the most famous men in British history – Oliver Cromwell.

ACTIVITY

1 Here are four statements about Cromwell. Use the information opposite to decide which period each statement belongs to.

A A great British hero who ruled very successfully.

C A complicated man who had both successes and failures.

B A murderous monster.

D A cruel military dictator.

2 Now complete the graph below, drawing either a thumbs up or a thumbs down sign on each period of your graph depending on whether Cromwell was seen as a hero or a villain.

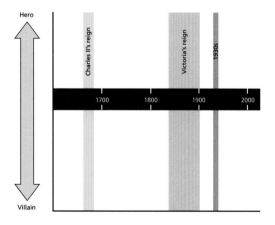

3 Around each thumb make brief notes to show why people had that idea about Cromwell.
4 Why do you think views about Cromwell have changed so much?
5 Why do you think people still disagree about Cromwell? (Use Source 2 to help you.)

SOURCE 1 *In 1899 Lord Rosebery paid for this statue of Cromwell to be placed inside the Houses of Parliament. But Irish MPs and members of the House of Lords angrily disagreed and his statue was placed, where it still stands, outside Parliament.*

SOURCE 2 *John O'Farrell is a journalist and a member of the Labour Party. He has stood as Labour Party candidate in two elections.*

It is probably because I come from an Irish family that I was brought up to regard Cromwell as a mass murderer, rather than the hero of democracy that he seems to be regarded as by some. I would put Cromwell in the same category of religious fundamentalists as the zealots who kill in the name of Islam today. He was a Christian fundamentalist but he considered Irish Catholics to be 'barbarous wretches to whom no mercy should be shown'. So in Wexford and Drogheda thousands were massacred by his soldiers. He was essentially a military dictator, a fascist zealot like Stalin or Saddam or the traffic warden who works my road.

There is a website run by the Cromwell Association, www.olivercromwell.org, if you want to find out more.

Charles II's reign (1660–1685)

After Charles II became king, the strict religious laws of the 1650s were changed. Music, dancing, horse-racing and gambling were allowed and became popular again. The theatres reopened. People could celebrate Christmas and Easter once more.

The men who had signed Charles I's death warrant (the Regicides) were hunted down, put on trial and executed. Cromwell's body was dug up, hanged and then his head was chopped off.

Writers made up stories to show that Cromwell had been evil from birth. They even said that the four-year-old Cromwell punched the two-year-old Prince Charles in the face and made his nose bleed in 1603. This cannot be true as the two never met as children.

The Victorian period (1837–1901)

By the 1800s Britain was ruled by a prime minister and the monarchy had lost its power. The Victorians were very proud of their democratic system of government. Britain also ruled a large overseas empire that made the country very wealthy. The Victorians were proud of their empire and the past rulers and soldiers who created it. In Yorkshire, people talking about times when ordinary people were well-off still said it was just like 'in Oliver's days'.

Most Victorian families were very religious and belonged to the Church of England. Many also disapproved of drinking and gambling, especially on Sundays.

In 1845 Cromwell's letters and speeches were published for the first time. Now people could study Cromwell's own words rather than what his enemies wrote about him.

> **SOURCE 3** *From* Cromwell's Place in History *by Samuel R. Gardiner, 1897.*
>
> No man ever defended more strongly the two bases of parliamentary government – freedom of thought and freedom of speech. It is time for us to regard him as the greatest, because the most typical, Englishman of all time.

The 1930s and 1940s

Several countries in Europe were ruled by dictators. In Germany Adolf Hitler hated elected governments and believed that his country needed a strong leader to make it powerful again. He won a lot of support from the army, then banned elections and other political parties.

He also ended religious freedom and controlled newspapers, film and radio. Millions of people were imprisoned or murdered (such as Jews) by the secret police. Hitler's invasions of other countries also led to the Second World War (1939–1945).

... and today?

Historians today try to look at Cromwell in a different way, as a man of his own time rather than an earlier version of a nineteenth- or twentieth-century ruler. They have also tried to reach balanced conclusions about his successes and failures. They see Cromwell as a puzzling and complicated man:

- an MP who believed in parliamentary government **but** a soldier who believed that the army did the work of God
- a revolutionary who supported the execution of Charles I **but** a conservative who wanted to protect the power of landowners
- a deeply religious man who was often tortured by doubt as he struggled to discover God's will for him and the country.

> **SOURCE 4** *Professor Barry Coward, in an article called 'Your Highness Cromwell', BBC* History Magazine, *2003.*
>
> How well did Cromwell and the Protectorate do? Given their inexperience, the answer must be that they did a fairly good job. It was a regime with visionary ideals. It was not a stereotypical Saddam Hussein-type military dictatorship, run by men who were determined to keep power only for their own ends. On the contrary, Cromwell and those around him were driven by a passionate desire to purify the lives and thoughts of their fellow countrymen.

DOING HISTORY: Change and continuity

CHANGE AND CONTINUITY   **Recap**

- At any one time there are things that are changing and things that are staying the same.
- Some changes happen quickly. Some happen slowly.

You used these two ideas last year. You have seen a lot of evidence of these two ideas in this section. Look at the following pairs of statements.

1530s

I have the power as king to change the whole country's religion. That's why I was able to leave the Catholic Church and set up the Church of England. That shows how powerful the king still is.

1530s

The king is still extremely powerful but the power of Parliament has changed, thanks to the king! We have been meeting regularly and passing laws on more important things, like religion.

1649

The country went to war in 1642 because some people wanted to change the King's ideas about government. We did not expect them to execute him – then suddenly we were discussing his trial and execution. It all happened really quickly.

1770

We have had a prime minister now for 50 or 60 years. Sometimes the King is more powerful, sometimes the Prime Minister. There has been no dramatic change in power – yet!

What information do the statements on page 174 tell you?

1 What has changed?
2 What has stayed the same?
3 Which of the changes happened most quickly?
4 Which changes happened most slowly?

Now here is a new idea.

Change and continuity

A key change in a pattern of events is often called a 'turning point'. A turning point is a time of great change, leaving things permanently different from how they were before.

5 Which of the two speakers below is describing a turning point?
6 What other examples of turning points have you studied in this section?

The prime minister and his ministers run the country now. George III's illness and George IV's laziness have put an end to the power of the monarchy.

Lord Liverpool

The execution of Charles Stuart changed things forever. England will never be the same again. Parliament will always be more powerful than the king.

LEARNING LOG

You will do more work on change and continuity later in this course. How will you record these big ideas so you can remember them and use them next time?

Now it is time to pull together your ideas about the Big Story of royal power.

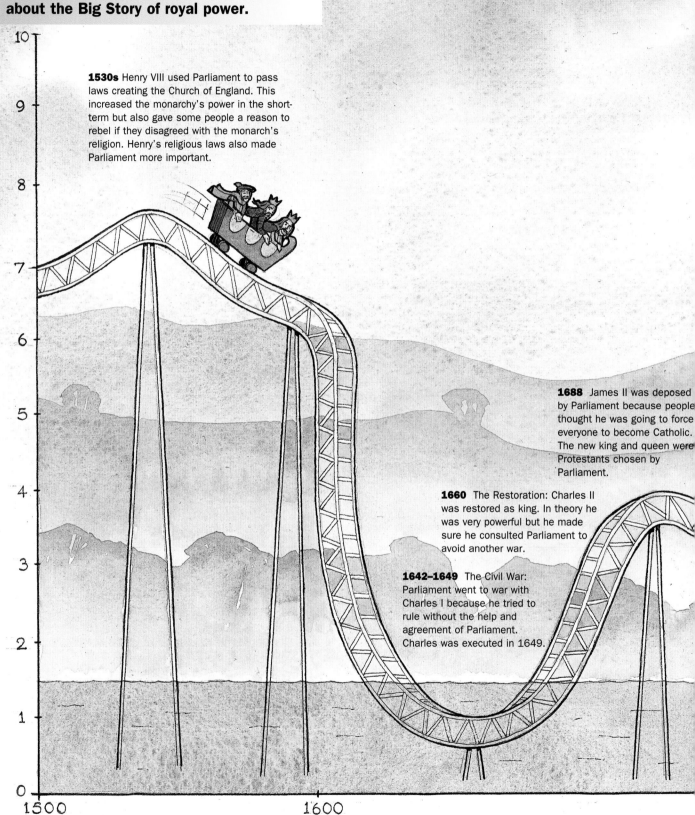

1530s Henry VIII used Parliament to pass laws creating the Church of England. This increased the monarchy's power in the short-term but also gave some people a reason to rebel if they disagreed with the monarch's religion. Henry's religious laws also made Parliament more important.

1688 James II was deposed by Parliament because people thought he was going to force everyone to become Catholic. The new king and queen were Protestants chosen by Parliament.

1660 The Restoration: Charles II was restored as king. In theory he was very powerful but he made sure he consulted Parliament to avoid another war.

1642–1649 The Civil War: Parliament went to war with Charles I because he tried to rule without the help and agreement of Parliament. Charles was executed in 1649.

DISCUSS

Your rollercoaster has been showing the story of the changing power of the monarchy. Compare yours with ours below. There are no right answers. Then discuss:

1 How was royal power developing in the 1500s? (Think about: Was this a major change or was there plenty of continuity from the Middle Ages?)

2 How great was the fall in royal power in the 1600s? (Think about: Did royal power disappear completely? Was the king as powerful after the Restoration in 1660 as he had been before?)

3 What were the continuities and changes in royal power in the 1700s and early 1800s? (Think about: Who was in charge in the 1700s – the monarch or prime minister? How great was the fall in royal power after the 1780s?)

4 Which period do you think was the greater turning point in royal power – 1642–1660 or 1780–1830?

LEARNING LOG

Your completed rollercoaster will be a good way of recording what you have learnt about royal power. Is there anything more you want to add to it? You could record an audio commentary to describe and explain the pattern you have shown.

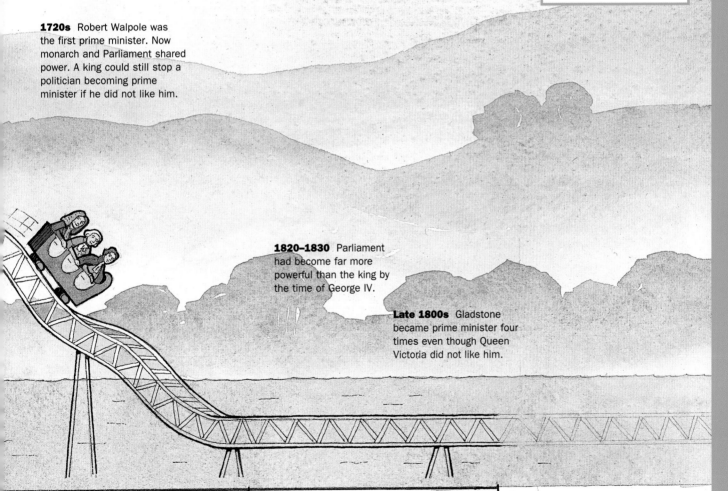

1720s Robert Walpole was the first prime minister. Now monarch and Parliament shared power. A king could still stop a politician becoming prime minister if he did not like him.

1820–1830 Parliament had become far more powerful than the king by the time of George IV.

Late 1800s Gladstone became prime minister four times even though Queen Victoria did not like him.

1800

1900

THE BIG STORY

Power

Looking back

There has been a lot of unfairness in history. Think of the peasants in the Middle Ages who had to serve their lord, had no right to leave the village or marry without his permission. Or remember the millions of Africans sold into slavery by traders and treated cruelly for the profit of others. Or the workers in Britain's cities – facing dangers at work and dreadful living conditions. In every country, ordinary people felt powerless to change things. Their grievances were ignored. What could they do to improve their lives?

Looking forward

You are going to look at an extraordinary period of history when the idea emerged that ordinary people had rights. People demanded a say in how they were ruled – in other words, they wanted democracy. We're going to begin it with …

A day that made history

When? 4 July, 1776

Where? Philadelphia, USA

Who are these people? Representatives from the thirteen British colonies on the east coast of North America.

What are they doing? They are going to sign the document on the table, declaring themselves independent from British rule.

Why? Because the British government was trying to tax them.

How did this happen?

From 1607, when the first successful British colony was set up in Virginia, more and more people had emigrated from Britain to America. They made a living as farmers, fishermen, merchants. In the south some were owners of plantations worked by slaves brought over from Africa.

At first the thirteen colonies were left alone by their British rulers – they were 3000 miles away, six weeks' hard sailing across the Atlantic. But as the British Empire in North America grew wealthier the British government felt that the colonists should pay more taxes. The colonists fiercely resisted these efforts because they had no say in the British Parliament about how much and how often they were to be taxed. Their slogan was 'No taxation without representation'. In 1776 they declared themselves independent from Britain and wrote the Declaration of Independence. War broke out between the colonists and Britain. With help from France, the colonists defeated British forces and in 1783 Britain admitted defeat. It had lost the most valuable part of its empire. The history of the USA had begun.

What did the Declaration say?

- *All men are created equal …*
- *They are given certain Rights by their Creator … Among these are Life, Liberty and the pursuit of Happiness.*
- *To secure these rights, Governments are set up … gaining their power from the agreement of the governed.*
- *Whenever any Form of Government becomes destructive of these ends, it is the Right of the People to alter or to abolish it, and to set up a new Government.*

Therefore, the colonists said, they were no longer citizens of Great Britain, but of a new country, the United States of America.

Why was this a turning point?

- **Before** this day they were British colonists, ruled from London.

- **After** this day they lived in a new country, the United States of America. It was the first time a colony had broken free from its European masters.

But the fact that it was a new country was not the really powerful thing. It was the **ideas**:

Before 1776, governments had said:
1 people are not equal
2 ordinary people do not have any rights
3 kings get their power direct from God
4 the upper classes run the government because they own lots of land
5 rebellion is a sin and a 'treason', which is the worst form of crime.

DISCUSS

1 How did the Declaration of Independence challenge each of the points in the 'Before' list?

2 These ideas were dynamite at the time: why do you think they were so explosive?

How can you change things for the better?

The American Declaration of Independence was about more than a new country. It was about the ideas of human rights and equality. It inspired many people in other countries to think that they too could do something. But there were disagreements about how to do this. Some believed in peaceful campaigning; others believed in armed uprising. As you study the turbulent events of 1789–1830s in France and in Britain (see timeline below) you are going to view these events through the eyes of two British people: James Fury and Sarah Patience.

Events outside Britain		Events in Britain
US Declaration of Independence.	1776	
Start of French Revolution.	1789	
	1791	Tom Paine published his book *The Rights of Man*.
Execution of French King Louis XVI – followed by the execution of tens of thousands of other innocent people.	1794	(1790s) Bad harvests: widespread hunger.
Napoleon crowned Emperor of France.	1804	
Monarchy restored in France.	1815	
	1819	The Peterloo Massacre. Pro-democracy demonstration in Manchester broken up by soldiers: 11 people killed.
	1831	Riots in many cities, especially Bristol, Derby, Merthyr Tydfil and Nottingham as ordinary people demand the vote.
	1832	Right to vote given to middle class men.
	1839	First Chartist petition demanding the vote for every man: rejected by Parliament. Armed rising in Newport, South Wales: 20 killed.
	1842	Second Chartist petition rejected.
Monarchy finally abolished in France.	1848	Third Chartist petition rejected.

YOUR CHALLENGE

James Fury and Sarah Patience are Chartists. They both want the same things to improve the lives of ordinary people. But they disagree about how to do it. They have to make a speech to this meeting. This is how they are going to start:

Your task will be to write a speech for James or Sarah. There is guidance for this on pages 208–209. You will use the 'double hamburger' to write a persuasive speech packed full of tasty evidence. But to get you ready you are going to gather evidence over the next 26 pages. You can see that both James and Sarah refer to past events to support their arguments. You will decide what else they can use.

What did the French Revolution achieve?

In 1789 France erupted in violent revolution. You are going to find out who won and who lost from this revolution and whether the protesters got what they expected. You will also find plenty of evidence to use in James' or Sarah's speech.

Why were the French angry?

France in the 1780s was the most powerful country in Europe, with the biggest population – 25 million. All of Europe admired French luxury goods, fashions and cuisine. Yet the country was in crisis. The chart on the opposite page summarises the reasons.

An absolute ruler

Louis XVI became king in 1774 at the age of 20. He ruled France from his palace at Versailles, which he hardly ever left. Louis made all the big decisions, for example when to go to war or levy taxes. He chose his ministers and sacked them if he didn't like them. He could put people in prison without trial. There was no Parliament to share the ruling of France.

A financial crisis

Louis' biggest problem was money. His annual income was only 475 million livres but his annual expenditure was 587 million livres. He had a debt of 1646 million livres. (The livre was the unit of currency in France at the time.)

▼ SOURCE 1
Louis XVI.

Structure

The First Estate: the Church (priests, monks and nuns), c.0.5 per cent of the population
The Church was rich and powerful. It owned ten per cent of the land. Churchmen, such as bishops and archbishops, had a huge income – up to 400,000 livres a year. Churchmen paid no taxes but they did make a gift to the King each year. The Church controlled what books and newspapers should be published and ran all the schools and hospitals so it had great control over ideas. Village priests were poorer. They received less than 1,000 livres and they often did a lot to help the poor when food prices were high. They wanted the King to make the Church fairer.

SECOND

The Second Estate: the nobility, c.1 per cent of the population
The nobility owned about 30 per cent of the land. They paid no taxes. They collected many taxes from the peasants who also paid them rent, in the form of money, farm produce or in unpaid work. People from the nobility also filled all the top jobs in the Church and provided nearly all the officers in the army. However, they did have to follow the King's orders. They could not change the laws or tell the King what to do. They wanted more influence over the King.

THIRD

The Third Estate: everyone else
The bourgeois: 8 per cent of the population
These were the middle classes: merchants, lawyers and bankers. They were becoming quite wealthy and were very important to the prosperity of France.

BOURGEOIS

Henri
I am a merchant in the port of La Rochelle. I have become rich from the trade in slaves with French colonies in the Caribbean. I pay taxes to the King but I cannot vote. Also I am a Protestant so in Catholic France I cannot worship freely. I admire the Americans who say that everyone has rights and that governments should be more democratic. The French monarchy is hopelessly out of date.

The sans-culottes: 5 per cent of the population
Unskilled workers formed only 5 per cent of the people of France, but they made up 75 per cent of the population of Paris and the other cities. They got their name from their clothes. Wealthy people who did no manual work wore knee-breeches, called culottes. Manual workers on the other hand wore trousers, which were more practical. Because they did not wear culottes they were called sans-culottes (without breeches).

SANS-CULOTTES

Edith
Our wages are low and we are poor. Most of what we earn goes on rent to pay for our homes and bread, just to stay alive. But rents and bread prices are rising. Many sans-culottes are starving.

The peasants: 85 per cent of the population
These people lived in the countryside and worked on the land. Some owned land. Together they owned about 40 per cent of the land.

PEASANTS

Gaston
We pay taxes to the King, tithes to the Church and more taxes to our lord. We also pay rents to our landlord, which are rising, and with the harvests so bad bread prices have rocketed. Many peasants are starving.

The Revolution begins 1787–1789

Stage 1: The bourgeois revolution

King Louis was desperate for money. In 1787 he called a meeting of a select group of nobles and asked them to pay taxes for the first time. Not surprisingly, the nobles refused. They wanted Louis to call a meeting of The Estates General, a gathering of representatives of all three Estates (see page 183) to discuss how to solve France's problems. It was over 170 years since that had last happened!

Henri

As a wealthy merchant, I was elected to be a member of The Estates General. Before meeting, we asked each community to draw up lists of their grievances, called cahiers. I took them with me when I went to Paris and hoped to be able to explain our region's problems.

When we met in May 1789, there was a row immediately. The First and Second Estates, the Church and the nobles, said that each of the three Estates had just one vote. This meant that they always out-voted us, even though we represented 98 per cent of the people. So in June we decided to ignore the other two Estates. We called ourselves the National Assembly and said that, as representatives of the people, we had the right to decide taxes. We abolished several hated taxes and ended the King's right to imprison people without trial.

Then, on 23 June, we were locked out of the room we had been meeting in. (We thought the King had done it to stop us from meeting, although in fact it was being prepared for him to make an announcement.) Instead we went onto a nearby tennis court and swore an oath not to go home until we had drawn up a new, more democratic constitution (a set of rules for governing a country) for France.

At first the King refused to accept the idea of a National Assembly but when some priests and even some nobles joined us, he gave way. But at the same time he called 30,000 soldiers into the Paris area. We were worried. Was he going to order the troops to arrest us and shut down the National Assembly?

 Now fill out your Revolution Chart for Henri.

Stage 2: The revolution of the sans-culottes

Because of bad harvests, bread prices in Paris were sky-high. The sans-culottes were starving – and angry.

Edith

In July 1789, to save ourselves from starvation, we broke into warehouses looking for grain. We had support. Some of the bourgeois members of the National Assembly were fearful of the King's soldiers, so they urged us on to look for weapons as well.

That's what led to one of the greatest days of the Revolution – 14 July 1789. We stormed the royal fortress of the Bastille, killing the governor. The Royal soldiers could not stop us! Some even changed sides and joined in.

Everyone was scared of us. In October we sans-culottes women walked to that useless royal palace at Versailles. We forced the King to come back with us to Paris. We even made him wear our revolutionary colours: blue, white and red.

 Now fill out your Revolution Chart for Edith.

▼ **SOURCE 2** *The storming of the Bastille, 14 July 1789. The day is now a French national holiday.*

Stage 3: The peasants' revolution

Gaston

So far we peasants had played no part in the Revolution. But the bad harvests meant we were hungry too. When we heard of the fall of the Bastille we knew things were changing. That's when we began attacking the barns belonging to the nobles and the Church which held the grain we had paid as taxes and tithes. Chateaux were burnt, although there were very few attacks on people – at that stage.

We put the fear of God into the nobles and the churchmen. In fact they called our rebellion 'The Great Fear'. They were so desperate to stop us that one night, 4 August 1789, the nobles and churchmen in the National Assembly queued up to renounce all their privileges: tithes, courts, tax exemption, the lot.

 Now fill out your Revolution Chart for Gaston.

The Declaration of the Rights of Man: 1789

After the events of August 1789, the Mayor of Paris was jubilant: 'We can see the dawn of a new revolution, when all the burdens weighing on the people are abolished and France is truly reborn. The National Assembly has achieved more for the people in a few hours than the wisest nations have done in many centuries'.

Now the members of the National Assembly, including the bourgeois and the sans-culottes, set about building a new France. They felt they were dragging their country out of its past to be the most modern nation in the world.

The Declaration of the Rights of Man was published in August 1789. This remarkable document laid out the principles for a new, democratic France. In summary, it said:

ACTIVITY

1 Add details to your Revolution Chart.

2 Who had achieved the most of what they had hoped for by this stage?

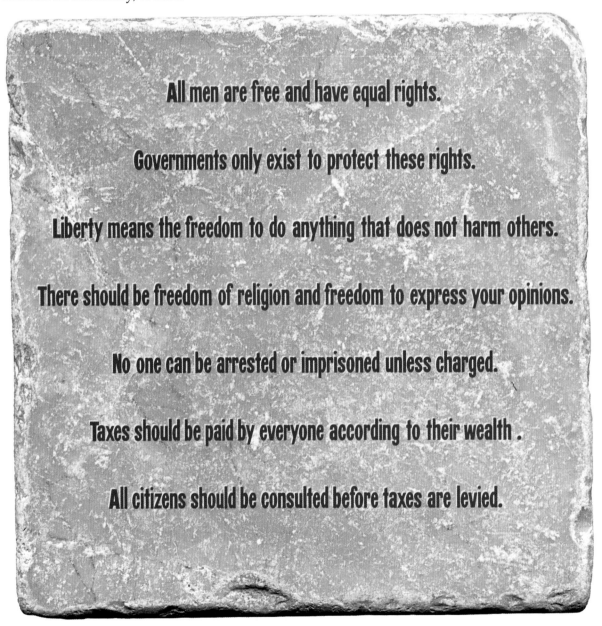

All men are free and have equal rights.

Governments only exist to protect these rights.

Liberty means the freedom to do anything that does not harm others.

There should be freedom of religion and freedom to express your opinions.

No one can be arrested or imprisoned unless charged.

Taxes should be paid by everyone according to their wealth.

All citizens should be consulted before taxes are levied.

Over the next two years the members of the National Assembly put these ideas into practice.

1 Local councils Anyone who paid tax equivalent to ten days' wages could vote. That was about 61 per cent of French men, including merchants, shopkeepers, lawyers and some better-off peasants but not women, sans-culottes or poorer peasants.

2 The Church All Church lands were sold. Now the Church had to pay taxes like everyone else. Protestants and Jews were allowed to worship freely.

3 Tax Everyone paid tax according to how much land or property they owned.

4 Law All French men were now equal in law and torture was abolished.

5 National government France was now a constitutional monarchy, governed by an elected Assembly. The king could choose his own ministers but the Assembly had the last word on taxation and foreign policy, including going to war. Almost all members of the new, elected National Assembly came from the bourgeois, middle-class, better-off members of the Third Estate.

The execution of the King: January 1793

Edith

Louis has turned traitor. He came to Paris – he did not dare refuse – but he did not keep his promises to support the Revolution. He said he did not need to because he was being treated like a prisoner by us, the Paris sans-culottes. Now his friends in Austria have declared war on us. Louis wants them to win so he can be set free. We were right not to trust him.

In June 1791 Louis and his family tried to escape. They made a headlong dash one night by coach, heading for the border. He was recognised at Varennes, caught and brought back to Paris. After that he was doomed.

In September 1792 Louis was removed from the throne and the National Assembly declared France a republic. In January 1793 he went to the guillotine. In October Queen Marie Antoinette too was guillotined.

But never mind them. Something more important happened. Our government, the Committee of Public Safety, fixed the price of bread at a level which made us, the sans-culottes, very happy. We no longer fear hunger – or the King!

▶ **SOURCE 3**
A painting, made at the time, of the execution of Louis XVI.

Henri

This is turning into a disaster, though I dare not say so aloud. Many nobles have fled abroad. They say that 60 per cent of all army officers have left, just when we need them most. We are at war with most of Europe! First Austria (remember Queen Marie Antoinette was Austrian) threatened war and invaded France from the east while Prussian troops invaded from the north. Then the Dutch and British joined in. This is terrible. How can I trade when my ships are intercepted by the British navy? My business is ruined.

The Terror: 1792–1794

Edith

From 1792 we ruled France. We were the ones with power, not the bourgeois members of the Assembly. We had started out wanting cheaper bread, but now we wanted real, radical change. Our slogan was 'Liberty, Equality, Fraternity'! We wore the red 'cap of liberty' and the revolutionary 'tricolour'. Red, white and blue colours were everywhere. We called everyone 'Citizen'. There were no more Dukes and Viscounts. We even changed the names of the months and the counting of years. Floréal was the month of flowers, 20 April–19 May. September 1792 was the start of Year 1.

And we believed in 'direct democracy'. We could change our representatives at any time if they didn't carry out our wishes. We kept our swords sharp. Violence is a grand way of winning an argument. We controlled Paris and the whole of France.

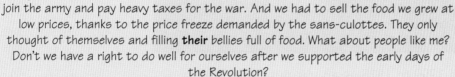

Gaston

I hated this Terror. I wasn't surprised when I heard of a rebellion in the Vendée region of western France in 1793. We peasants were angry at having to send our sons to join the army and pay heavy taxes for the war. And we had to sell the food we grew at low prices, thanks to the price freeze demanded by the sans-culottes. They only thought of themselves and filling **their** bellies full of food. What about people like me? Don't we have a right to do well for ourselves after we supported the early days of the Revolution?

That revolt in the Vendée was savagely put down: 800 peasants were shot without trial at Toulon; 1000 were shot at Angers; 1800 were put on barges from Nantes and taken out to the mouth of the River Loire where the barges were sunk. Women were raped, crops burnt, animals mutilated. And these sans-culottes talk about the Rights of Man!

The Terror lasted from 1792 to 1794, the bloodiest period of the Revolution. A new election was held on the basis of one man one vote and a Committee of Public Safety, led by Citizen Robespierre, was set up to rule France. He could do what he liked as long as he had the support of the sans-culottes.

Why was it called 'The Terror'? Simple. Anyone who opposed the Revolution or supported the King was arrested. It was a crime to be a member of the First or Second Estate, or to be rich. Trials were brief. No evidence was heard. Every day the sans-culottes gathered to watch the tumbrils [open carts] bring the victims for execution. Around 2700 people were guillotined in Paris and 15,000 more in other towns and cities.

DISCUSS

1 Think about what Henri, Edith and Gaston had wanted back in 1789. Who is most/least pleased with the outcomes?

2 Remember you are also gathering evidence for a speech. What is there here that James and Sarah could use in their speech?

The Emperor Napoleon

The Terror could not go on. In 1794 Robespierre was overthrown. Now France was run by a Directory of five men and only property-owners could be representatives. Rebellions broke out, two by sans-culottes, another led by royalists. France was in chaos. Then, in 1799, Napoleon Bonaparte, France's most successful general, seized power.

▼ SOURCE 4 *Napoleon crowns himself Emperor.*

Napoleon ruled France from 1799 to 1815 as an absolute ruler (like a modern dictator). There were elections, but the representatives had no power. In 1804 he crowned himself Emperor. At home Napoleon continued the process of building a new France. He

• issued a new set of laws, the Code Napoleon, which is still the basis of French law
• reformed education and ordered a National Curriculum to be drawn up
• set up an efficient civil service and a police force
• standardised measurements on a scientific basis: metres, litres, centigrade, grams
• divided France into 96 'départements' and he appointed a prefect to run each one. The prefects did what he said.

Napoleon also created a new, national army. It was popular, patriotic and successful. Soldiers believed in the revolutionary ideals they were fighting for. Officers were promoted democratically, by ability, not on how important your noble relatives were. Promotion could be rapid: some reached the high rank of Marshal while only in their 30s. Napoleon was the army's unbeatable commander, leading his forces to astonishing victories over all the great armies of Europe. In 1805 Napoleon had his army and ships ready to invade England (see pages

122–127). At its peak, in 1812, France controlled most of western Europe: Holland, Belgium, Spain, Italy, Germany, Austria and Poland. Everywhere they went, French forces brought with them their revolutionary ideals of Liberty, Equality and Fraternity, as proclaimed in the Declaration of the Rights of Man.

Napoleon was only defeated and exiled in 1815 after the battle of Waterloo. Although he was replaced by a new king, the last king of France was removed – peacefully in 1848. There has not been another king of France since.

What did the revolution do for me?

Henri
Although Napoleon's wars were very bad for my trading business, we bourgeois gained a lot from the Revolution. We could buy Church and noble lands cheaply when they had to sell them. Our children were educated, so could now make careers in the government service which were previously only open to nobles. And you had to be fairly well off to vote, so we were the biggest group of voters and controlled the National Assemblies through the nineteenth century.

Edith
There were times in 1793 and 1794 when I thought we sans-culottes were going to get what we wanted. After all, it was we who stormed the Bastille and then dragged the King and Queen to Paris. The Committee of Public Safety gave us decent wages and control of prices. I enjoyed sitting with my knitting by the guillotine watching the tumbrils bring the nobles to be guillotined. But we were bitterly disappointed in the end. Wage and price controls were stopped after 1795. When we could not make ends meet or got ill, we starved, whereas before the Revolution the Church looked after the poor. We sans-culottes rose in revolution three times in the nineteenth century, but were crushed each time.

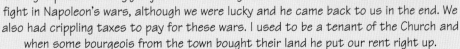

Gaston
My wife hated the Revolution because she is a devout Catholic and was shocked to see the Church attacked. I disliked the controls on the price of grain under the Committee of Public Safety as it stopped me charging the right price. I strongly objected to sending our son to fight in Napoleon's wars, although we were lucky and he came back to us in the end. We also had crippling taxes to pay for these wars. I used to be a tenant of the Church and when some bourgeois from the town bought their land he put our rent right up.

On the other hand, we no longer had to pay tithes, or feudal taxes. I ended up buying a little bit of Church land myself, which helped. I had the right to vote and was an elected member of our local council for years. All in all, I am still puzzled about how I feel about the Revolution – was it worth all that blood?

ACTIVITY

Add final details to your Revolution Chart. Compare your two charts. Do you agree with each person's judgement above?

Consequences of the French Revolution

ACTIVITY 1

Here is a Power-ometer to show who was most powerful at various stages of the French Revolution. On your own copy, mark where power lay:

a) in 1786

b) in 1788 after Louis met the nobles

c) in June 1789 after the Tennis-Court Oath

d) in July 1789 after the storming of the Bastille

e) in August 1789 after 'The Great Fear'

f) in 1794 at the height of the Terror

g) in 1800 after Napolean seized power.

If you think power is shared then put the marker between the points.

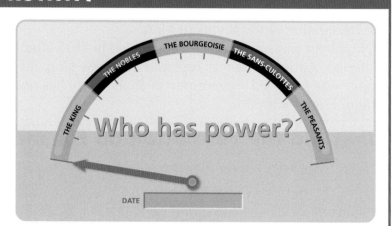

Who has power?

THE KING · THE NOBLES · THE BOURGEOISIE · THE SANS-CULOTTES · THE PEASANTS

DATE

ACTIVITY 2

All the events and situations on these two pages are linked to the French Revolution. Some helped cause the revolution; others are consequences of the revolution.

1 Using the set of cards you are given or on your own copy of this page highlight causes in one colour and consequences in another. Leave any that you are not sure about.

2 Some of the consequences are linked to each other – one thing led to another. Draw lines to show these links and write notes to explain the link if necessary.

3 What do these exercises tell you about consequences?

France was declared a republic

A bourgeois National Assembly took over governing France

Governments in other countries cracked down on protesters for fear of a revolution

France was at war with much of Europe

Louis XVI did not have enough money to run France

Louis XVI called a meeting of the Estates General

During the Terror, thousands of opponents of the Revolution were executed

Many French people lived in great poverty

Napoleon crowned himself Emperor of France

Many sans-culottes and peasants were better off

Nobles lost their power and wealth

Peasants in the Vendée rebelled, leading to thousands of deaths

Poor and powerless people in other countries were inspired to protest

Revolutionary ideas spread from France to other countries

The American Declaration of Independence gave other countries a thirst for liberty

The French King and Queen were executed

The Declaration of the Rights of Man was published

ACTIVITY 3

Remember you are also gathering evidence for James and Sarah.

Peaceful protest is the only way to be sure you achieve your aims. You never know what will happen if you are violent. Look at what happened in France: they ended up with a tyrant.

Violent protest is the only thing that causes big changes. Rulers will not give up their power unless we make them.

Choose at least two events or situations that either James or Sarah could use to support their arguments.

Could it happen here?

After the French Revolution the question on many lips in Britain was 'could it happen here?' For some people this was a hope. They would welcome this happening in their country: the ordinary people taking over government and making Britain fairer. For others it was a fear: it would spell disaster – the old order overthrown followed by violence and war. You are going to examine why some Britons were fearful and others were angry.

What did the government see?

1793
FRENCH KING EXECUTED
Louis XVI goes to guillotine

The Terror claims thousands more lives

1795
ATTACK ON PRIME MINISTER WILLIAM PITT
Stones thrown at Downing Street home
Mob chants 'No war, no famine, no Pitt, no king'

1812
PRIME MINISTER ASSASSINATED
Prime Minister Spencer Perceval shot in House of Commons by bankrupt merchant

Crowds celebrate in Midlands towns

1813
LUDDITES SMASH FACTORY MACHINES
Unhappy workers in Yorkshire
Machine breaking spreads across country

1815
DOWNING STREET ATTACKED AGAIN
Stones thrown at Prime Minister's home
Crowds demand jobs and bread

1816
MOB RIOTS IN LONDON
Peaceful meeting turns to chaos before Henry Hunt can even speak
Drunken crowds try to seize guns from Tower of London

1817
REVOLUTION IN DERBYSHIRE?
Spies reveal plot to overthrow government
Rebellion feared all over north

1817
PROTEST MARCH ON LONDON
Unemployed march from St Peter's Fields, Manchester
One killed, several wounded as soldiers stop marchers

A *SOCIETY* OF **LOYAL BRITONS,**
Instituted the 10*th of* OCTOBER, 1793;
At the NEW CROWN, in BLACKMAN STREET, *Southwark.*

Whereas

… we have seen with great concern, the RUIN and MISERY that now pervades every Province in FRANCE, in consequence of the REBELLIONS and TREASONS lately perpetrated there, …

… The ideas of LIBERTY and EQUALITY, were pleasing sounds to the ears of the less discerning and lower orders of the French Nation … [but] in the end, those deluded People were led insensibly to commit RAPINE [plundering], ROBBERY and MURDER; and to complete the measure of their wickedness, to glut themselves with the *BLOOD of their SOVEREIGN.*

… Those Despots in power, according to their *Levelling Plan,* next proceeded to destroy and annihilate every Species of Commerce, Trade, and Property …

… those REGICIDES are now amusing themselves with the LIBERTY of cutting each other's Throats, an employment worthy of a people who not only sacrificed their KING, but have also openly declared War against their GOD, by defiling and profaning his Temples and murdering such of the Clergy as have unfortunately fell into their hands …

…[now] by their Agents and Emissaries, have endeavoured to introduce and propagate their pernicious Doctrines, for the infamous purpose of exciting in this Country, the like state of Insurrection and Revolt.

[Therefore]

… this Society of LOYAL BRITONS, will … aid and assist the Executive Government upon every occasion, and discountenance, deter, and prevent, to the utmost of our Power, the circulation of Inflammatory Pamphlets, Papers, or Conversation.

ACTIVITY

Use the information on page 194 and in Source 1 to prepare a memo to the Prime Minister warning him of the risk of revolution in Britain and what he should do to prepare for it.

◄ SOURCE 1 *A notice produced by the Society of Loyal Britons in 1793. This organisation was set up to oppose French revolutionary ideas coming into Britain.*

Why did ordinary people want change?
Long-term problems

Working conditions were hard
- Hours were long. It was not unusual to work 5a.m.–7p.m. with only short breaks for meal times or toilet stops. When people were desperate for jobs employers could easily find workers who would accept these long hours.
- Factories were full of dangers – unfenced machinery, toxic materials and dust.
- Conditions in the mines were even more dangerous.
- There were no official limits on working hours. People were campaigning for a Ten Hours Act – limiting working hours to ten hours per day.
- Jobs were insecure. When the order book dried up workers were laid off.

Living conditions were awful
- Towns had grown quickly and houses had been built so fast that they were poor quality, full of damp.
- Sanitation was basic. There were toilets in the yard and a bucket in the corner of the room.
- Houses were overcrowded. A family lived and slept in one room and sometimes sub-let to other people to earn more money.
- The factory machines were steam-driven, so the air was full of smoke from the furnaces.
- There was no system of refuse collection so rubbish piled up in the streets.
- People often kept animals in town so there was the noise and smell of cows, pigs and chickens.
- Drinking water was from a standpipe (which might not be very clean) or from a stream which would almost certainly be polluted.

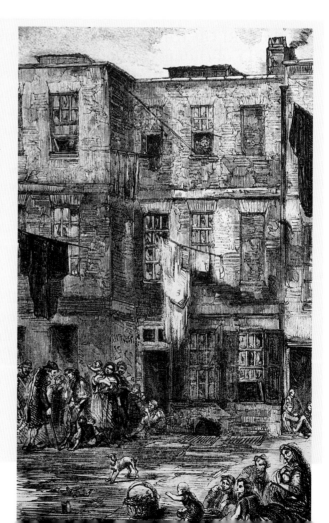

Short-term problems in 1815–1820

People had lived with these problems for years. They were prepared to accept them as long as they got good wages and could eat. But in the years after the Napoleonic Wars …

- There was unemployment. During the Napoleonic Wars many industries had boomed because they were supplying the army with kit or weapons or rations. After the war, orders dried up so people were laid off; thousands of ex-soldiers and sailors were looking for jobs as well.
- Factories were introducing new machines that were taking the place of skilled labourers.
- Food prices were sometimes low, but sometimes very high. When prices rose almost all workers had difficulty affording enough food for themselves and their families.
- Far from helping ordinary people in these times the government taxed them. The government had spent too much money fighting the Napoleonic wars and to pay its debts it had increased all kinds of taxes – including those on food.
- The government also passed a Corn Law that kept the price of wheat artificially high. So ordinary people had to pay more for their bread.

▼ SOURCE 2 *Protest leaflet circulated at a meeting at Spa Fields in 1816.*

BRITONS TO ARMS!

The whole country awaits the signal from London to fly to arms!

Haste, break open gunsmiths and other likely places to find arms!

Run all constables who touch a man of us; no rise of bread; no Regent; no Castlereagh, off with their heads; no placemen, tythes or enclosures; no taxes; no bishops.

> Everything that concerns their subsistence or comfort is taxed. Is not their loaf taxed? Is not their beer taxed? Are not their coats taxed? Are not their shirts taxed? Is not everything that they eat, drink, wear and even say, taxed?

▲ SOURCE 3 *Radical democratic speaker Henry Hunt, a politician who campaigned for reform in Britain (see pages 200–201).*

ACTIVITY

List the three most important reasons why people protested for change after 1815.

What was wrong with British elections?

In a modern democracy there would be a simple way of dealing with the problems on pages 196–197. People would take their concerns to their MP and if enough MPs heard similar complaints they would pressure the government to change things.

But in 1815 there was a problem with British democracy.

ACTIVITY

1 Work with a partner. List all the things that were undemocratic within the voting system in Britain in 1815.

2 Choose the two biggest problems from your list and prepare a table like the one below.

Major problems	How it should be changed	Why the government might oppose this
1		
2		

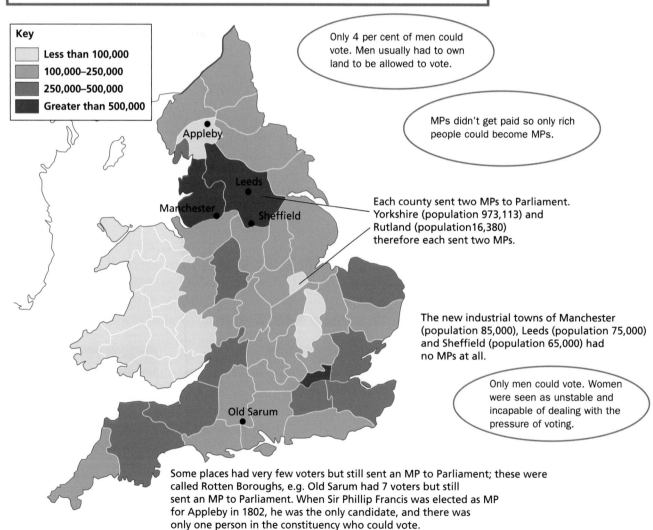

Key
- Less than 100,000
- 100,000–250,000
- 250,000–500,000
- Greater than 500,000

Appleby

Leeds

Manchester

Sheffield

Old Sarum

Only 4 per cent of men could vote. Men usually had to own land to be allowed to vote.

MPs didn't get paid so only rich people could become MPs.

Each county sent two MPs to Parliament. Yorkshire (population 973,113) and Rutland (population16,380) therefore each sent two MPs.

The new industrial towns of Manchester (population 85,000), Leeds (population 75,000) and Sheffield (population 65,000) had no MPs at all.

Only men could vote. Women were seen as unstable and incapable of dealing with the pressure of voting.

Some places had very few voters but still sent an MP to Parliament; these were called Rotten Boroughs, e.g. Old Sarum had 7 voters but still sent an MP to Parliament. When Sir Phillip Francis was elected as MP for Appleby in 1802, he was the only candidate, and there was only one person in the constituency who could vote.

▲ **SOURCE 1** *Map showing distribution of voters in 1815.*

▼ **SOURCE 2** The Polling Station *by William Hogarth.*

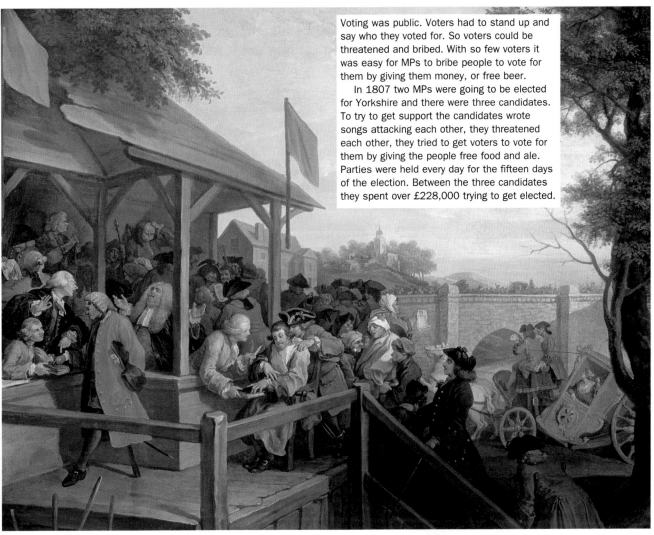

Voting was public. Voters had to stand up and say who they voted for. So voters could be threatened and bribed. With so few voters it was easy for MPs to bribe people to vote for them by giving them money, or free beer.

In 1807 two MPs were going to be elected for Yorkshire and there were three candidates. To try to get support the candidates wrote songs attacking each other, they threatened each other, they tried to get voters to vote for them by giving the people free food and ale. Parties were held every day for the fifteen days of the election. Between the three candidates they spent over £228,000 trying to get elected.

Our system is fine. It has lasted for centuries. Only the landowners should vote. We have a vested interest in Britain doing well. We should control the government. Those French revolutionary ideas will be our downfall. These reformers need to be put down, by force if necessary. Otherwise we will go the way of the French – thousands guillotined just for being rich.

If we ordinary people could vote then Parliament would have to pass laws that helped us, rather than the rich just passing laws that help them.

Peterloo 1819: what did they want and did they get it?

It started out as a peaceful protest but it ended as a bloodbath. What happened at St Peter's Fields in Manchester and did it help to win anyone the vote?

What happened at St Peter's Fields?

The atmosphere in Britain in the years after 1815 was tense, especially in northern England, with angry, hostile groups on both sides. Already there had been large protest meetings in Leeds, Birmingham and London. The speakers called for reform of Parliament; for reduction of taxes; and for votes for all adults.

The meeting at St Peter's Fields on 16 August 1819 was due to be addressed by Henry Hunt. This is what happened.

Reform leaders in Manchester call a big public meeting.

Manchester has no police force. Magistrates are worried about law and order so they call in soldiers, including the Manchester and Salford Yeomanry.

Demonstrators arrive from all around Manchester, perhaps 50,000 people, many in their Sunday best. They march with brass bands playing.

As soon as Hunt begins to speak, magistrates order the Yeomanry to arrest him.

Yeomanry cut their way out through the crowd with their swords.

Eleven people are killed, including two women, and 400 injured.

What were the consequences?

The next day a newspaper, in a sarcastic reference to the famous battle of Waterloo four years earlier, calls it 'The Peterloo Massacre'.

The government congratulates the Manchester magistrates on their handling of the situation.

Henry Hunt is charged with 'assembling with unlawful banners for the purpose of exciting discontent' and sentenced to two and a half years in prison. Other speakers are sentenced to one year. A magistrate tells one reformer 'Some of you reformers ought to be hanged – the rope is already round your neck'.

The government bans meetings of more than 50 people and gives magistrates power to search houses for weapons.

The tax on newspapers is greatly increased to try to stop workers reading them and getting 'dangerous' ideas.

The answer is no. There was no change in who had the right to vote in elections.

ACTIVITY

1 Complete columns 2–4 of this chart.
2 After Peterloo, the government had two options. It could have
   a) listened to the protests and given more people the vote; or
   b) punished the protesters and refused to change the voting system.
   Why do you think the government chose option **b**?
3 Who do you think was most to blame for the deaths at Peterloo – the protesters or the magistrates?
4 Now fill in the final column of the chart.

	Aims What did the protestors want?	Actions Did they use peaceful or violent methods to achieve their aims?	Outcomes What were the consequences of what they did? Did they get what they wanted?	Lessons from history What evidence could James or Sarah use in their speeches?
Peterloo protesters 1819				

The reform riots of 1831: the same story?

In the picture below you can see more protesters, more soldiers. Does it look as if these protesters were any more successful than those at Peterloo?

▲ SOURCE 1 *Contemporary illustration of the Bristol reform riots of October 1831. The city jail and many houses were burned down. Soldiers were sent in to restore order. Twelve people were killed and over a hundred were injured.*

Reform

For ten years after Peterloo the violence died down. The economy was recovering; food prices had fallen sharply and there were more jobs available. The harsh treatment of the protesters had scared off many people.

In the 1830s, however, protest was back on the agenda. There were riots in the countryside: farm workers destroyed machines they thought were putting them out of work. In Parliament there was a big change – the election of 1830 had brought in some new MPs who were in favour of reform. Against this background the 'Reform' movement got going again. Meetings were held all over the country to demand changes to the voting system so that ordinary men had a say in how the country was run.

The reformers had the wind in their sails. They got Parliament to agree a reform bill but when it went to the House of Lords to be approved it was rejected. The next day in Nottingham …

Nottingham

Rioters stormed Nottingham castle, the home of the Duke of Newcastle. The Duke was well-known for influencing elections by bribing and threatening voters. He owned many houses in Nottingham and people who dared to vote against his wishes were turned out of their homes onto the streets. Many protestors were arrested following the riots. Three were executed and six were transported to Australia.

Bristol

Two weeks later in Bristol …

SOURCE 2 *Reverend J. L. Jackson describing the Bristol riots in a letter, 31 October 1831.*

During the whole of Saturday Bristol was in a state of considerable ferment from the arrival of Sir C. Wetherall, the Recorder (Judge). In the evening the multitude assembled before the Mansion House in Queen Square, and smashed the windows by a volley of stones in the front of the building. Yesterday morning when I was going to Bristol to serve the church of a friend, I learnt that the populace had actually broken into the Mansion House, and forced the cellars and were destroying and gutting the house. Three individuals were killed by the soldiers and more wounded. In the afternoon we heard the multitude was assembled in much greater masses, and about four o'clock we saw the new City and County Gaol in flames; afterwards the Bridewell and prison in the Gloucester Road, about a mile from Bristol. In the course of the evening Queen's Square was fired and the Bishop's palace. Of Queen's Square two whole sides have been burnt down, including the Mansion House. Other property to an immense amount is also destroyed. This morning an actual slaughter has taken place; it is supposed, though of course nothing precise can be known at present, that about seventy persons have been killed, besides a large number who have been wounded. The military charged through some of the principal streets, cutting right and left.

London next?

Rumour spread that 200,000 protesters would march from Birmingham to London and not leave until Parliament agreed to more people having the vote. In response, the government ordered a regiment of soldiers to 'rough-sharpen' their sabres to stop the march – but the soldiers refused to obey!

An anonymous message arrived:

> 'Depend upon it the country is ripe for revolution … then goodbye to England's King and Ministers!'

The government took this very seriously. In June 1832 the voting system was changed.

The Reform Act	But 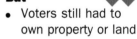
• Gave the right to vote to men who owned, leased or rented property over a certain value • Increased the number of men who could vote to 8 per cent of the population • Large cities such as Leeds, Manchester and Bradford got MPs for the first time	• Voters still had to own property or land • Working men could not vote • Women could not vote • Voting was still in public so bribery and fear still played a part in elections • The countryside and south still had more MPs than the north and industrial towns

ACTIVITY

1 Add a new row to your chart from page 201 for the Reform riots of 1831.

2 Complete columns 2–4: aims, actions and outcomes.

3 Discuss:
   a) Why were so many people disappointed by the 1832 reform?
   b) Do you think the threat of more violence in 1831 had been successful in forcing the government to make changes or had it prevented greater changes?

4 Now fill in the final column of your chart.

How did the Chartists try to win the vote?

The voting system had been changed but working men still could not vote in elections. They were very disappointed. They had worked with the middle classes to change the old system but now felt they had been let down. Their struggle for the right to vote went on.

What was Chartism?

In 1836 a group of London working men drew up a Charter with six political demands.

▼ SOURCE 1 *The Charter.*

ACTIVITY 1

1 Summarise each demand in one sentence.
2 How was each of the six points in the Charter meant to make the voting system fairer?

The Six Points
OF THE
PEOPLE'S
CHARTER.

1. A VOTE for every man twenty-one years of age, of sound mind, and not undergoing punishment for crime.

2. THE BALLOT.—To protect the elector in the exercise of his vote.   **i.e. a secret ballot**

3. No PROPERTY QUALIFICATION for Members of Parliament —thus enabling the constituencies to return the man of their choice, be he rich or poor.

4. PAYMENT OF MEMBERS, thus enabling an honest trades-man, working man, or other person, to serve a constituency, when taken from his business to attend to the interests of the country.

5. EQUAL CONSTITUENCIES, securing the same amount of representation for the same number of electors, instead of allowing small constituencies to swamp the votes of large ones.   **i.e. equal sized constituencies**

6. ANNUAL PARLIAMENTS, thus presenting the most effectual check to bribery and intimidation, since though a constituency might be bought once in seven years (even with the ballot), no purse could buy a constituency (under a system of universal suffrage) in each ensuing twelvemonth; and since members, when elected for a year only, would not be able to defy and betray their constituents as now.

Peaceful protest or violent action?

There were two main groups of protesters. Both groups wanted the six points of the Charter but they went about getting them in different ways.

Moral force

William Lovett was the leader of the 'Moral Force' Chartists. They believed that the way to get the government to agree to the Charter was to show them that Chartists were worthy of the vote. They held meetings, wrote letters to persuade the government, set up schools to help people learn to read and write and encouraged Chartists not to drink, in order to show that they were worthy of the vote.

SOURCE 2 *William Lovett writing in 1839.*

Let us, Friends, unite together the honest, moral, hard-working and thinking members of society. Let us obtain a library of books. Let us publish our views, so that we create a moral, thinking, energetic force in politics.

Physical force

Feargus O'Connor on the other hand was prepared to use force to get the government to introduce the six points of the Charter. He was leader of the 'Physical Force' Chartists. He held large meetings and made passionate speeches urging Chartists to fight for what was their right. A lot of the language he used in his speeches was violent.

SOURCE 3 *One of Feargus O'Connor's closest allies, George Harney, wrote in the Chartist newspaper* The Northern Star, *February 1839.*

We will make our country one vast howling wilderness of desolation and destruction rather than the tyrants shall carry out their infernal system. Believe me, there is no argument like the sword, and the musket is unanswerable.

ACTIVITY 2

1 On pages 206–207 we tell the story of the Chartist movement. Use this information to fill out a new row for your table: The Chartists.
2 Why do you think the Chartists were split over how to win the vote?
3 Why do you think the government did not agree to the changes the Chartists wanted?

The story of Chartism

7 1842 Mills back at work
Strikers arrested by troops

Prison for those who will not go back to work

8 1848 Fears of revolution
Third Chartist petition to go to Parliament – 5.7 million signatures

Commons rejects petition by 222 votes to 17

5 1842 Second Chartist petition rejected
3 million people sign new Chartist petition

Petition rejected again – 287 votes to 49

3 1839 Chartist petition rejected
House of Commons rejects petition by 235 votes to 46

MP says 'we cannot ever give the vote to the lower classes'

6 1842 Strikes and more strikes
50,000 on strike in Lancashire

Chartists say 'No work until we have the Charter'

1 May 1839 The People's Charter
1.2 million sign petition supporting the Charter

Meetings held up and down the country

4 1839 Rebellion in Newport
7000 miners and ironworkers march on Newport

Soldiers kill twenty

Leaders to be transported

2 July 1839 Chartist riot in Birmingham
Police and soldiers clash with crowd

6000 troops sent to the North

1848 – the Chartist revolution?

The government was worried stiff. There had already been revolutions that year in Paris, Baden, Vienna, Berlin, Dresden, Budapest, Warsaw, Milan, Venice, Bologna and elsewhere. Would London be next? Would the mass of people on Kennington Common (see Source 4) storm Parliament and seize power? The Commander in Chief of the British Army, the 79-year-old Duke of Wellington, feared the worst. How do we know?

- He sent Queen Victoria for safety to her palace on the Isle of Wight!
- He banned the Chartist procession from going into the centre of London (which they had no intention of doing).
- Cannon were placed on London's bridges in case the Chartists tried to attack Parliament.
- Key buildings – the Bank of England, the Post Office and the Guildhall – were barricaded.
- 85,000 special constables were appointed.
- And just in case, there were 4000 police and 8000 soldiers standing by!

ACTIVITY

Write some headlines for various newspapers for 11 April 1848. Include some that are meant to be read by important government officials and some that are read by working men. What will be their angle on the meeting?

In fact, the great Chartist demonstration was a peaceful affair. Thousands of people gathered to hear speeches. The event ended in pouring rain. A huge petition was carried to Parliament in a series of horse-drawn coaches, then everybody went home. Parliament overwhelmingly rejected the petition.

▲ SOURCE 4
On 10 April 1848 thousands of Chartists met on Kennington Common, London.

What is the best way to win the vote?

You have been collecting evidence from history to write a speech. This page and the next one will help you to organise it.

How to write your speech

Your speech should persuade your listeners that you know the best way to win the vote. That means making your arguments clear and interesting and using evidence to back them up. A good speech presents your argument but also attacks your opponent's argument. The Double Hamburger will help you.

Starting and finishing

The buns at the top and bottom of the hamburger are your introduction and conclusion. These are critical parts of your speech. They should be

a) clear so your listeners know exactly what your opinion is

b) short and punchy to grab your listeners' attention. Think carefully about which words to use so they get attention.

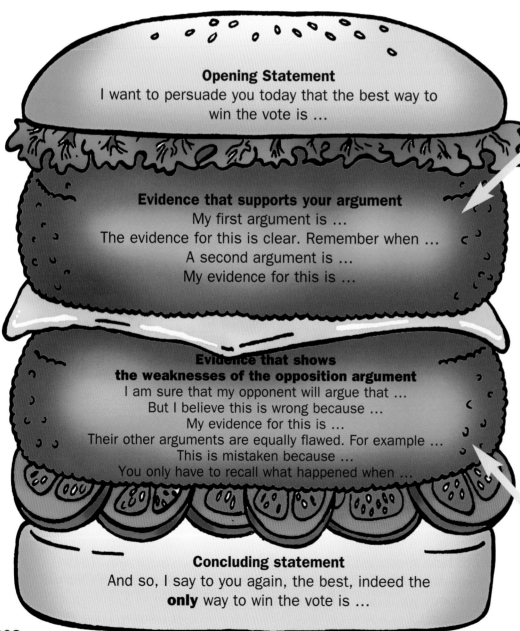

Opening Statement
I want to persuade you today that the best way to win the vote is …

Evidence that supports your argument
My first argument is …
The evidence for this is clear. Remember when …
A second argument is …
My evidence for this is …

**Evidence that shows
the weaknesses of the opposition argument**
I am sure that my opponent will argue that …
But I believe this is wrong because …
My evidence for this is …
Their other arguments are equally flawed. For example …
This is mistaken because …
You only have to recall what happened when …

Concluding statement
And so, I say to you again, the best, indeed the **only** way to win the vote is …

The top burger

is your viewpoint. You need to include:

a) your argument. The activity on page 209 shows arguments you could use. Use at most two of these.

b) your evidence to show that your argument is true. Use the evidence you have collected through pages 194–207 to help you.

The bottom burger
Challenges your opponent's argument(s). You need to be as hard-hitting as possible.

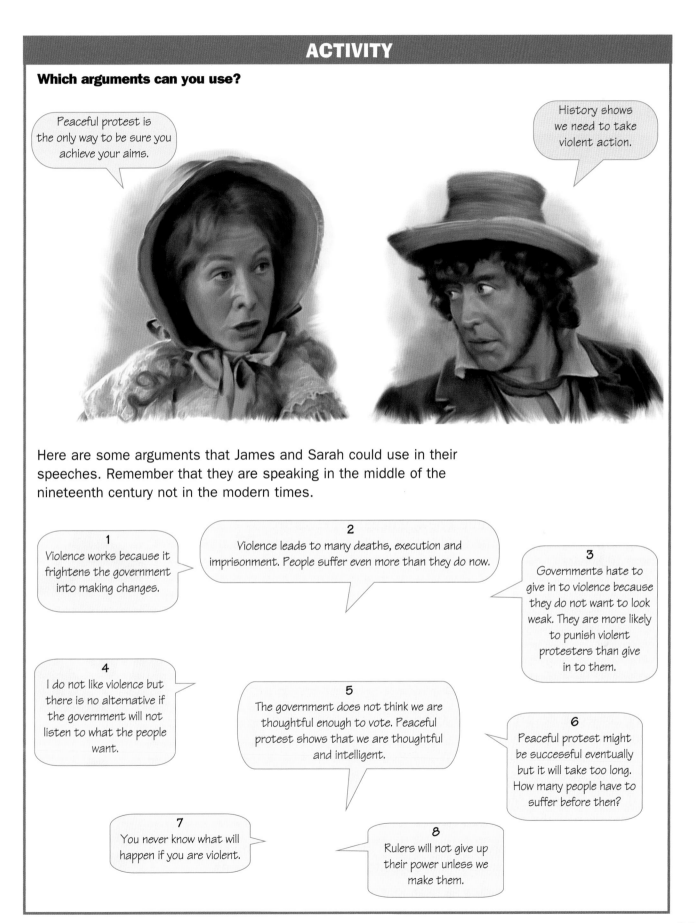

ACTIVITY

Which arguments can you use?

Peaceful protest is the only way to be sure you achieve your aims.

History shows we need to take violent action.

Here are some arguments that James and Sarah could use in their speeches. Remember that they are speaking in the middle of the nineteenth century not in the modern times.

1 Violence works because it frightens the government into making changes.

2 Violence leads to many deaths, execution and imprisonment. People suffer even more than they do now.

3 Governments hate to give in to violence because they do not want to look weak. They are more likely to punish violent protesters than give in to them.

4 I do not like violence but there is no alternative if the government will not listen to what the people want.

5 The government does not think we are thoughtful enough to vote. Peaceful protest shows that we are thoughtful and intelligent.

6 Peaceful protest might be successful eventually but it will take too long. How many people have to suffer before then?

7 You never know what will happen if you are violent.

8 Rulers will not give up their power unless we make them.

This section has been about how people tried to win rights such as the right to vote but it is also about consequences: the results of decisions and events.

Consequences

A single event or decision can have many different consequences

You mean we caused all that? Incroyable!

For example, the consequences of the first protest in France included:
- the execution of the King and Queen
- the Terror – the execution of opponents of the Revolution
- the Declaration of the Rights of Man
- many sans-culottes and peasants were better off
- France was at war with much of Europe
- revolutionary ideas spread to other countries.

Consequences

Consequences can be of different kinds, for example short-term and long-term consequences

Gee, that's great. We got to be independent but people are still thinking about what we did a hundred years later. That's what I call a long-term consequence.

For example, the American Declaration of Independence had consequences which were:
- short term – the USA became a new, independent country
- long term – the ideas in the Declaration motivated protesters for the next 100 years.

Consequences

Some consequences are intended, some are unintended and so cannot be predicted

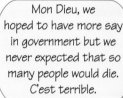

Mon Dieu, we hoped to have more say in government but we never expected that so many people would die. C'est terrible.

For example, the revolutionaries in France in 1789 intended to make France more democratic but an unintended consequence was the Reign of Terror.

1 Choose at least one more example of each key idea from your study of events in Britain. The panels on the opposite page will give you ideas.

2 Would any of these examples be useful for your speech?

Peterloo 1819

- The speakers at Peterloo were put in prison

- Eleven people were killed and many more wounded

- The government banned meetings of more than 50 people

- The government was frightened that if they gave in this would only encourage more violence

CONSEQUENCES

The Reform Riots of 1831

- The destruction of buildings in Bristol and Nottingham

- Ringleaders were executed or transported to Australia

- Middle-class men were given the vote

- Working people felt betrayed and were more determined to win the vote

The Chartist movement in the 1830s and 1840s

- Chartist groups were set up all over the country and many working-class people became interested in politics

- Chartist miners tried to take control of Newport but failed and many were killed

- Millions of people signed the Chartist petition

- Chartist strikers were jailed and leaders transported

- Again, the government was frightened that if they gave in this would only encourage more violence

LEARNING LOG

You will do more work on consequences later in the course. How will you record what you have learned so you can remember it and use it again in the future?

So who was proved right?

Maybe the collapse of the Chartist movement felt like an anti-climax to you. It certainly did to the Chartists. But they didn't just give up. They worked in other ways to win the vote. And less than twenty years later they got it – or some did. So in this final enquiry you have two questions: Who was right about how to get the vote – James or Sarah? And were the Chartists right that once they got the vote their lives would change for the better?

ACTIVITY 1

In 1867 MPs were again debating whether to give the vote to working men. If you had dropped in at the MPs' club on the night before the vote here are some viewpoints that you might have heard. If James and Sarah could listen in too which one would say 'I told you so'?

1 I'm impressed by how many of these working men have educated themselves at evening classes. They are not wild revolutionaries any more. They're hard-working decent men. They deserve the vote.

2 This country is much more prosperous. People don't want revolution. They want their reward for working hard and making Britain great. These hard-working men deserve the vote , but there should be some restrictions – only the educated ones should get it.

3 The days of the French Revolution are long past. Nobody can remember that now. We aren't afraid that revolutionaries will set up a guillotine in the centre of London these days.

4 If we give them the vote now we will be able to control them. There were those riots in Hyde Park, remember. The trouble died down quickly but we don't want to look as if we are being forced into changes. Then those who don't get the vote might think violence wins.

5 We need working men's votes to beat the other lot in Parliament. If we give them the vote, they will vote for us in the next election and we will win.

6 You lot won't admit it but all those Chartist riots played their part. If you hadn't felt threatened you wouldn't even have discussed giving working men the vote.

7 I'd never have believed it! But now they are talking about working men – what about me? Don't ignore the women.

What were the consequences?

In this section you have been looking at consequences. Working men believed that the consequence of getting the vote would be improvements in their lives. Were they right? Look at the timeline below and decide. How did voting change things?

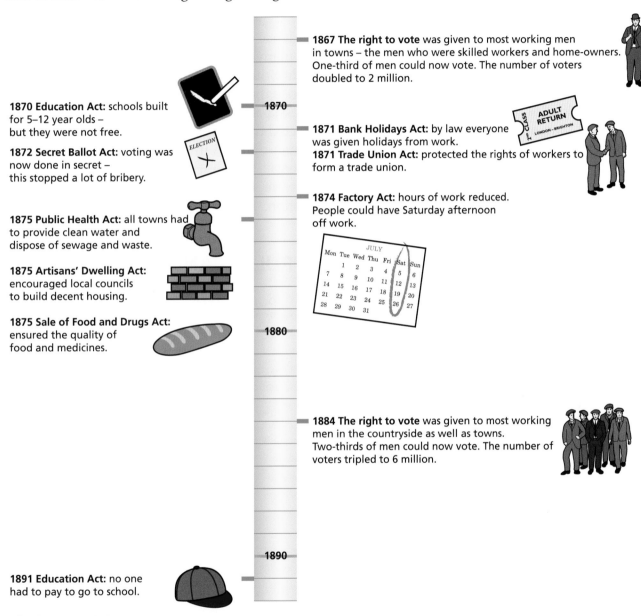

1867 The right to vote was given to most working men in towns – the men who were skilled workers and home-owners. One-third of men could now vote. The number of voters doubled to 2 million.

1870 Education Act: schools built for 5–12 year olds – but they were not free.

1871 Bank Holidays Act: by law everyone was given holidays from work.
1871 Trade Union Act: protected the rights of workers to form a trade union.

1872 Secret Ballot Act: voting was now done in secret – this stopped a lot of bribery.

1874 Factory Act: hours of work reduced. People could have Saturday afternoon off work.

1875 Public Health Act: all towns had to provide clean water and dispose of sewage and waste.

1875 Artisans' Dwelling Act: encouraged local councils to build decent housing.

1875 Sale of Food and Drugs Act: ensured the quality of food and medicines.

1884 The right to vote was given to most working men in the countryside as well as towns. Two-thirds of men could now vote. The number of voters tripled to 6 million.

1891 Education Act: no one had to pay to go to school.

1870

1880

1890

ACTIVITY 2

In Y9 you will study many protests for democratic rights in the twentieth century.
- In Britain, women campaigned for the vote.
- The people of India wanted independence from Britain.
- Black Americans and black South Africans wanted their civil rights.

Write three Golden Rules for these campaigners based on your knowledge of the French Revolution and how men won the vote in Britain.

THE BIG STORY:
Power Part Two – democracy

How had ideas and beliefs about democracy and human rights changed by 1900?

Nowadays voting is something we take for granted. Many people do not even think it's very important, but in the past people died to win the right to vote and the period you have been investigating saw some of the most crucial changes. The American Declaration of Independence and the French Revolution set an example which led people in many countries to rise up and try to make a better world for themselves. In Britain, this led to a struggle for democracy which lasted 150 years and since then there have been revolutions in many other countries, including Russia and China. The idea that all human beings have rights also deeply affected the campaign to abolish slavery (see Section 2) and the struggle for human rights in the twentieth century which you will find out about next year.

This timeline shows what the hot issues of the time were. Often the attitudes had been common for centuries without question.

THE IDEAS AND ATTITUDES OF THE RULERS AND GOVERNMENT

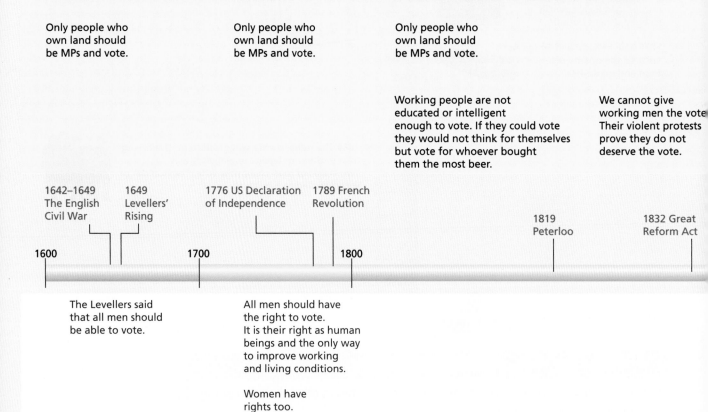

Only people who own land should be MPs and vote.

Only people who own land should be MPs and vote.

Only people who own land should be MPs and vote.

Working people are not educated or intelligent enough to vote. If they could vote they would not think for themselves but vote for whoever bought them the most beer.

We cannot give working men the vote. Their violent protests prove they do not deserve the vote.

1642–1649 The English Civil War

1649 Levellers' Rising

1776 US Declaration of Independence

1789 French Revolution

1819 Peterloo

1832 Great Reform Act

1600

1700

1800

The Levellers said that all men should be able to vote.

All men should have the right to vote. It is their right as human beings and the only way to improve working and living conditions.

Women have rights too. Men and women should be able to vote.

THE IDEAS AND ATTITUDES OF ORDINARY WORKING PEOPLE

LEARNING LOG

Next year you will continue the story of human rights and democracy, building on your studies up to 1900. To help you with the final part of this story, record your answers to these questions in whatever way will help you remember them and re-use them next year.

1 Which of these people had won the right to vote in Britain by 1900?
  a) all men over 21
  b) most men over 21
  c) all women over 21
  d) married women over 21

2 What was still unfair by today's standards about Britain's voting system in 1900?

3 How had people won the vote by 1900?

4 Which events do you think had been the major turning points in the struggle for human rights before 1900?

Middle-class men have shown they deserve the vote. They own property and business so have a stake in the country, are educated and hard-working – and if they have the vote they will not join the workers' protests.

Many working men now deserve the vote. They have educated themselves and shown they are hard-working and respectable and if they have the vote they won't join violent protests.

Women should not have the vote. They are not educated and are too emotional to take intelligent decisions. Every year there is a vote on this in Parliament and every time we vote against it.

1839–1848 Chartists' petitions

1867 Vote given to most working men in towns. One-third of men could now vote.

1884 Vote given to most working men. Two-thirds of all men could vote.

1900

All men should have the right to vote. It is not fair that middle-class men have been given the vote. We workers are the ones making Britain rich and powerful.

There are many Chartist Womens' clubs too. Women deserve the vote as much as men.

Most working men have won the vote – but there are still many men who cannot vote. The struggle is not over yet.

Men have the vote but not one woman has, not even women who have trained as doctors. We want votes for women!

Women teachers and doctors have shown they can do responsible jobs. Parliament needs to address women's issues: a Parliament of men will never do this. We want votes for women!

... about sources?

We find out about the past by using sources. Sources give us evidence of what life was like. As we get nearer to modern times, there are more sources, and more types of sources, available.

ACTIVITY

Look at the sources A–J. Some are from what we have called 'the Early Modern period' (1500–1750); some from 'the Industrial period' (1750–1900). Some other sources are 'misfits': they were not available to historians until after 1900.

1 Decide which period each source comes from and what category of source it is. Record these examples in a table like this – we have done one for you. Don't include the 'misfits'.

2 Find other examples to add to your table. You might need to add extra coulmns.

	Surviving buildings	Objects	Pictures	Writing	Photographs
'Early Modern period'					
'Industrial period'		C – old piano			

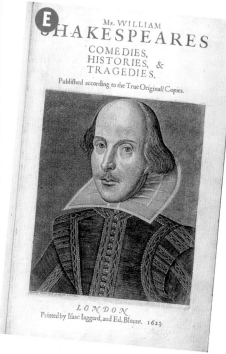

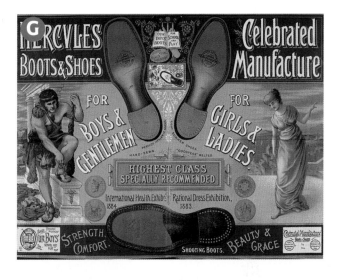

217

... about significance: what and who should be remembered?

ACTIVITY

1 The Post Office wants to issue two new sets of stamps. One set of stamps is to commemorate five important historical events; the other, five people. Which events or people from 1500–1900 do you think they should choose? Use the ideas below and on the next page to help you make your choices. You can find out more via the index. You could choose

- events or people that were the most significant (see the Recap box about significance)
- events or people that have surprised, shocked or interested you in History this year.

2 If we had to add **one** new annual national holiday to remember an event or person, what would it be and why?

1536
Pilgrimage of Grace
Rebels in northern England join mass protest mainly against Henry VIII's religious policy

1539
Dissolution of the Monasteries
Henry VIII closes down over 600 monasteries and nunneries

1588
Spanish Armada
Spanish attempt to invade England fails

1620
Pilgrim Fathers
Puritan refugees found colony in New England

1649
EXECUTION OF CHARLES I
England becomes a republic for the next 11 years

1660
Restoration
Charles II becomes king after 11 years of republic

1689
The Glorious Revolution
James II removed from the throne. William of Orange invited to become king

1707
Act of Union
England, Wales and Scotland form one kingdom

1805
Trafalgar
Napoleon's attempt to invade
foiled by British naval victory at Trafalgar

1807
Abolition
of slave trade

1819
Peterloo
Soldiers charge democracy
protest meeting in
Manchester: 11 people killed, 400 injured

1830
**Liverpool to
Manchester railway**
First passenger-carrying
railway in the world

1839
First Chartist Petition
Huge petition demanding
greater democracy
in Britain presented
to Parliament

1847–1849
Potato crop in Ireland fails
Famine results in
over 1 million dead

1870
Education Act
State schools are set up
for every child from 5 to 12

1871–1872
**FA cup
first held**

1893
British seize land in
southern Africa from
Lobengula, the African king,
making the colony
of Rhodesia

1875
Public Health Act
Every local government had to provide
clean water, proper drains and sewers and
appoint a Medical Officer of Health

219

... about people: who would you like to meet at the History party?

Edward I

Cortes

Rhodes

William Wilberforce

Olaudah Equiano

Toussaint L'Ouverture

Thomas Clarkson

Robert Aske

Richard Whiting

John Pym

Thomas Jefferson

Henry Hunt

Robespierre

Nelson

Napoleon

Philip II of Spain

Francis Drake

Charles I

Oliver Cromwell

Elizabeth I

Henry VIII

Michael Faraday

Isambard Kingdom Brunel

James Watt

A sans-culottes

Pilgrim Father

Peterloo casualty

Civil war soldier

ACTIVITY

1 Here are a few people you have met in this book, plus a few you have not. Use the index, your memory or your research skills to work out what the people in each group have in common.

2 Who would you most like to talk to? What would you ask them? Choose one character, decide on some questions to ask them, and then role-play an interview.

ACTIVITY

You are going to construct a human Connections Diagram. You will need tabards, string, paper, clothes pegs and Blu-tack.

Step one
Each group takes one theme. Look at the other themes and use your string to make links to other groups/themes.

Step two
Now you need to set out the evidence to justify these links. For each link you have made, take a piece of paper and write, in a few words, the evidence to support your link. Then clothes-peg them to the string.

Step three
Now you need to record your conclusions. Get a sheet from your teacher and record the details of the links or use a digital camera to photograph your links.

... about ideas and beliefs?

Into the mind of ...

History is not just about events and who did what. It's about what kinds of ideas, beliefs and attitudes people had. They lived in different kinds of homes, wore different clothes, did different things for fun – but were their ideas and thoughts all different too?

ACTIVITY

1 Who is thinking each of the thoughts on these two pages? Fill in a grid like the one below with the letters of the thoughts but be careful – some thoughts go in more than one column!

Thoughts of people from the 1300s (the Middle Ages)	Thoughts of people from the 1500s and 1600s	Thoughts of people from the 1800s

2 Which do you think are the **two** most important differences between the thoughts of people in the Middle Ages and people in the 1500s and 1600s? Explain why you chose them.

3 Which do you think are the **two** most important differences between the thoughts of people in the 1500s and people in the 1800s? Explain why you chose them.

4 Choose **one** similarity and **one** difference between the ideas of people in the 1800s and the ideas of people today.

5 Choose **one** of the thoughts from the past that interested or surprised you. Explain why you think it is interesting or surprising.

A Only another week and we can get the harvest in. We must pray it doesn't pour with rain now and ruin the crops. If we have another bad harvest many people will go hungry this winter. Some poor folk may even starve to death if it's really bad.

B Men should have the right to vote in elections for Parliament but I don't think women can be trusted to do that. They are too emotional.

C Thanks be to God for the good monks at the monastery. If there is no work, or food prices are high, we can depend on the monks to give us help.

D Our empire is vital for making Britain rich. We need to defend it from other countries — by force if we have to.

E My brother's worried about losing his job. He works as a weaver but he thinks this new weaving machine in the factory will take over and put men like him out of work.

F Catholic, Protestant, now Catholic again. If the king or queen does not choose the right religion then will everyone burn in hell?

G The King is a traitor. He has betrayed his people and deserves to die. We will not just make another man king but get rid of kings completely. England does not need a king.

H My sister's got terrible toothache. It's been really bad all week. She's used honey and tried a herbal remedy our mother gave her but nothing's doing any good.

I It's so hard to find work at home that I've decided to emigrate to America on one of the new steamships.

J We have one of these new Bank Holidays coming up soon. I'm off on a train to the seaside for some sunshine.

K Governments should help the needy — the poor and elderly, the sick and unemployed. Not everyone agrees but I think it's the government's duty to help people in need.

L It's back-breaking work bringing the harvest in but at least there's plenty of holidays coming up. It's a good time of year for celebrating Saints' days.

M I think it is time to abolish slavery. It is inhuman to keep people in chains and deprive them of their freedom.

COMING SOON IN
THE BIG STORY OF...

...HUMAN RIGHTS

...CONFLICT
War goes global

...ORDINARY LIFE
Fighting the giant of poverty around the world

ACTIVITY

Work in groups. Look at the topics on these two pages. You will be investigating them in the rest of Key Stage 3 History.

1 Use the Doing History ideas to list as many good history questions as you can about these topics.
2 Swap your list with another group. Can you identify which topics the other group's questions are about?
3 Which of the topics are you most looking forward to investigating? Why?

...POWER
Twentieth-century dictators crush democracy

...EMPIRE
The end of the British Empire

...MIGRATION
Making modern Britain

...EVERYTHING
What can the Olympic Games teach us about history?

EMPIRE WINDRUSH

LONDON

The book with no name!

You are now going to sum up some of the big ideas from this course by making improvements to our book cover (see pages 2–3).

The title
This book has no descriptive title so it's up to you to choose one. Think of a title that
- grabs people's attention
- sounds intriguing
- but also sums up what you think are the important changes in this period.

The pictures
You might not agree with our choice of pictures so you can choose your own if there are people who you think better represent the period.

Once you have created your covers (you can get a template to work with on the computer) you can then take a class vote on which one best conveys the period.

Here is one person's idea for the Year 7 book that you may have used last year:

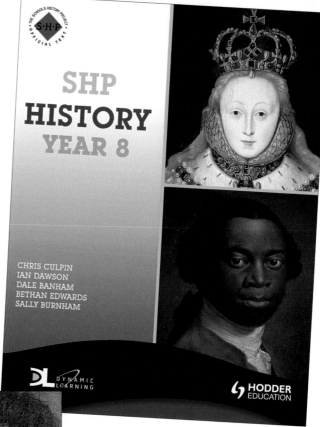

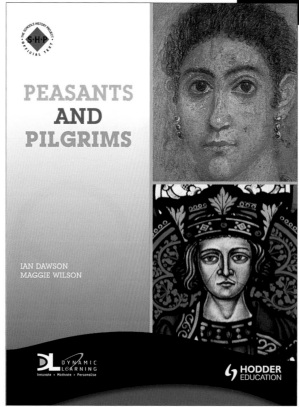

Index

Acknowledgements

Cover t © National Portrait Gallery, London, UK/The Bridgeman Art Library, b © Royal Albert Memorial Museum, Exeter, Devon, UK/The Bridgeman Art Library; **p.3** cl © Corpus Christi College, Oxford, UK/The Bridgeman Art Library, cr Michael Holford, t By permission of the British Library (MS Add. 42130 f.171v); **p.4** Getty Images/The Bridgeman Art Library; **p.6** © Bettmann/CORBIS; **p.8** The Bridgeman Art Library/Getty Images; **p.22** t Guildhall Library/COLLAGE/London Metropolitan Archives; **p.23** b © Cheltenham Art Gallery & Museums, Gloucestershire, UK/The Bridgeman Art Library; **p.24** bl © Fotomas/TopFoto, br © Cheltenham Art Gallery & Museums, Gloucestershire, UK/The Bridgeman Art Library, tc Bibliothèque des Arts Decoratifs, Paris, France/Archives Charmet/The Bridgeman Art Library, tl & tr The Bridgeman Art Library; **p.27** © Mary Evans Picture Library 2008; **p.28** © Manchester Art Gallery, UK/The Bridgeman Art Library; **p.30** b Ann Ronan Picture Library/HIP/TopFoto, t Broadlands Trust, Hampshire, UK/The Bridgeman Art Library; **p.32** Mary Evans Picture Library; **p.33** bl Mary Evans Picture Library/Alamy, br © Mary Evans Picture Library/Francis Frith, t © Royal Holloway and Bedford New College, Surrey, UK/The Bridgeman Art Library; **p.34** b Museum of London, t Amoret Tanner/Alamy; **p.35** bl General Photographic Agency/Getty Images, br © Mary Evans Picture Library 2008, tl © Mary Evans Picture Library 2008, tr Museum of London/HIP/TopFoto; **p.36** b Mary Evans Picture Library/Alamy, tl Greenwich Heritage Centre, tr John Thomson/Getty Images; **p.37** b National Fairground Archive, University of Sheffield, c London Stereoscopic Company/Hulton Archive/Getty Images, t © Mary Evans Picture Library; **p.38** b Reproduced by permission of English Heritage/HIP/TopFoto, t Amoret Tanner/Alamy; **p.39** b © Museum of London, UK/The Bridgeman Art Library, t Wellcome Library, London; **p.40** © Mary Evans Picture Library 2008; **p.41** Reproduced by permission of English Heritage/HIP/TopFoto; **p.42** © Chris Culpin **p.50** © Bettmann/CORBIS; **p.51** © Bettmann/CORBIS; **p.55** l The Art Archive/Bodleian Library Oxford/The Bodleian Library Arch Seld A1 fol 21v, r The Art Archive/Bodleian Library Oxford/The Bodleian Library Arch Seld AS1 fol 67r; **p.56** bl The Art Archive/Bodleian Library Oxford/The Bodleian Library Arch Seld A1 fol 61r, r Newberry Library, Chicago, Illinois, USA/The Bridgeman Art Library, tl © Bettmann/CORBIS; **p.57** b © Boltin Picture Library/The Bridgeman Art Library, br The Art Archive/Templo Mayor Library Mexico/Dagli Orti, t The Art Archive/Bodleian Library Oxford/The Bodleian Library Arch Seld A1 fol 60r; **p.58** © Bettmann/CORBIS; **p.59** b CarverMostardi/Alamy, t The Art Archive/Museo del Templo Mayor Mexico/Gianni Dagli Orti; **p.61** The Art Archive/National Palace Mexico City/Dagli Orti; **p.65** t Shelfmark RCS/Fisher 4/585; reproduced with permission of the Syndics of Cambridge University Library, b The Bridgeman Art Library; **p.68** bl The British Library/HIP/Topfoto, br Roger-Viollet/Topfoto, t © Wilberforce House, Hull City Museums and Art Galleries, UK/The Bridgeman Art Library; **p.69** b North Wind Picture Archives/Alamy, c Topfoto, tl www.topfoto.co.uk, tr © Mary Evans Picture Library 2008; **p.74** Ministere de l'Outre Mer, Paris, France/The Bridgeman Art Library; **p.75** Wilberforce House, Hull City Museums and Art Galleries, UK/The Bridgeman Art Library; **p.76** © Wilberforce House, Hull City Museums and Art Galleries, UK/The Bridgeman Art Library; **p.77** © Wilberforce House, Hull City Museums and Art Galleries, UK/The Bridgeman Art Library; **p.78** b & t © Wilberforce House, Hull City Museums and Art Galleries, UK/The Bridgeman Art Library; **p.79** b North Wind Picture Archives/Alamy, t MPI/Getty Images; **p.81** © Philip Mould Ltd, London/The Bridgeman Art Library; **p.82** © Wilberforce House, Hull City Museums and Art Galleries, UK/The Bridgeman Art Library; **p.86** British Library, London, UK/© British Library Board. All Rights Reserved/The Bridgeman Art Library; **p.87** Bibliothèque Nationale, Paris, France/Archives Charmet/The Bridgeman Art Library; **p.88** l

Alex Smailes/Colors, r Georgina Cranston/Anti-Slavery International; **p.92** b Bob Thomas/Popperfoto/Getty Images, c Shelfmark RCS/QM 24/38; Reproduced with the permission of the Syndics of Cambridge University Library, t Shelfmark RCS/Fisher 4/585; Reproduced with the permission of the Syndics of Cambridge University Library; **p.93** bl The Bridgeman Art Library, br Shelfmark RCS/GBR/0115/Y3043C96; Reproduced with the permission of the Syndics of Cambridge University Library, c www.topfoto.co.uk, t © 2005 Roger-Viollet/Topoto; **p.94** Yale Center for British Art, Paul Mellon Collection, USA/The Bridgeman Art Library; **p.95** b Punch, t Eye Ubiquitous/Alamy; **p.99** By permission of The National Library of Wales; **p.104** Courtesy of St. Andrew's Society of Winnipeg Pipe Band; **p.105** Hulton Archive/Getty Images; **p.106** Edwin Levick/Getty Images; **p.107** b © Punch Limited/TopFoto, t © Bettmann/CORBIS; **p.114** Glasgow City Council (Museums); **p.116** Mansell/Mansell/Time & Life Pictures/Getty Images; **p.117** l © TopFoto, r His Grace The Duke of Norfolk, Arundel Castle/The Bridgeman Art Library; **p.118** b & t National Maritime Museum; **p.124** © TopFoto; **p.127** © Skyscan/CORBIS; **p.128** City of London/HIP/TopFoto; **p.129** © Hulton-Deutsch Collection/CORBIS; **p.134** © Stapleton Collection/Corbis; **p.140** © Ashmolean Museum, University of Oxford, UK/The Bridgeman Art Library; **p.141** © 2003 Fotomas/Topham; **p.144** b © The Print Collector/Alamy, t © TopFoto; **p.147** Private Collection/The Bridgeman Art Library; **p.156** bc The Art Archive/Handel Museum Halle/Dagli Orti (A), bl © Burghley House Collection, Lincolnshire, UK/The Bridgeman Art Library, br © TopFoto, tc The Bridgeman Art Library/Getty Images, tl & tr © The Gallery Collection/Corbis; **p.158** © The Gallery Collection/Corbis; **p.159** National Portrait Gallery, London; **p.160** The Bridgeman Art Library/Getty Images; **p.162** © The Gallery Collection/Corbis; **p.164** © Burghley House Collection, Lincolnshire, UK/The Bridgeman Art Library; **p.165** Time Life Pictures/Mansell/Time Life Pictures/Getty Images; **p.166** The Art Archive/Handel Museum Halle/Dagli Orti (A); **p.167** National Army Museum, London/Acquired with assistance of National Art Collections Fund/The Bridgeman Art Library; **p.168** b Rafael Valls Gallery, London, UK/The Bridgeman Art Library, t © TopFoto; **p.169** Hulton Archive/Getty Images; **p.172** © Stu/Alamy; **p.175** l © Burghley House Collection, Lincolnshire, UK/The Bridgeman Art Library, r © Michael Nicholson/CORBIS; **p.178** Hulton Archive/Getty Images; **p.182** © The Gallery Collection/Corbis; **p.185** © The Gallery Collection/Corbis; **p.188** Art Media - Carnavalet, Paris/HIP/TopFoto; **p.190** The Bridgeman Art Library/Getty Images; **p.196** b Hulton Archive/Getty Images, t © Mary Evans Picture Library; **p.197** Mary Evans Picture Library; **p.199** Courtesy of the Trustees of Sir John Soane's Museum, London/The Bridgeman Art Library; **p.202** www.topfoto.co.uk; **p.204** © 2003 Fotomas/Topham; **p.205** b & t Hulton Archive/Getty Images; **p.207** © Alan King engraving/Alamy; **p.216** l © Robert Harding Picture Library Ltd/Alamy, r © TopFoto; **p.217** bl Ingram, br © Steve Prezant/Corbis, ct © Historical Picture Archive/CORBIS, rc The National Archives/HIP/TopFoto, tc Getty Images/The Bridgeman Art Library, tl © Leeds Museums and Galleries (Lotherton Hall) U.K./The Bridgeman Art Library, tr © TopFoto, cl © Jim Belben; **p.226** br SHAH MARAI/AFP/Getty Images, l Illustrated London News, tr Gerald Hoberman/Hoberman Collection UK; **p.227** bl Keystone/Getty Images, br Printed with kind permission of the International Olympic Committee, tl © ullsteinbild/TopFoto, tr © Bettmann/CORBIS

c = centre, l = left, r = right, t = top, b = bottom

Every effort has been made to trace all copyright holders, but if any have been inadvertently overlooked the Publishers will be pleased to make the necessary arrangements at the first opportunity.